Pagan Visions

for a SUSTAINABLE FUTURE

About the Editors

Ly de Angeles is a witch and High Priestess of the Covenant of Wild-Wood Gate, Australia, and is the author of several books, including *Witchcraft: Theory and Practice, When I See the Wild God,* and *The Quickening* (St. Paul, Minn.: Llewellyn Publications). Clear communication, history, mythology, and all the magic of a "Celtic" inheritance have been her companions on a "Grail Quest": seeking respect for the rights of indigenous people to self-determination and the earth's release from plunder.

Bobcat (Emma Restall Orr) is a priestess, author, poet, and singer who has spent the last fourteen years working as a teacher, theologian, and ritualist in Britain and around the world. Bobcat's work emphasises the roles of both the feminine and the shamanic in Druidry and offers a vision of the world which honours the cycles of life and death through an active engagement with both the land and the ancestors.

Thom van Dooren is a Pagan and a philosopher with a passionate interest in the intersection of political issues and people's lifeways. He lives in Australia and is currently undertaking a PhD that explores the political and philosophical dimensions of modern food production.

EDITED BY:
Ly de Angeles, Emma Restall Orr & Thom van Dooren

FEATURING:

Ly de Angeles, Dr. Douglas Ezzy, Akkadia Ford,

Dr. Susan Greenwood, Gordon MacLellan, Dr. Val Plumwood,

Emma Restall Orr, Marina Sala, Dr. Sylvie Shaw,

Starhawk, Thom van Dooren

Pagan Visions

for a SUSTAINABLE FUTURE

Llewellyn Publications
Woodbury, Minnesota

First Edition
First Printing, 2005

Book design and layout by Joanna Willis
Cover design by Ellen Dahl
Cover image © 2005 by Comstock
Editing by Valerie Valentine
Illustration on page 131 by Llewellyn art department

Llewellyn is a registered trademark of Llewellyn Worldwide, Ltd.

Library of Congress Cataloging-in-Publication Data
Pagan visions for a sustainable future / Ly de Angeles, Emma Restall Orr,
   Thom van Dooren, editors ; other contributors, Douglas Ezzy ... [et al.]. —
   1st ed.
       p. cm.
   Includes bibliographical references.
   ISBN 0-7387-0824-0
   1. Paganism. 2. Religious ethics. 3. Human ecology—Religious aspects.
   I. De Angeles, Ly, 1951- II. Van Dooren, Thom, 1980- III. Restall Orr,
Emma, 1965- IV. Ezzy, Douglas.

   BL432.P34 2005
   299'.94—dc22

                                                              2005045099

Llewellyn Worldwide does not participate in, endorse, or have any authority or responsibility concerning private business transactions between our authors and the public.
   All mail addressed to an author is forwarded, but the publisher cannot, unless specifically
instructed by the author, give out an address or phone number.
   Any Internet references contained in this work are current at publication time, but the
publisher cannot guarantee that a specific location will continue to be maintained. Please
refer to the publisher's website for links to authors' websites and other sources.

Llewellyn Publications
A Division of Llewellyn Worldwide, Ltd.
2143 Wooddale Drive, Dept. 0-7387-0824-0
Woodbury, MN 55125-2989, U.S.A.
www.llewellyn.com

Printed in the United States of America

contents

contributors

EMMA RESTALL ORR (aka Bobcat) is head of The Druid Network and former Joint Chief of the British Druid Order, priestess, author, poet, and singer. She is author of *Druid Priestess* (formerly published as *Spirits of the Sacred Grove*) (Thorsons, 1998), *Principles of Druidry* (Thorsons, 1999), *Ritual: A Guide to Life, Love and Inspiration* (Thorsons, 2000), and most recently, *Living Druidry* (Piatkus Books, 2004). Emma is also the author of two collections of poetry entitled *Black Lizard Forest* and *Tides of Dying*. She is co-writer of *The Druid Directory*, and has had articles published in countless journals and magazines worldwide. Her current works-in-progress are *Pagan Ethics*, exploring the nature of morality within Neo-Pagan society and theology, and *Kissing the Hag*, an exploration of the unacceptable nature of woman.

AKKADIA FORD holds master's degrees in both Egyptology and visual art and has travelled extensively into the ancient Egyptian religious beliefs. She is the author of several books, including *Isis, Afrikan Queen* (Capall Bann, 1999), *The Powers That Seek—Unlocking the Magick Within*

Ancient Egyptian Creation Legends (Capall Bann, 2001), and *Egyptian Animals—Guardians & Gateways of the Gods* (Capall Bann, 2005). In 2000 Akkadia was invited to contribute a chapter for a book entitled *Egyptian Art—Principles and Themes in Wall Scenes*, published in Cairo by the Egyptian Government, Ministry of Culture. Her writing encompasses both Egyptological and magickal perspectives, and she maintains an ongoing practice within the Egyptian temple.

DR. SUSAN GREENWOOD has BA and PhD degrees in anthropology and teaches undergraduate courses on shamanism and altered states of consciousness at the University of Sussex, UK. She has written widely on magic, taking a critically sympathetic approach to issues of identity, gender, feminism, morality, and the environment. She is the author of *Magic, Witchcraft and the Otherworld* (Berg, 2000), *The Encyclopedia of Magic and Witchcraft* (Lorenz, 2001), and *The Nature of Magic: An Anthropology of Consciousness* (Berg, 2005).

MARINA SALA holds a master's degree in international relations and has researched the theory and practice of conflict resolution at PhD level. She has written articles and poetry focused on breaking down the prejudice about magic and feminism in everyday life. She is also the writer of *Magic Happens in the Strangest Places*, a fairy tale for all ages, and "Who Cares About Human Rights?", an article written against apathy in the West.

LY DE ANGELES has been High Priestess of a tradition of Witchcraft for over thirty years and has lectured and taught throughout Australia for many years. She is the author of several books, including *The Way of the Goddess* (Unity/Prism, 1987), *Witchcraft: Theory and Practice* (Llewellyn Publications, 2000), *The Feast of Flesh and Spirit* (WildWood Gate, 2002), *Genesis—A Legend of Future Past* (WildWood Gate, 2002), *When I See the Wild God* (Llewellyn Publications, 2004), and *The Quickening* (Llewellyn Publications, 2005).

DR. DOUGLAS EZZY is a senior lecturer in sociology at the University of Tasmania, Australia. His research focuses on the way people find meaning and dignity in social life. This question has been worked through studies of unemployment, living with HIV/AIDS, contemporary witchcraft, and environmental sociology. His books include *Narrating Unemployment* (Ashgate, 2001), *Qualitative Analysis* (Allen & Unwin, 2002), and *Practising the Witch's Craft* (Allen & Unwin, 2003).

DR. SYLVIE SHAW has a PhD in sociology which has a focus on nature religion and ecopsychology. She lectures in sociology at Monash University in Melbourne. Her passions are sacred ecology and shamanic studies, and she is currently undertaking research on people's social and spiritual relationships with the sea.

GORDON MACLELLAN works as Creeping Toad, creating celebrations with groups of people that explore and rejoice in the relationships between people and the places where they live, work, and play. He is the author of *Talking to the Earth* (Capall Bann, 1995), *Sacred Animals* (Capall Bann, 1997), and *Shamanism* (Piatkus Books, 1999). He is currently working on *Celebrating Nature: A Manual for Creating Community Celebrations.*

STARHAWK is the author and coauthor of ten books, including *The Spiral Dance: A Rebirth of the Ancient Religion of the Great Goddess* (Harper-Collins, 1979), long considered the essential text for the Neo-Pagan movement, and the now-classic ecotopian novel *The Fifth Sacred Thing* (Doubleday, 1993). Her works have been translated into German, Danish, Dutch, Italian, Portuguese, Spanish, French, and Japanese. She is also a veteran of progressive movements and deeply committed to bringing the techniques and creative power of spirituality to political activism. She travels internationally teaching magic, the tools of ritual, and the skills of activism. Starhawk's latest book is *Earth Path: Grounding Your Spirit in the Rhythms of Nature* (HarperSanFrancisco, 2004).

DR. VAL PLUMWOOD is an Australian Research Council Fellow at the Australian National University. She has published four books and over one hundred papers, mostly in environmental philosophy. Her books include *Feminism and the Mastery of Nature* (Routledge, 1993) and *Environmental Culture: The Ecological Crisis of Reason* (Routledge, 2002).

THOM VAN DOOREN has a BA with first-class honours majoring in philosophy and religious studies. At present Thom is at the Australian National University working on a PhD dissertation titled *Strange Seed: A Political Philosophy of Food in the Global Village*, which focuses on environmental philosophical issues in modern food production.

foreword

I welcome this book as an excellent gathering together of passionate portrayals and evocations of what it means to be Pagan now. *Pagan Visions for a Sustainable Future* embraces a rich community of writers who represent many of the diverse trends that make up Paganism. Reading these chapters together, in any order, reveals something of the intensity of debates about what it means to be human now. It is all too easy to complain about the state of the world, but it is hard to proffer encouragements and empowerments of ways of living in this beautiful, wonderful, and threatened world that may yet make it a better place. The editors and contributors deserve high praise, especially for those moments that sparkle with beauty and spark with challenge.

The book, like Paganism itself, is as full of potential and paradox as life itself. For example, this is a new religion but is inspired by ancient knowledges. It evolved in Britain but is unmistakably similar to many indigenous religions around the world. It is among the fastest growing, globally spreading religions, but it is homely and everyday. It entails powerful transformative encounters but celebrates ordinary life. It excites people interested in their own personal growth and those out to change the world. It has no scriptures, but has generated a large and growing library of books, magazines, and websites. It focuses attention on the physical world of nature, bodies, and materiality, but it has generated and consumed much of the imaginative literature of recent decades. It includes intensely private and personal experiences, but also causes people to participate in activism and protest. At its heart is a simple matter of affection for the world into which we are all born and with which we are all inescapably in touch, but it has rapidly evolved into a myriad of diverse groups, traditions, styles, and flavours.

Further evidence of the vitality and significance of Paganism can also be adduced from the considerable interest in it shown by academics. There are important and interesting books and articles about Paganism researched and written by historians, anthropologists, sociologists, psychologists, philosophers, theologians and thealogians, and scholars of religion, culture, gender, performance, and more. Scientists interested in consciousness, ecology, brain chemistry, and beyond have been interested in aspects of Paganism. Every year sees more PhDs and books written about Pagan worldviews and lifeways, ideas, and practices. Of course, none of this academic interest means that Paganism is "true," but few Pagans or academics think that's important or interesting. It isn't the role of academics to say that one way of being human or one way of living is the right way. Sadly, it is more common to hear academics being destructive and dismissive of particular cultures and religions that they fail to appreciate. But it's easy to be negative; the hard task is always to suggest something better. Paganism may not be better or worse than any other religion, and Pagans may not be better or worse people than other religionists. But Paganism does have considerable advantages if you agree that living in the world and liking it is important. Paganism is of considerable interest in relation to some of the most interesting, important, and imperative issues of today, for example, ecology, gender, power relations, and sustainable living. It is, therefore, far more than just another small-but-growing alternative religion. Its existence, diversity, interests, and engagements can speak to us (whoever we are) about the world in which we live—the human world, and the more-than-human world.

But this book does not leave it to academics to talk about Paganism. It certainly includes academics and other well-read, thoughtful, and scholarly people. But the sense of passion and engagement conveyed by all the writers comes from each writer's commitment to particular visions and practices—to *living* Paganism—not just thinking about it. This makes it not only an interesting book, but a good one.

For my own part, I most value the chapters in which Paganism is presented as a response to a world full of life. Some of the following chapters talk about "spirit," "energy," or "archetypal forces." These generate poetic and enchanting visions that might greatly enhance people's pleasure and purpose in being alive now. They might aid and enrich the quest for well-being, not only for individuals, but also for communities, and not only for humans, but for the widest community of living beings. Indeed, they reach towards planetary well-being because, at heart, they are about living at home—here in our planet home, here in our particular locations. That is a large part of what "ecology" means. Of course, we must not forget that it is not only home to us humans. It is home, too, to those who would eat us (viruses and crocodiles, to name but two of our neighbouring predators). Because of this, there are exciting chapters ahead by those who think the label "Pagan" properly applies only to radical engagements with the wider community of life.

If every contributor to this book celebrates life in the here and now, some make clear that if we don't get out into the world and stop the destruction of threatened ecosystems and living communities there is little point in being happy to have been born. If we don't find ways to live respectfully (i.e., both cautiously and constructively, as Mary Black says of Ojibwa engagements with the world)[1] with *all* who live—including those we don't like, those who threaten us, and those who say "no" to our desires to make the world cosier for ourselves—there is little point in seeking greater self-knowledge and self-empowerment.

I've read and reread a number of these chapters, gaining more each time. But I have also gone back again to the chapters that did not resonate with me. I do not pretend to be without preferences and predilections. I recognise in the mingling of all these chapters into this important book much of what I value about Pagan spirituality, Pagan activism, and Pagan people. Pagans are wonderful at confounding expectations other people (especially academics) might have of them. This book manages to portray this unexpectedness wonderfully. The contributors, when read together, challenge all categories, labels, sketches, and constructions that others (myself included) might want to place on them. They do so simply by writing about what they do, what motivates them, inspires them, calls them, provokes them, captivates them, forms them, and pleasures them. They write about what they would like to do; they write about the world as they see it, and the world as they would like it to be. This vision makes the anthology particularly good as an example of real Paganism. These *are* the kind of people Pagans are.

Reading is somewhat like a journey that makes strange places familiar and familiar places strange. It is all too easy to go again and again to places where we feel at home; but the best moments of all journeys happen in serendipitous encounters and conversations. In the greatest adventures, you turn a corner and the world shows itself to be different than what you thought before. There are plenty of such moments ahead in this book; you only have to turn the pages.

GRAHAM HARVEY
Author of *Contemporary Paganism: Listening People, Speaking Earth*
(New York University Press, 1997)

Note

1. Mary B. Black, "Ojibwa Power Belief System," in *The Anthropology of Power,* eds. R. D. Fogelman and R. N. Adams (New York: Academic Press, 1977), 141–51.

introduction

There was no one "spark" of inspiration that lead to the creation of this book; rather, it is the result of a growing uneasiness about what is happening in the world today, and the general response to those happenings from Pagans around the globe. Anybody reading this book who mixes in Pagan circles will appreciate that there is a wealth of knowledge, insight, and inspiration in the wider Pagan community. As a "group" (if that is what we are), Pagans must surely represent one of the most diverse, open, and accepting (not to mention a touch radical and critical of the status quo) communities on the planet today. When Pagans meet, the topic of discussion often quickly moves to politics and world events, or animal rights and ethics, or sometimes, with my friends, philosophical issues about the nature of time, space, and reality. Where, though, are these conversations in print? Of course there is a wealth of literature to be found on all of these topics, but where is the specifically Pagan thought dealing with these topics? Surely, these are all Pagan issues.

By this I mean that Paganism (which I understand not as an abstract spiritual "quest," but rather as a "lifeway," a "way of the sacred," as Ly de Angeles terms it) encompasses all of these issues and more. It encompasses every aspect of what it is for each of us to live as an embodied individual on this planet, issues that include the politics and ethics of what we eat, drink, wear, and how we generally go about our lives. These are, for many of us, *essentially Pagan issues.* At a point in time, however, at which these issues are getting more and more complex, and the situation on this planet in getting graver and graver, a tiny number of writers are becoming solitary voices crying in the wilderness, in the midst of an ever increasing surge of popular Pagan literature.

Much of this literature, which in today's world of generally profit-governed publishing, is churned out year after year, adding nothing new to Pagan thought or practice, being produced purely and simply for the satisfaction of the egos and the bank balances of a group of self interested "superstar Pagans." This situation insults and degrades all of us. I struggled for a long time to become comfortable with the label "Pagan," not because I am ashamed of my practices or way of life, nor because I am ashamed of my incredibly beautiful, gifted, and passionate Pagan friends, but rather because the popular perception of Paganism has become something that any self-respecting individual must surely shy away from.

I have met people who I am certain are involved with Paganism for no other reason than the steady supply of young women that it can provide for them. I have heard tales of the thousands and thousands of dollars that go missing from large Pagan groups, and seen the prices that some groups are charging for "teachings," prices so far exceeding "covering costs" that any suggestion that this is their motivation is simply insulting. We make jokes about it in Australia—we talk about "superstar Pagans" and "cash-register Druids," and all the while these people are becoming more and more common, both here and overseas. What is so significant about these people, though, is that they are coming to *define what Paganism is.* Not to those of us who already know, who already feel it deep down in our stomachs, in our blood and our bones, but to a public that is greedy for anything even slightly sensational, and, from my perspective far more importantly, to future generations of Pagans who will have to deal with the messes that we, both as a general society and as a Pagan community, are creating and adding to every day.

The current generation of newly "outed" Pagans, many of whom are still young children, are often growing up on a diet of pure glamour that completely sensationalises what I have always taken to be the most grounded spiritual path that there is (so grounded, in fact, that the term "spiritual" seems largely inappropriate). This situation is not only eroding the essence, the heartbeat, and the dance of the Pagan paths, but it is also often exposing these people to situations in which they are taken advantage of and seriously hurt, both emotionally and physically.

The thing that shocks me most about this situation is that I thought (very naively as it now turns out) that Paganism would inherently reject this commodification, that it would fight tooth and claw against the very concept of a superstar. Guru worship has never been a part of our traditions. As always, though, it seems that "they" have found a way to market and sell back to us a diminished version of what we already had. Paganism has, for many people, become another "new age" spirituality (in fact, this is how everyone from academics to some publishers and the media characterises and classifies it). There are T-shirts, jewelery, TV shows, movies, bumper stickers, music, and cookbooks. Soon we'll have our own board game (unless there already is one?). Perhaps there is nothing inherently wrong with most of these products; there is, however, a big problem with them being used to define *what we are*, with marketing teams and manufacturers getting together and manipulating and utilising our stories, symbols, and beliefs—hell, even our gods—just to turn a quick buck. I thought that Paganism would resist this trend more successfully.

Perhaps it sounds as though I'm scapegoating these superstar Pagans, when really the problems of the world are not their fault any more than they are the fault of the rest of us. What is undeniable, however, is that these people, with the aid of large corporations, have begun to dilute and distort the essence of Paganism. They have become yet another voice that soothes us into the comfortable oblivion of conformity and acceptance of the status quo. In my mind, however, Paganism has the opportunity to be much more than this—to begin the re-sacralisation of the world in the Western psyche. In order to do this, however, we need to begin to engage with issues—not just within universities (because the gods know there are a lot of Pagans studying, writing, and teaching in universities!), but in a popular context as well. We need to begin a more open dialogue on these issues and share our unique perspectives with the wider world.

This open public dialogue will in itself do a great deal to address a lot of the more prevalent popular opinions about Paganism, but in addition to this fact, perhaps we also need to openly become more critical of one another. There are Pagan books out there in which the historical facts are just plain wrong, the reasoning is shot full of holes, the spells and ritual directions are dangerous, and everything else is either fluff or the same stuff that was published last year with a different title. This is not simply a matter of academic or scholastic professionalism—it is primarily a matter of pride and integrity, of preserving a meaningful Paganism into the future, and clearing a respectable place for it in the realm of popular discourse. We don't need to share everything—there is a great deal that cannot, and I would add, *should not* be put into writing—as I understand them, secrecy and silence are essential parts of Paganism. But again, this does not mean that we can say nothing meaningful at all.

In this book, we tried to say something meaningful. You will have to read it to see if you think that we have succeeded. For myself, I think that we have taken a big first step in the right direction. This is not supposed to be a definitive guide for Pagans living in the twenty-first century. It is simply supposed to invigorate a much-neglected realm of discussion for the printed Pagan word, to web together some scattered issues and explore the way in which they may not be scattered after all, to take a look at them from within Paganism, to take a look at the world and its problems from a perspective that honours and acknowledges the sacred aspects of our lives. If we have succeeded in doing these things, then we will have achieved our goal—we will have helped in the important task of further opening Pagan discourse into the twenty-first century; we will have inspired people to begin to dream an alternative future, and to dance and sing their visions through the veil, into a world that could really use a touch of magic.

THOM VAN DOOREN

The Ethics of Paganism
The Value and Power of Sacred Relationship

EMMA RESTALL ORR

Not so long ago, it was possible to define a community by the physical boundaries of a village, reaching out across the fields to include all that directly supported those who lived within it. For some time, even growing urbanization didn't induce much change in this respect; human perspectives remained tight, seldom stretching beyond the familiar, the tangible, and the understood. Those who did travel, leaving the close comfort of community, were conspicuously alone, without the silent affirmation of others to support their actions.

Yet over the course of the last few-score years, the reach of community has changed radically. With sudden ease of travel and global communication—telephone, satellite, internet—available to the strata of human society with the resources to use it, clearly defined communities have emerged that have nothing to do with geography or environment. Instead of boundaries laid down by physical horizons, communities are increasingly delineated by nothing but overt and specific common interest. Even in this era when people of quite different cultures and creeds might be sharing the same concrete and brick neighbourhood, no longer is there a need for those living within close proximity to affirm or even tolerate each others' beliefs. Furthermore, with our past and our dreams now often leading our focus elsewhere, no longer is behaviour informed by the local environment.

Immediately it is possible to see advantages from the new reality: individuals released from the constraints of parochial convention are better able to free their potential in self-expression and innovation; extrinsic information allows broader perspectives that rise above isolated self-interest. As quickly, though, we can perceive the counterbalancing disadvantages; there is now little need to find agreement or forge understanding with our neighbours. Self-defining communities, asserting their own ideas of acceptable behaviour, can positively affirm intolerance, narrow-mindedness, selfishness, and perversion on a global scale.

To my mind, the issue of ethics has consequently become of critical interest and concern. As the practical application of our beliefs and values, the way we judge right and wrong, the way we manage our passions, shared ethics are the glue that bonds a community; ethical disagreements tear people apart.

From my perspective as a priest of the modern Druid tradition, and as a Pagan facing this new century with all its environmental and social complexities, there seems little of more importance than just how we each behave, and why.

Although disagreements abound among academics, politicians, scientists, religious elders, and the media, each with their own agenda of personal investment, it can be globally accepted that there are questions about how humanity is using and abusing the natural wealth of this planet upon which it depends. In every direction we turn, there is doubt about the tenability of resources, from fresh water to rainforests, wild fish to fossil fuels. We could note the issues of global warming and rising sea levels, invulnerable viral strains emerging in response to our chemicals and medicines. I could load words with judgement and speak of the rapacious greed of consumerism, the insecurity of personal and political paranoia; I could look deeper into human need and the cravings for safety, familiarity, belonging, and acceptance that influence actions.

It is not in the debate on causes where we find most disagreement, however, but in the spread of solutions. Nor is it simply that I find myself unconvinced by most solutions presented. Where only problems are argued and the issues are torn apart to find clarity, yet no solutions are offered at all, the value of debate seems negligible. The critical issue now is surely not in the details of what is going wrong, but how we can get the vast tanker of humanity to turn before it wrecks itself and everything around it, smashing onto the rocks of its own evolutionary dead-end.

The solution lies, simply, in how we behave. On what basis of beliefs are we making decisions and prioritising? How are we judging value in order to justify the way that we live? What tenets are we and should we be using? And why?

As is in the nature of such debate, some of the words used here will need clear definition. However, my understanding of these key words will be given as an integral part of the chapter, for in many ways it is these definitions that express the solution I would offer.

When facing issues of behaviour, the first array of answers presented can be found beneath banners that assert some category of authority.

Primarily, the government, backed by its police and armed services, lays down and enforces laws regarding individual and collective (say, corporate) behaviour. An individual follows laws according to both awareness of the regulations and fear or respect of the authority. These rules deal with most—but not all—issues in ways that many can accept as just; however, the foundation of much of the legal system and legislation is motivated by political power and economic growth, not ethics. For example, in Britain, council tax (the amount paid to the local authority) may constitute 7 percent of the income of a family living in a tiny, crowded house, while someone with ten times the income, living in a house of luxury, could be paying a fifth of that percentage. What system of belief and value, what ethical base, does this legislation reveal in those who make up the government?

Beneath another banner of authority are the dictates of religious stricture. While politics may not always claim to be ethically sound, by their very nature religious organizations overtly claim the moral high ground, despite their beliefs and values often being complicated by political and historical issues.

Authority is embedded in the system, particularly within those religions based on the revealed word of a supreme deity. However, obeying the laws requires one to have allegiance to the religious hierarchy, from the priesthood to the ruling god, and thus to adhere to the dogmas. The danger emerges, furthermore, when a people's struggle to believe fully in an invisible, intangible, supernatural being leads them to transfer that belief, with its unquestioning allegiance and obedience, onto the dictates of a priesthood that is as humanly flawed as they are themselves. Without sufficient belief, many of those laws are easily broken. The Christian Bible's eighth commandment, "Thou shalt not steal," is a fine example, for most people eagerly get away with what they can, taking a little from the tax man, the hotel bathroom, the restaurant bill; fear of divine judgement stops some fingers pilfering, though for many even an underlying threat of eternal damnation is not enough.

My New International Version of the sixth commandment states, "You shall not commit murder." This is a good deal easier to keep to than the King James's I was taught as a child, "Thou shalt not kill," which deeply confused me: I knew the history of the Crusades, I'd seen the priest swat a wasp clean dead, and after church everybody openly savoured the meat that was their roasted Sunday feast. The original Hebrew uses the word *ratzach*, meaning "murder," but from a standpoint outside the Judeo-Christian faith, watching world events century upon century, it is clear that the killing of another human being can be acceptable if the religious authorities are on your side.

Taking just one of the 613 commandments that make up the canon of Judaic law, we could perceive the ban on eating shellfish as mere common sense in a desert climate. In fact, abstinence based on reason, science, or secular ethics is not acceptable within the core of that faith, nor is blind compliance with this or any other command- ment. The tradition asks specifically for conscious devotion to God, and as such clearly revels in the more obscure and irrational laws, for adherence here can only then be attributed to that devotion.

Of course, any law is open to interpretation, and most adjust their understanding to suit their own convenience. However, questioning and interpreting is not usually promoted. At the time of this writing, the new appointment of a gay man as a bishop in the Church of England is enraging many in that faith community, especially outside the context of British culture, for the Bible states sodomy to be an "abomination." However, the original Hebrew word in the context of Judaic law is considerably less disapproving of homosexuality than it is of gossip, deceit, and slander: far worse crimes. Furthermore, within these same scriptures can be found support for slavery, geno- cide, subjugation of women, capital punishment for adulterers—each attitude set within its own cultural and historical context. Questioning one thing can lead to all kinds of instability.

Moreover, questioning the laws is not something many would wish to do. To be given the law as a framework within which to live, laid out not by another human but by some supreme authority, allows unquestioned living. Faith communities develop, offering holistic support and affirmation backing that framework of laws. Where there is simply a low capacity to think, religious laws followed blindly with no understanding of their source will often degenerate into the irrational shudders of superstition—yet these, too, are beliefs affirmed by community.

Blind faith makes me uncomfortable; as a Pagan, I feel happier with an emphasis on consciousness and questioning. In the New Testament, Jesus does cry out for self-awareness, clarifying his perspective of the old sixth commandment teaching, elucidating that simply to be angry with someone is tantamount to murder in the eyes of the divine. However, this can easily take us back to the problem of behaviour being guided by the fear of a god one must believe in; without that belief, the precepts can be abandoned as meaningless restrictions.

As a priest myself, it might be expected that I would give equally clear rules based on my own understanding of the principles of Pagan Druidry. However, one of the many characteristics that so clearly distinguishes Paganism from the revealed religions is the lack of necessity to believe blindly in anything at all. As a spiritual tradition founded on the power of nature, the tenets guide the individual not into belief but into genuine experience, in order that each person may savour life's sanctity through his or her own physical, emotional, and spiritual senses. The emphasis is on personal reality within a web of connectivity.

It could be argued that this is simply mysticism, and so can be found at the heart of every faith. As a spirituality crushed by persecu-

tion for centuries, remaining true to itself only amongst dedicated individuals, Paganism in part has avoided corruption by the politics and
platitudes of everyday life. As it continues to grow at speed, though, it
is already possible to see its ideals being dulled by both secular and institutionalised spiritual values.

Even with this steady dilution, my hope is that the key difference
remains ever sharp: the lack of a divine command. This absence of
supreme authority is significant in my motivation to explore the subject of ethics within the tradition. Where around me, in the ethical
landscape, behaviour is guided or affirmed by an authoritative force,
asserted regulations, and religious fear, a Pagan mind like my own instinctively seeks out and questions the current of nature beneath the
rule. Curious to find the flow of nature's power that drives the need
to do or not do, I am perpetually troubled by what seems to be a
yawning gap in reason. It is the lazy parent's reply to a child's waking
wish to understand: "just because."

To the Pagan mind, rules are there to be questioned. It is never
sound simply to follow, for to do so is to abdicate our personal and
sacred responsibility as an individual and also as a part of society.
Sharing the existentialist's suspicion of the individual's submersion
into the collective, the Pagan emphasizes retaining personal moral responsibility. That's an uncomfortable path for many to walk. However, if we question and we agree, we are making a personal choice
as to how to respond and behave in each situation from an informed
position. If we disagree, we have still been through the process of
considering another's perspective and needs. Some rules exist simply
to express this general level of social consideration and common
sense, clearly delineating for those unable to see for themselves, such
as young children. There are many rules, though, that are the result of
somebody else's fear, and fear is never an intelligent motivation.

Where there is no religious or secular authority to guide our behaviour, in areas of life that are not considered socially, politically, or economically dangerous, we may use instinct to close that gap. These are decisions made without thinking, decisions that express deep beliefs and values. For example, a child who repeatedly tortures a pet cat for no apparent reason is considered psychotic, unable to empathize with the cat's pain and therefore unable to behave ethically towards it. For someone who is socialized within Western culture, it *feels* wrong to torture a cat.

It's an approach that leaves the issue wide open. We might declare it rational not to belch at the dinner table, divert a river, clear-cut an area of old-growth forest, nor eat a guinea pig, but such thought processes are culturally specific. Local priorities and insularity together with historical attitudes and justifications create the pathways of reason on which instincts are based. Like the interpretation of law, our instinct works in our own favour (as individual or community). We can use instinct to buy a cheap carpet, so protecting our own resources and securing our own survival, regardless of the child/slave labour used in its production.

A good deal of our behaviour, though, is based not on divine or secular rules nor on instinct, whether justified by logic or not; it is simply habit. Habit is the easy road of using attitudes and actions that have never been—or are no longer—fully considered; we could define instinct as evolved habituation, within a culture or an individual.

As human beings, we live by a subconscious blend of personal success tactics (what we can get away with) and institutionalized values, behaviour that is sufficiently acceptable within our society for us to get away with it. We are happy in our developed nations to condone the killing of lambs for food, but not puppies; we sustain the reality of marital infidelity, but can't cope with the idea of consensual polyamory. Society stamps its acceptance, and we need do nothing but respond fittingly and unquestioningly.

Not only does this allow us again not to have to think, but also sanctions our own comfort above ethical consideration. It leaves us again able to deny personal responsibility for our actions. Here, instead of the church or the government, society itself can take the blame as we shirk behind the asserted impotence of our tiny individuality amongst the masses. If someone else can do it, we can surely feel justified in doing it, too.

We do need habituation. Certainly, we often don't have time (or feel we don't have time) to consider every little thing we do. However, when we aren't evaluating each decision, it is even more important that those habituated responses and behaviours are based on *good* habits and on sound values (as yet here undefined), not just on social acceptability. For, in practice, not only do we do all we can get away with—and that, too, is socially acceptable—but we also learn about behaviour through observing what society accepts. In other words, social acceptability becomes a proxy for ethics.

So while I am not satisfied that sufficient reason is used to justify behaviour beneath the shadows of authority, the gap seems bridged here by little more than momentary conceit outside that shadow: instinct, intuition, and individual feelings of security. Most of the time, the reasons are deeply hidden in or even absent from the subconscious mind. We are still doing what we want to do, unthinking, "just because."

To assert an ethical code that extends beyond the self based on any of these things makes me uncomfortable, yet ethics are a critical part of every society. Even where the rules are unspoken, we depend upon an agreed ethical standard. It is this agreement that glues people together into what we call community, providing a sense of security, predictability, and comfortable expectation. Yet, it is also the comfort and safety of this agreement that engenders the overconfidence of pedantry and dogma, of overt, insidious, or subconscious prejudice, the cut-and-dried dualistic attitudes of good/bad, right/wrong. It induces arrogance, where one person or community believes itself in some way superior to another, an arrogance that has brought about wars throughout history.

In Paganism, the fundamental pluralism and focus on life as it is naturally lived leads to the acknowledgement of individual experience—and so an acceptance of individual realities, priorities, and visions. Living within different cultures, landscapes, and climates, rooted in different histories, bloodlines, and experiences, the spread of humanity is considerable. Individually, we are each a unique and complex tangle of beliefs and values; our tribal instinct reflects how clumsily and cautiously we bring individual idiosyncrasy into the behavioural agreements that create the communities within which we choose to live.

How can we make an ethical code that has any universal validity?

Religions try.

Let's return to the idea of religion and its role in ethical coding, but begin by offering a definition. With a broad view, religion is the way in which a culture engages with its concept of superhuman entities or powers. A religion offers the language, imagery, and laws relating to what is not understood. While death may be one of the few fundamental powers of nature still beyond our grasp, to our distant ancestors the mysteries of fire, fertility, birth, healing, and so on were also completely in the hands of the gods. For modern Pagans celebrating nature through both scientific knowledge and religious mystery, these gods *are* those powers of nature.

The word *Pagan* can itself be poignantly defined by reaching back into the Roman context of the word *pagus*, a village community, one that was reliant upon the cycles of nature for its wealth and well-being. Such communities required intricate understanding of natural lore/law for survival and guidance. The alternative source of law is through human authority.

Where religions become powerful, their politics comes not from connection with the environment but directly from law sourced in humanity's social mind, law that is so distinctly different from that of the pagus. Although some in the Pagan tradition would object to my words, the foundation of my definition of Paganism itself means that spiritual and religious paths that do not look clearly to the flows of nature for guidance are not Pagan.

The use of religious authority is pervasive: priests and other proponents use their apparent status with the "superbeings" (those who have or are attributed even more power) as an indirect form of communicating control over the people. So do they establish and maintain ethical standards that are no more than restraints on behaviour: means of controlling the community that has been led into belief.

When the ruling class of a society feels at ease, those controls become looser. In Classical Rome, albeit a patriarchal culture, the moral codes were at their most flexible at the height of the empire; as threat moved in, required morality became tighter. Class boundaries became more important, with the ruling elite needing to affirm bloodlines, hold wealth more securely, and control more brutally. Happening at the time that it did, it can be said that the conversion to Christianity of the Roman Empire simply instilled into the new faith a morality born of the fear of decline and fall.

The Genesis quote that is most used by Pagans in conflict with Christian morality is that God gives man "dominion" or "mastery" to "rule over" the earth and every living thing.[1] It is an issue I have raised many times with priests and students of the Christian tradition, asking about the original text and the historical flow of its translation and interpretation. Few have any idea, which leaves me feeling that, whatever the writers meant, the modern usage appears more important to Christians now. In fact, the Hebrew is complicated, but perhaps the most powerful word used is *kev'shehah*: the word translates as "conquer it." It is an unambiguous command, having a grammatical ending that makes the task a male fighting obligation.

There are now apologists amongst liberal and organic Christians who are keen to retranslate the word into acceptable language, speaking of humanity as *caretakers* or *stewards* of creation. The pre-eminent Jewish rabbi Maimonides speaks considerably on this issue, pushing the point that this gift of nature given by God to humanity does indeed require a tremendous responsibility of care, and I can accept this as a theologian's intelligent interpretation. With imagination, too, I can place the phrase into its historical context of prescientific struggle against a changing and harsh climate, an untamed environment. However, such words are now surely irrelevant; the situation has changed. Humanity certainly has sufficient wit to be dominant, but does it have the wisdom not to destroy?

To Pagans, the difference between mastery and stewardship with care is barely relevant, for both still affirm a hierarchy within the natural world, with human beings somehow on top. The Christian word *sin* can be defined from its roots as action consequential to a spiritual separation from God; from the Pagan perspective, the biblical concept of human dominion over nature is the epitome of sin, for it expresses clearly an asserted separation between humankind and nature.

The Islamic *fitra* feels, at first, easier to accept. Conveying the idea of a state of being that is perfectly placed within time and space, in total connection with God's creation, its boundaries exist to actively hold back the human instinct to dominate. However, the constraining force is the religious allegiance to Allah; the Pagan perceives not only an unnecessary concept of authority, but submission provoked by fear of the deity and his priests' reaction to transgressions. On a day-to-day level, this may reflect institutionalised values, not Islamic mysticism, yet to the Pagan, the separation from nature is still seen as fundamentally intrinsic to the faith.

Are ethics possible without God, without the ultimate authority of a single supreme deity? Do we have to use the force of threat from a governing body, human or superhuman, in order to ensure that we behave well?

My Pagan mindset perceives monotheism as just another part of the human craving for monism: one nation, one god, one code of morality. The simpler the rules, the simpler it is to understand them and stay out of trouble. Equally, the simpler it is to rule with one sweep of the brush, to have to judge an action within a cultural context that is different from one's own with validity, can be impossible. Table manners, relationship ethics, business etiquette and terrorism all fall into this complex box. Monist leaders—whether of governments or households—pay no attention to the context of others' behaviour.

Such acceptance, however, is inevitable within Paganism. Understanding that each person is utterly individual, holding within himself the history, strengths, and weaknesses of his ancestors, the wisdom of his home environment, the Pagan does not look to the authority of the creator, nor the subject and subjected of creation; instead his focus is on the flow of ongoing creativity. Within this pluralist mindset, polytheism is a natural idea: instead of one supreme power, the energy of life, independently conscious, purposeful, and even caring, the universe to the Pagan is a weave of innumerable forces—currents, tides, and cycles, each creating the ever-changing pattern of nature, each spirit playing with the creativity of matter. Pagan gods may have names given them from myths told and retold, but essentially they are no more than spirits of nature, of thunder and fertility, anger and rebirth, lakes and germination, love and moon, and so on.

Not dependent on revealed nor channelled scriptures outlining codes of behaviour, to someone of a monotheistic or mainstream religion Paganism can appear anarchic, held together by such loose threads it seems simply a poetic vision that declares it coherent. Yet what holds it together is as loose and as potent as the lay of the land, as hills that slide into valleys and beyond. Its diversity, which of itself teaches acceptance of diversity, is exactly what gives it its subtle strength of coherence. Encouraging us to find our own truth and to live by it, is an official sanction for anarchy; yet, the philosophy is held within a framework of connectivity, for landscapes meet landscapes, energy flows into energy, rivers meet and merge, nature touches nature.

Paganism doesn't address the human craving for simplicity by streamlining society down one path of acceptability. It seeks to move beyond fear by facing life in its light, darkness, and shadows, making relationships that are enriched with those definitively human tools of art, language, and ritual.

Not only do I feel that ethics are potentially valid without God, but I feel that the monotheistic system actually hampers the way individuals are able to understand or live ethically. The very issue of force of authority limits or negates any need for personal investment or responsibility.

I speak as a priest, yet I welcome the question that must be raised as to whether there can be a valid ethical code without religious backing at all. In the eighteenth century, the German philosopher Immanuel Kant declared that all morality had to be built not only on belief in God, but also on a social framework within which the moral law is asserted. Thomas Hobbes, perhaps the first materialist of our heritage of philosophy, denied the existence of God in the seventeenth century and declared that the only way society could function, alleviating the acute human fear of death, was for individuals to submit to the greater human power of government. I disagree with both: morality is possible without a superhuman authority, as is it possible without any other kind of authoritarian governance. Yet is it possible without the power of mystery?

Using the logic of René Descartes in the late seventeenth century, Benedict Spinoza brought the concept of the infinite power of God out of the limitations of dualism, expressing ideas that are easier for most Pagans to understand: those of pantheism. Focused with a mathematical precision, much of Spinoza's specific ideas now feel out of synch with twenty-first-century perspectives, but his best-known and well-quoted phrase, *sub specie aeternitatis*, inspires us to perceive our own reality through the wider vision, from the standpoint of eternity, where every thread and touch of connection is in view. This is what we so often fail to do.

Humanity's ignorant and anthropocentric mentality is fast driving us into crisis. Our inability or unwillingness to abstract a broad enough vision of time and space, of cause and effect, holds us on that dead-end course. Animal instincts of survival, combined with the chattering of the fearful, self-conscious mind, create behaviour patterns that are locked in selfish, short-term visions.

Yet, to bridge the insufficiency in our vision, we do not seek the wider mystery; we impose human/superhuman laws. They aren't working.

Rights are a powerful issue: human rights, animal rights. Though entirely a human construct, this fact is often mislaid, the one advancing the case often behaving as if he were presenting the perspective of some higher and incontrovertible authority. Such ideas, too, come from minds that dwell some distance from the edge of trauma, where there is time to consider what should be done for or to those actually in the thick of crisis; for when we are balancing on the precipice, much lower instincts kick in. When we need to survive, we make quick decisions that can easily trash any thought-out ideas of "rights."

Furthermore, rights are based entirely on decisions made about what deserves consideration. As such, integral within their makeup are the deepest prejudices of a society or individual. Science steps in to guide us as to whether something physically responds as if it "feels pain." We contemplate, too, whether it might feel desire, as if desire and pain were sufficient measures for us to acknowledge whether something has enough consciousness to deserve consideration. The modern philosopher Peter Singer, who is credited with the term "animal liberation" from his 1975 book of the same name, declares that all animals are entitled to equal status. Yet even he draws a line, determining what he perceives has no consciousness and is therefore without rights and open to human consumerism.

Rights codify the personal, creating a social framework of rules on which we can rest easy. It is an attempt to universalise a human perspective on life. With ethical behaviour based on rights, then, we face the countless problems of social and personal history that form beliefs about what deserves to live and in what conditions. Attitudes towards live-animal export, slave labour, circumcision, and fox hunting are changing in Britain; battery hens, animal experimentation, and the "collateral damage" of modern warfare are still widely accepted.

The assertion of rights can be seen as a way of establishing new social values: ethics that can be accepted without much thought or comprehension. Where we are in the midst of the trauma, we might respond instinctively; at a distance, we may be able to retain a sense that the issue is not our business, not our responsibility, and therefore we are beyond culpability. We let others decide who or what has rights and sate our greed on the rest.

My scepticism about the ethics of "rights" is evident.

Consent is another way of dealing with the issue. Agreement made between two sane adults can override expectations, conventions, and even instinct, allowing a behaviour that might be deemed unethical by others. Euthanasia is a key example, as are DNR ("do not resuscitate") orders and living wills that allow a dying person to pass away without further medical intervention. While to some the idea of mercifully and consensually ending a life is sound, others may feel that ethics (whether social or divine) transcend consent.

Abortion lies on the same tack; however, the problem may be posed that the consent is between doctor and mother to end the potential life of the foetus, not with the foetus itself. Does this negate the idea of consent? Where there is not sufficient sharing of consciousness or understanding, consent is not possible. Could a calf consent to die in an abattoir? Overwhelmed by force, in the hands of killers, with the only options being brutalisation or death, perhaps I would consent, too.

Further flawing consent between human beings is that sanity and clarity of cognisance cannot be scientifically measured; we can be (self-)destructive, (self-)negating, crippled by insecurity and lack of (self-)value. When a man agrees or even offers his body to be whipped by a dominatrix, is he making a journey into self-discovery or expressing self-loathing?

In addition, where we may believe we share understanding, too often we are simply perceiving through projections of our own needs, attitudes, and assumptions.

Emmanuel Levinas, the twentieth-century French thinker, criticized philosophy as being solely concerned with how humanity views the world, when clearly those perceptions are taken into and lost in the mind. Only is it in the exploration of ethics, he wrote, that there is acknowledgement of an "other" outside the self; the study of ethics is about consideration of how to deal with that other.

Some argue that very many psychoanalytical and psychotherapeutic models promote the same mistake. Indeed, there are also some within religious communities, including Paganism, who perceive the divine, spirits, and ancestors to be figments of our imagination, simple tools of personal development and inner healing. This idea does not lie within my definition of Paganism, nor is it conducive to sound behaviour: there is no connection, thus no communication, and no opportunity for respect.

Empathy is the next word I would raise here, an important word within Pagan vision and important, too, where lack of communication disallows behaviour based on consent. Between adults across cultures, where language and customs limit understanding, there can still be a natural human empathy: we recognise expression of pain, grief, and joy, and we feel it, too. With children unable to express their needs, and even with animals, we can perceive emotional responses and respond sympathetically. Even with creatures without faces, we can observe: the lobster dropped into the pot of boiling water, the tree creaking under the scream of the chainsaw; some of us feel the pain. Inherently what we want for ourselves (safety, comfort, assurance, freedom . . .) we want for others with whom we feel somehow connected.

But what of those aspects of creation with which we can't relate?

Is it acceptable to abuse or condone the abuse of people whom we don't know or understand? Our culture turns its blind eye to the likes of Nestlé, Nike, and Gap, because those being abused for our luxury items are generally across the world and are of a different race and culture. Those who support these companies aren't admitting to unethical behaviour; they are presenting their own brand of ethics based on money, an ethical code that clearly reveals a complete lack of connection or empathy.

In the same way do we accept abuse of animals in laboratory testing for pharmaceutics and toiletries, for the dairy industry, for pet foods? Once again, our culture turns away from the reality of chimpanzees perforated with wires and tubes, the screams of the milking cows as the calves are taken from them to be slaughtered or sold into the horrific life of the veal crate, because if we were to witness such scenes and empathize we could not benefit from the products their torturers sell us.

Our culture condones the killing of people in wars across the world, our elected governments playing their violent games of power; we condone the slaughter of animals for medicines, meat, and leisure, and the myriad trades that pollute and consume the natural world; we support the annihilation of forests by clear-cutting trees, causing the extinction of species by the hour. The only way this is humanly possible is without empathy, without connection.

Yet what about the mussels thrown into the bouillabaisse, the rat that dies twisted in the poisoned trap, the cockroach crushed underfoot, the old mahogany or sequoia crashing to the ground? Everyone's empathy runs out somewhere.

In our language we use euphemisms to maintain the lack of connection needed for us to continue within the comfortable limits of our blinkers: the "collateral damage" of war doesn't describe the screeching of a mother holding her dismembered child, nor does the clean, plastic-wrapped hunk of bacon reveal to us the squeal of terror, the smell of burning flesh and bristle, the pig's severed muscles running with blood. Values are altered, allowing us to feel we are not to blame. The culinary use of the French term *fruits de mer* ("fruits of the sea") for a plate of boiled marine mollusks and crustaceans tells no truth whatsoever.

Empathy as a source of ethics relies on care, and care requires connection. Yet we are so skilled at denial and selective ignorance, all empathy truly shows is once again the reality of our prejudice and judgement, determining what is conscious and deserving of consideration.

So do we return to rights. Where consent and empathy work as guidelines for behaviour, they are still based on personal interaction. Where there is insufficient caring on a personal level, our society fills the gap with rights.

My discomfort with this is acute. Offering certificates of moral territory, rights become causes of conflict at every boundary. The farmer may claim his right to defend his livelihood from predation; the hunt saboteur claims the right of the fox to life. Yet, necessarily anthropocentric (the fox has no notion of this right fought on his behalf), the authority of that territory is sourced in human judgement.

From the spiritual perspective of my religion, all life is sacred and equally so. While valuing one life to the detriment of another can be necessarily a part of life's prioritizing, too often such decisions are based on greed and selfishness, on unnecessary personal gratification, most often pompously disguised for the sake of pacification and coercion.

As a Pagan and a priest, however, I would not be protesting the killing of a rabbit in a pharmaceutical lab, a calf in the meat industry, or an innocent citizen in some foreign war on the ethical grounds that life is sacred. Life *is* sacred. The Pagan animistic vision perceives all the world to be imbued with life energy. Where that energy flows, it forms patterns of spirit, each eddy and current finding its own identity, its individual journey, its intention of flow; the cohesion of its being, we might call its "soul" or "consciousness," albeit perhaps far removed from anything we might humanly perceive. As the soul journeys, upon its way it leaves footprints: trails of its creativity, of its physicality and mortality. Every body of water, of bones, fur, or feathers, of bark and sap, every mountain and breath of wind, is an expression of spirit, utterly sacred.

But the argument is brittle. Because I see all life as sacred creativity, I may believe it is wrong to kill unnecessarily; yet any person of any other belief could very easily and quickly disagree.

Where is the universal ethic? Using religious ethics of any tradition—even my own—is of no more use than political or cultural values; another rational argument can just tear it apart.

Abandoning religious tenets, the secular base of rights, legalities, and instinct, the quest brings us to personal responsibility upon yet another tack: sustainable relationship is a concept increasingly raised.

Most often presented in terms of cause and effect, this perspective declares that if we behave in a certain way we have more chance of maintaining the tenability of a situation. With reference to environmentalism, the ideas most widely used are human-centred; we must not destroy the rainforests because in doing so we would negatively affect our own survival through global warming and loss of natural resources for medicine and technologies. Where human behaviour is addressed to ensure the survival of a penguin or sticky green beetle, the logic may be just as strong, but the argument less persuasive. Reflected on a personal level, we can clearly see the self-interest: care for your partner or she might walk out on you, taking the house and the kids.

In sustainable relationship, the word *sustainable* is the one usually emphasized and, as a result, it argues logic; like any consequentialist perspective, someone else can always take the same facts and manipulate them to back another view. Enlightened self-interest may be a powerful motivation for ethical behaviour, but finding agreement is hard, for political, social, local, and personal priorities are just too diverse. In the end, a judgement is inevitable. We see it in poignant and painful decisions about damming rivers, allocating medical funding, and the custody of children.

Even where the logic is flawless, it seems to me that we are simply returning to a fear-based, metareligious standpoint, where the powers of nature will overwhelm us (human, superhuman, nonhuman) if we continue doing wrong. Gaia becomes a modern Yahweh, threatening to annihilate humanity if we don't behave, if we don't do what we're told. In this way, governments and protest groups are using science instead of divine judgement to guide or control our behaviour through fear of consequences.

That may reflect a passive and reactive human mentality, the more objective logical view stating simply that human mismanagement may lead to human extinction without need for any concept of a punitive higher force. However, that fearful reaction is a strong part of our psyche; an instinct within us seeks out the one in charge—the parent, boss, or deity, the one who holds the power and the culpability: the ape higher up the tree. We need someone to take responsibility for what has been done.

My argument is that fear is never a tenable motivation for ethical behaviour. Regardless of any good intention, clarity of vision, or caring, if fear is involved on any level, the guidance is flawed. As human beings, we are forever seeking ways to sneak away from fear by using the escapism of drugs and alcohol, or through the stupefying power of screen entertainment. We are always finding ways to rebel and to cheat the fear-inducing authority. Indeed, beating the fear is more important than following the rules or erasing the cause of the fear; immediate relief is the primary focus.

This is particularly true when the cause seems too big for one person's actions to make a difference, either positively or negatively. We know it is illegal to avoid paying taxes, and most would agree that taxes are an efficient way of collecting funds for general social services; however, the majority would also cheat the system at any glint of an opportunity, simply because in doing so we gain a moment's increase in ease.

Socrates, much of whose philosophy lies so fundamentally beneath modern Western society, when judged to be against the Athenian state with his constant questioning of ethics, chose to accept the punishment meted out to him, drinking the hemlock rather than escaping. In clear contrast, few in our society of pathological comfort are willing to live by an ethical standard if it means making an effort; a good number would jump at the chance of beating an authority or winning a little coup on the side.

Any utilitarian basis for behaviour is always going to be complicated with the fear of possible effects, prioritizing judgements, lo-
calized self-interest, and denied culpability. Not many of us have
Socrates's integrity.

I have laid out a number of solutions and guidelines for ethical behaviour, all of which are in active play, all of which are failing. I return to the question: is it possible to have a code of ethics that is inclusive, universal, and effective?

In Paganism, particularly in Pagan spiritualities based on the oral
tradition, the emphasis on the uniqueness of the individual is paramount. Each situation, in its distinct location, witnessed by the spirits
of place, the gods, the powers of nature, the elements, the ancestors,
sliding through a unique moment in time, further adds to the context
within which that individual's action might be judged. It might seem
that this is hardly the place to find a broad-spectrum code of ethics.
However, simply because diversity is such an integral part of the philosophy of the tradition, this is exactly what we do find.

On what basis does the Pagan make his choices?

What are his defining ethics?

At this point, I speak from my own tradition of Paganism: Druidry,
within which there is no stated code of ethics. At the heart of its
teachings, instead, lies a powerful word: *honour.* For those who first
encounter it, the word is pretty hard to grasp; in time, perhaps, we
come to feel we understand its guidance, but the deeper we get into
our studies, the more elusive its core truth once more becomes. Like
love, it is a part of the mysteries and, as such, as a label on the outside of the spiritual box its usefulness is almost notional.

I risk here a simple explanation in this context. Our behaviour
expresses clearly our attitude to nature within and around us. There

is only honour in our interaction with those around us—and with ourselves—when we recognize the essence, the spirit or life energy.

Thus, relationship is the word emphasized in "sustainable relationship." In Pagan Druidry, relationship is paramount; it is relationship based on the acknowledgement of spirit.

Within that animistic vision of reality, where every part of creation shimmers with life, a current of energy flows with its own purpose, so giving individual identity—as oak tree, river otter, easterly wind—no spirit is isolated. Energy isn't held inside boxes of flesh or bark or stone. Naturally, continually, spirit touches spirit. Our human insecurity encourages us to be separate, to hold in tight and be safe, yet a deeper craving is for connection. The animistic teaching simply guides us to wake to the way that we are ever touching and touched, each one of us naturally integrated into the web of life. Myriad golden threads hum with the sacred song of life; it is a magical vision. As a simple, prosaic scientific perspective, it offers the individual a profound sense of belonging, of acceptance. On a social level, it is an attitude that instills a quiet strength, confidence, and cooperation within a culture.

In religious terminology, perceiving the spirit wakes us to the sacred nature of life. However, if that language cannot be translated from the jargon, it is valueless beyond the bounds of that religious perspective. Spirit is not some ethereal meta-angelic entity; it is simply the power of life, energy held temporarily within a cohesive, coherent form. We need no metaphor or mythology (though many may love the poetry of such), for the idea in itself is awe-inspiring enough.

Nor do we need some psychic vision to perceive the energy of spirit. We see it in the glint of a young girl's eye. We feel it in the vibrance of a blackbird's song, in the kick of a hare's dash, the leaves of a tree bathing in sunshine. We are usually just too busy, preoccupied, or apathetic to notice.

The words *animism, pantheism,* and *polytheism* carry with them connotations of primitive society, yet this is simply residue of the militant arrogance of political Christianity and Islam. As natural spiritual philosophies and perspectives of life, the essential tenets of these ideas have evolved with human thought, while not losing their fundamental principles. Sourced in human awe at the powers of nature, scientific discovery only goes to deepen the profound respect for nature that is integral to these traditions. Rooted in the value of ecosystems, localism, diversity, natural balance, an understanding of the cycles, of influence and impact, of decay and regeneration, the principles of these philosophies are acutely pertinent to human society today. They address issues of sufficiency and sustainability, of respect for nature, community, and culture; they question all that is based on greed and unnecessary consumption and growth.

Poignantly, the significant value of relationship that evolves from this perspective is that behaviour is no longer motivated by fear. The quest is not to store up supplies and favours (with neighbours or superbeings) in case that ever-perceived threat does collapse into fact; the Pagan Druid is seeking ways to deepen and strengthen his every relationship, better understanding the currents, tides and eddies of nature's energy, so enabling him to live more effectively in harmony—in both winter and summer, with birthing and dying, growth and decay. Not pushing against the flow, he learns to ride it, finding inspiration in the challenge of life on calm or wild rivers, ecstasy of attunement to the high seas and deep water. He finds freedom, an inner serenity, beyond friction.

While we are conventionally taught that our actions inevitably have effects that we must deal with, either by ducking the negative or grabbing the positive, the Druid is not anticipating feedback resulting from his behaviour. Making decisions based on the wider vision of integral connection, he accepts responsibility for the impact of behaviour, yet his personal gain is entirely based on the sense of immediate internal satisfaction that comes of walking in perfect harmony.

A term I use for interaction based on this wakefulness both to spirit and the web of connection is "sacred relationship," and I see it as fundamental to Druidic and Pagan vision, and to the issue of ethics. It brings us back to three issues raised here already: consent, empathy, and sustainability. These, however, are now no longer the focus in the search for a solution; instead, they are the effects of sacred relationship, the successful result. How?

When we are open to perceiving our own life energy, we cannot help but feel our true state of health and well-being. Our ego, fed on insecurity, may allow us a dram of self-delusion temporarily; if it persists, it is a measure of how little we are truly open, and as our general culture is one of escapism and denial, it is not surprising that to open is considered difficult, dangerous, and strange. It can be hard to face our own truth after a lifetime's conditioning. It can take a lifetime of small steps to reach a place where we feel ourselves completely. It is a poignant responsibility to teach our children not to shy away and hide their truth.

Awake to ourselves, feeling our own honesty in its brilliance and tenderness, with our feet upon the ground, our perception of others' truth and lies rises equally. We see others for who they are beneath the guise they try to present; we see their shimmering, trembling spirit, the ebb and flow of their desire and their fear. We see what nourishes and strengthens. So are we better able to use consent as a guide for behaviour.

In the same way, seeing another's soul or intention more clearly, the purpose as the current of the spirit energy, our ability to empathize increases. As we learn to glide high winds, to raft white water, in harmony, spirit to spirit, so can we step into the flow of another soul for a moment, with our minds, sensing the quality of the currents and pressures, allowing us to journey for a while in peace, in pace beside them.

In acutely seeing the spirit and flow of another soul, our ability to behave appropriately is also increased. We can communicate in a way that touches the other, the level of relevance and respect reflecting in the efficacy of the interaction. By holding a stronger focus on the relationship than on the yield and profit, the sustainability of the relationship is always going to be better, both parties honouring each other in the balance of harmony.

The issue of sustainable relationship is further improved, because the key flaw in human-based ethics, the individual's selfish/survival instinct, is put into the wider perspective of the whole web of spirit. Our consciousness of the broad picture is increased simply by perceiving the essence, the life energy or spirit.

Certainty is something that we have always sought in terms of the decisions we make about our behaviour and about the ethics of what we do. Prevarication and doubt undermine instinctive reactions as much as they allow other consequentialist arguments to break up our own rationale. However, seeking moral certainty on a personal level is not based on causality or blind faith in Paganism, nor through discipline, rules and restraints, denial and dictates. Moral certainty is found through positively-motivated sources, in awareness of connection, acceptance, and belonging based on good relationship; it is found in and reflects back into enthusiasm for life and active presence. It is about opting in, not opting out.

In Pagan terms, moral certainty is a principle utterly rooted in the wisdom of the ancestors and the songs of the earth. In other words, it consciously seeks out all we have learned as a species, living between our forefathers and our descendants, living in the valleys and hills of our homelands, in relationship with the earth that feeds us, the skies and the seas, and distilling that understanding into one vision: honour.

To then transfer the individual vision effectively into a social value is essential if we are to initiate the changes needed to create a tenable future for humanity. Yet the only way that this can be done is through the action of individuals. So how does the Pagan behave? The nature of the oral tradition requires that he "walks his talk." The value of any mysticism or philosophy is only discovered if it is lived. That is why Levinas spoke of ethics as the only valid school of philosophy; only through ethics do we move beyond self-focused pondering and into arenas of interaction.

To lay out a list of rules here that a Pagan would aim to follow would be anathema, and in contradiction to all I have expressed. All I can give with any validity are examples of how Pagans (within the context of how I have defined modern Paganism) might affirm their values, expressing the inspiration they have sourced in sacred relationships as a part of ongoing honourable interaction.

Fully perceiving a landscape, the spirits that populate that place, those we see as trees, plants, and grasses, insects and animals, birds, winds, water courses, rocks and mud, human beings, and so much more, and those perhaps we can't see, as air spirits, ancestors, the Pagan wholly engages with that place. He also has a more acute perception of how places differ, not only physically, but energetically; by more poignantly feeling the particular and distinct beauty, the power and the fragility of a place, the Pagan honours, stepping more gently, respectfully, making no unnecessary impact. He is not likely to drop litter, to break branches or knock the heads of the flowers, nor to create noise or light pollution needlessly—not because of some legislation or social law, but simply because it would be disrespectful to those affected, seen and unseen. Nor would he vandalize property, deface buildings or damage walls, without good reason and clearly communicated intent (e.g., objection to forest clear-cutting sprayed over the timber company's machinery).

The acceptance of cultural diversity is a further result of acknowledging local spirits of place, for amongst those spirits are a community's tribal ancestry. The stories of a place, still humming in the wind, in memories and mythologies, in the cut of a field or the placing of a building, tell the history of all that has lived in that locality. Understanding the twisted roads of history helps us to accept the present, guiding us as to how to respond. So would a Pagan study the old stories, the past, in order to evaluate what would be ethical and appropriate behaviour now. Celebrating the depth of cultural language and tradition in his own community, the Pagan celebrates and honours the differences he encounters in others, too.

Honouring individuality, of course, comes from this perception of spirit, also. Acknowledging the important influences of landscapes and ancestry, along with the inimitable blend of physical elements and chemicals, as well as each individual's singular life experience, every person is expected to be idiosyncratically unique. The restrictions of convention are not entertained by the Pagan. Freedom of personal expression, of soul-truth, is perceived as glorious. All that might hold that freedom in check should be clear and wakeful consciousness of the web, of energy touching energy, and of integrated connectivity that allows a vision broader than self-centric greed and protectionism.

One of the key taboos in our Western culture is still about sex and sexuality. Gender identity to the Pagan is an essential part of personal creativity, and if that leads to transvestism or transsexuality there would be no judgement, but instead a celebration of a soul's true expression. As the spirit is considered more important than the physical body, the issue of sexuality is irrelevant; whether the lovers are of different genders or not matters not a jot to the Pagan. A Pagan would honour the tenderness of a person who over-asserts his or her sexuality due to needs of (majority or minority) group identity in order to protect his or her own fearful soul, for such behavior is sad to witness. However, Pagans make no judgement on those who express their sexual identities purely as celebration.

Honesty to oneself and to others is always valued more highly that keeping to the rules (of government or society). So while infidelity would be considered unethical to the Pagan, consensual polyamory is likely to be easily accepted. In the same way, the social expectations about having a partner, having children, and so on, are equally dismissed as imposed restrictions and potentially irrelevant to the individual.

The distinction between personal sacred relationship and political relationship is important in Paganism, too, returning to the issue of authority raised earlier in the essay. In political circumstances, our relationships are far from spirit to spirit; instead, we are communicating, directly or indirectly, with an abstract. We might perceive that abstract to have more or less power than ourselves, but either way we respond accordingly without seeing distinct individuals. We rant and complain and hurl abuse at government, officialdom, and authority: whoever we feel is in control. If an individual representing that abstract authority does come before us, we use him as a target, a tangible front for the untouchable power behind, not reaching to touch his spirit, but attacking the authority behind. In the same way, if we feel we have enough power not to have to care about individuals, we might abuse the workers, the voters, the consumers, the taxpayers: in short, the faceless masses.

Political relationship is ineffective communication and dishonourable interaction. It is untenable, mercenary, and capricious. Changes might be made, but not on account of any positive motivation; the impetus for change in the underdog is fear of the authority's power, and in the authority itself, the impetus is simply fear of losing that power. Behaviour based on political relationship is never in line with Pagan ethics.

By honouring the web of connection, we might acknowledge the power of an abstract, but decisions and communication are ethically made only through personal and sacred relationship. Only in this way can we be sure that those decisions, that behaviour, is life affirming and honourable.

We can see here a reflection in the Pagan understanding of deity— for deity in Paganism is not about authority, neither as monotheistic dictatorship nor as polytheistic oligarchy. The gods are powers of nature, wind, earth, sea, and thunder, energies about which we build understanding. We don't submit, cowering in fear; we stand in our own strength and laugh, sharing the energy of who we are, with profound respect (without which the natural world easily kills) but also with joy, confidence, and dignity, connecting and cooperating.

The stronger our relationships with the gods become, and the stronger our ability to live in harmony with the flow of nature, the more confidence we gain, the more strength to share and laugh and stand in our stillness. In consequence, too, not only do we feel more able to express our own truth in freedom, but our vision of the web of spirit grows clearer, allowing us a broad perspective that we might see the effects of our actions, shimmering across the web.

Pagan ethics relating to the food industry can be meticulous. In Britain, the majority of Pagans are vegetarian or vegan, and those who do support dairy or meat farming do so without blinkers, buying only free-range and organic products. I myself am vegan, as my own ethical standard does not allow me to invest in what seems to me flagrant abuse of other creatures. While my code does not declare the killing of animals to always be wrong, to kill unnecessarily is beyond my ability to accept.

The social habituation of Western culture that celebrates the slaughter of calves but not puppies is to me an expression of a blinkered lack of ethics. Peter Singer's statement that all creatures deserve equal consideration is entirely Pagan; the Pagan would take it further, to include forests, landscapes, and the earth itself. The riposte to "Where do we draw the line?" is one that reflects lack of understanding in the questioner, for there is no line—there is only relationship. If a line is drawn it simply marks the limitation of our human perception.

With an animistic vision, it is possible to reach the spirit that flows in each item that we touch. In an apple, we can feel the energy of the tree: vibrant, sweet, and tempting us to eat. In nuts, seeds, and grains, we are aware of the intention to reproduce. Processed foods with chemical additives make no sense to the Pagan, ethically or spiritually.

The animist feels the environment, too, the specific web of an ecosystem from which the food has come. To buy genetically modified crops, or agroindustrial crops sprayed with environmental toxins developed by companies that are polluting landscapes and water courses, using animal testing, and abusing their workforce is to the Pagan as unethical as eating battery-farmed eggs. Thus, organic food become the ethical choice: food grown on small farms, on local farms, or in one's own garden.

Human slavery is rife, notably in cocoa, coffee, sugar, and cotton industries, and companies that promote the horrors of this abuse of humanity with pitiful trade agreements, child labour, and inhumane conditions are all avoided by the wakeful Pagan.

Killing for food is ethically dubious; killing for beauty is beyond tolerance. The Pagan would be ethically unable to buy any toiletries, from lipstick to shampoo, that had been tested on animals or contained animal products. The pharmaceutical industry is one of the dirtiest in the world, in terms of ethics, and the Pagan would carefully have to weigh up priorities before taking any drugs forged by these companies. Petrochemical companies, the car industry, electrical appliances—all these the Pagan would think twice about supporting, always looking to find the most renewable, recyclable, low-consumption alternatives.

As he honours the spirit of others around him, so does the Pagan honour his own health and well-being. Here, ethics are about stepping beyond the self-destructive habits that our secular society considers acceptable, from drugs and alcohol to overeating and apathy. The Pagan will celebrate his own body as an expression of his creativity, regardless of how others might judge it. As he takes responsibility for his own living, so would the Pagan take responsibility for his own dying, retaining the right to end his life if he should choose, though ever-conscious of the web of relationships to which he is connected. He honours that others have that same right, most usually when disease makes living too painful to bear. Once again, ethical decisions are based on acknowledging the pure spirit of life.

What causes us to fail to make ethical choices is often lack of information or understanding, and an important part of the Pagan's spiritual journey, therefore, is education. Conscious choice is critical, and so is continual learning. We must keep our minds open to watching, questioning, engaging, ever-seeking understanding. The Pagan ethic here is based on the responsibility of the individual to be aware and act appropriately.

As a parent, the Pagan doesn't delegate responsibility for his child's education, but takes care that the child is in environments that nurture her growing vision, allowing her the confidence and self-esteem to express her own truth and creativity. For me, that means home education, ensuring that my son has opportunities to explore and discover in his own way, following personal interests in his own time, at his own pace, unbattered by the culture of competitive bullying.

Beyond our own direct actions, what could be more important than to bring up our children as human beings who are awake and responsible, who will care for this earth and bring beauty to others?

Finding this animistic vision of shimmering spirit, of life energy in everything, is an integral part of the journey of the Pagan. As a tradition that was originally only practised by a priesthood, the proportion studying the deep mysteries rather than simply living as a part of the faith community is greater than usual in spiritual and religious denominations. Perhaps also common to most Paganisms, the seeker does not have a priest whose role it is to act as medium between himself and the gods or the divine: he is expected to make that connection himself, creating a relationship that is personal, often very private and intimate.

For some, seeing the energy of spirit is instinctive; for some, it has been nurtured by parents and life experience. However, for most people living in a secular consumerist world, "the Pagan vision" is hard to grasp as an intellectual concept, let alone as a way of life. It requires the breaking down of inner barriers of belief and internalized social judgement. Slowly, confidence grows in our own perspective, independent and idiosyncratic, without the need for others' approval or acceptance.

The Pagan vision requires us to open ourselves in trust to the natural world. In this way, we see a parallel with the trust required within a monist faith like Christianity, where the adherent is asked to have faith in God. For the Pagan, however, the sense of deity or the divine is not existent beyond creation: the divine is the flow of nature, both within us and around us. Furthermore, where the God in question is described as caring, loving, and just, finding faith might be a good deal easier than for the Pagan who is all too aware that the currents of nature are far from merciful, devoid of justice, and fully red in tooth and claw. What he opens to is not some loving parental figure, some benevolent authority; he opens to truth, to himself, to the wonder of life, growth, love . . . and death, anger, decay: it can be as brutal as beautiful. Yet in his opening, he utterly affirms his own soul freedom, together with the power of his connectedness through those golden threads of energy into the web of spirit. For a moment, perhaps extending into the timeless, he finds his perfect place in the universe.

The very action of opening oneself to vision is in tune with the mysticism of every religious and spiritual tradition; it is where we come together. Regardless of cultural diversity, there is always that craving within some human beings to lose themselves into a higher, broader, depthless energy, to merge, breaking through the limitations of mortality and the conscious self into an eternal boundlessness. That energy may be understood to be a deity, a universal force, or nature itself; in Paganism, it is the latter. Shattering the coherent and cohesive form of our minds, our identity, we become a part of everything there is—rain, mist, leaves, wind, flowers, dew, cat, beetle, light and darkness—and in doing so, we sense more profoundly the nature of all creation.

This mysticism integral to the entire philosophy of Paganism distinguishes it from other traditions. Pagans do not reach to deity beyond life, but directly and more powerfully into life's essence. Released from our own limitations, truly touching and breathing spirit, we become one with that energy, experiencing its own soul-intention, flowing through the myriad currents of its creativity and its physicality. Most often the gateway into this mystical "oneness" is intensely intimate: it may simply be me and a drop of newly fallen rain, me and a rose that is bursting with life; me and a dying crow, silent at the road's edge; me in the moonlight, like water meeting water. In touching the spirit of another being, the "me" touches all life, and touches life itself.

Emerging from the pool of completeness, our wonder is only greater. In the act of dissolving, our ability to make sacred relationship is deepened. Our ethics grow stronger.

Sacred relationship, then, is the key. How we achieve that depth of connection is a part of the path we walk within the tradition, a part of our quest for motivation, inspiration, and peace, reaching for more effective and profound communication and understanding.

Each individual walks that path in her own way, in her own time. We each have our own gait: running, striding, and stumbling; meticulous, broad, watching, listening; too eager or too cautious; reaching for expectations and finding surprises, revelations. Diversity of practice and experience is an essential layer of the foundations we share, the earth beneath our feet: clay, sand, chalk, mud, and stone. Diversity expressed as wakeful individuality, integrally woven into a conscious connection with everything, is the heart of Paganism.

As a spirituality that is effectively an extremely broad spectrum of ideas, sourced in myriad landscapes, climates, and histories, what holds it together beneath that one word is this focus on connectedness, relationship, and belonging. The effect of such a spiritual practice is a natural code of ethics shared, a code that is based simply on the power of true relationship.

Pagan ethics are not sourced in an authority, codified by humanity, nor attributed to a superhuman force or deity. They have emerged, as Druidry and other nature-based, indigenous Paganisms around the whole world, out of the simple yet respectful interaction between the human mind and the environment. Responding out of wonder, our ancestors learned, as we learn now, that living in harmony with the currents of nature brings peace and abundance; reacting out of fear, casting up defences, and laying down laws produces only a people chained to their ignorance and barricades.

The ethics that will inspire and guide humanity into the future must be those that have evolved from the oldest religions and spiritualities. Born of a desire to understand, not to dominate, of exquisitely nourishing relationship, they encourage within each soul all that they most desire: freedom within belonging, peace within creativity.

Ethics are the study and practice of how we as human beings will best survive and thrive. Only by honouring the sanctity of relationship itself can we hope to do so. With love and respect, with wonder and the vision that comes from touching the web of spirit, with honour, we can live life to the full, awake.

Note

1. "And God said, Let us make man in our image, after our like-
   ness: and let them have dominion over the fish of the sea, and
   over the fowl of the air, and over the cattle, and over all the
   earth, and over every creeping thing that creepeth upon the
   earth." Genesis 1:26, King James Version.

Magickal Ecology

Future Visions from Ancient Egypt

AKKADIA FORD

The ancient Egyptian philosophy of living ethically is enshrined within a foundation sacred text known as *The Negative Confession*, also called *The Declaration of Innocence*. In the context of ancient Egyptian temple traditions, this text is central to a larger body of material called the *peret em heru*, or *Coming to Day*, a funerary papyrus popularly known as *The Book of the Dead*.

Utilised by an individual during their journey through the otherworldly realm, the *Tuat*, *The Negative Confession* encodes what is

39

arguably the earliest written record currently known that bespeaks the need for mankind to exist in harmony with the natural world.

Initially, the collection of spells and hymns within this papyrus originated within texts inscribed inside the pyramids of the Old Kingdom (Dynasties V and VI, c. 2400 BC) for the benefit of the king in his afterlife journey. Over time, through a gradual revealing of what had previously been kingly prerogative, by the New Kingdom (c. 1550 BC) these same texts had become widely available to whoever could afford a personalised version of this funerary papyrus.

With visionary foresight, *The Negative Confession* outlines a clear statement of the primary areas that require care in order to maintain a healthy existence in balance with life upon earth:

> Behold, I have come to you, I have brought you truth,
> I have repelled falsehood for you.
> I have not done falsehood among men,
> I have not impoverished my associates,
> I have done no wrong in the Place of Truth,
> I have not learnt that which is not,
> I have not wrought disorder,[1]
> I have not made labour in excess of what was due to be done
>   for me, my name has not reached the offices of those who
>   control slaves,
> I have not deprived the orphan of his property,
> I have not done what the gods detest,
> I have not vilified a servant to his master,[2]
> I have not caused pain,
> I have not made hungry,
> I have not made to weep,
> I have not killed, I have not commanded to kill,
> I have not made suffering for anyone,
> I have not lessened the food-offering in the temples,
> I have not destroyed the loaves of the gods,
> I have not taken away the food of the spirits,
> I have not conducted myself improperly in the presence of the
>   gods,[3]

I have not behaved in a harmful manner,[4]
I have not lessened food-supplies,
I have not diminished the aroura,[5]
I have not encroached upon fields,
I have not laid anything upon the weights of the hand-balance,
I have not taken anything from the plummet of the standing
    scales,
I have not taken milk from the mouths of children,
I have not deprived the herds of their pastures,
I have not snared geese in the goose-pens of the gods,[6]
I have not caught fish with bait made of the bodies of the same
    kind of fish,[7]
I have not stopped water when it should flow,[8]
I have not built a dam on flowing water,
I have not extinguished a fire when it should burn,[9]
I have not neglected the dates for offering choice meats,
I have not withheld cattle from the god's offering,
I have not opposed a god in his procession,
I am pure, pure, pure, pure, pure!
My pure offerings are pure offerings.

> *The Negative Confession*
> *Theban Recension & Papyrus of Nu* (composite translation)[10]

These timeless principles of right conduct recorded in Egyptian
terms accord with the nature of the Goddess Maat.

> "Each statement of *The Negative Confession* . . . implied a code
> of behaviour to be followed during life . . . without an exem-
> plary and moral existence, there was no hope for a successful
> afterlife."[11]

Outside of this "code of behaviour" lays in wait *Isfet*—Chaos, disorder. The triumph of Order (Maat) over Chaos (Isfet) is a recurrent
theme in Egyptian magick, which holds implications for the present
and future as powerfully as it did in ancient Egyptian times.

Ensuring that Maat is maintained may be of even greater urgency
for us in the twenty-first century. As the natural order is increasingly

denuded of vitality, the opportunity for Isfet to break through correspondingly emerges.

Chaos in nature manifests as a dissolution of the known and knowable—as irregularity of the seasons and their cycles, disruption of natural rhythms, and unseasonable drought and flood. From mankind's direct interventions to Maat, such as genetic engineering, comes Isfet most perilous—infertile plants incapable of seeding their own kind—a horrific labyrinth of nature rendered sterile in the quest to satiate corporate greed.

Not satisfied with ignoring Maat in even the most essential of natural laws—the necessity for nature to remain fertile—Isfet has been unleashed in the hideous and barbaric "science" of transgenics experiments. Disordering nature in the quest to create an "improved nature," that is, a more profitable nature, species are being mutilated into abominations.

Animals are now being systematically and deliberately deformed on a genetic level. Many well-documented cases of genetic mutation exist with regard to domesticated animals. Not content with this, transgenics experiments are now also reported to be taking place or being theoretically considered in other contexts. These include experiments aimed at producing such "useful" future animals as dolphins with hands.[12]

Whether this is possible or not does not preclude those with vested interests in attempting such distortions of life. In the interests of potentially destructive military applications, or to serve short-sighted political ends, plants and animals are excluded from ethical consideration. Future generations in all realms will have to deal with the physical and ethical Chaos unleashed in the present.

If ever there is a time when the environmental and personal ethics spoken of in *The Negative Confession* are needed, surely it is now. This text speaks across the ages with a clarity of vision and an integrity of worldview. It bespeaks the ancient Egyptians' deep connection to and understanding of the interconnection of all life. That this text was continually recopied by scribes into unknown numbers of personalised papyri over thousands of years is a testament to the sustaining nature of the vision. From this text a future vision of how to practically sustain life may still be granted.

A Vision of Maat: Ancient Egyptian Ethics

The primary aim of life within philosophies of the Egyptian tradition is to be in harmony with that which is Maat.

Maat is a powerful Goddess, the underlying right Order of the universe in existence at the First Time—when the universe and its emanations came into being.

She is the invisible, undying, dynamic force which maintains the balance of life. Maat is the source of the timeless sacred lore uniquely expressed within *The Negative Confession*.

As a blueprint statement of future intent, this text provides insight into the key areas which require ongoing attention, maintenance, and acceptance of personal responsibility, in order to sustain life in balance upon earth.

Embodied within the form of ostrich feather, Maat teaches the sacred lore that the heaviest thing known is also paradoxically the lightest. That is, Truth—which is an evocative translation of Her name.

Also closely associated with weighing scales, Maat is a force capable of bestowing upon mankind what it has earned.

To comprehend the significance of the scales to the ancient Egyptians, consider how their economy was not based upon money as we know it—but based upon a system of fixed copper weights and measures. Everyone was paid a wage of weighed foods and drink, symbolic of an individual's status and worth. Thus, to the Egyptians, the image of weighing scales evoked both the absolute sustenance of life and knowledge of who a person was in life. This reveals why an individual was so keen to swear at the end of their life that they had not made the weights of a scale read falsely. Inherent within this was the issue of balance: between living and sustaining life, and between the present and the future, which are ultimately one.

Significantly, the ancient Egyptians recognised the need for humans to live in harmony with the laws and rhythms of nature and with other living species. Within *The Negative Confession,* equal emphasis is given to the rights of animals and their natural habitats, balanced with the rights and responsibilities of humans in relation to each other and their environment. Humane regard for animals is expressed, especially when the lives of animals are taken as a necessary food source.

This careful and ethical approach to nature should come as little surprise given the reverence that the Egyptians had for their environment, expressed through the dominance of both sacred animals and plants as embodiments of the *neterw*—the Gods and Goddesses.

Everything that exists is *djeserw*—a manifestation of the sacred. There is no distinction between forms of life. A mountain is as *djeser* as a river, tree, animal, or human. All are acknowledged to contain indwelling spiritual essences. Within the *Papyrus of Ani* it is affirmed that every part of an individual's life is connected to one of the neterw.[13] To protect and sustain the world about us is nothing more or less than to protect, sustain, and respect the fabric of one's own life.

The Negative Confession speaks from the past with a clear vision, identifying key ways in which we humans may sustain life in the present and future, thus maintaining the continuous flow of life force throughout realms.

Speaking of Truth

Maintenance of Justice

Protection of the Sacred

Extension of Peace

Strength of Personal Honour

Noninterference with Other Beings and Realms

Seeking the Wisdom of Nature

Primary Personal Responsibility for Living

These key areas may in turn be expressed as powers that each person holds, and that may be consciously utilised in the service of life:

Power of *truthful speech*.

Power of *doing that which is right*.

Power of *being honourable in dealings with othe*rs.

Power of *preservation of life* (human, animal, plant).

Power of *maintaining the sacred in our lives.*

Power of *permitting life to exist as it is* without interference.

Power to *dwell in peace* with one's gods, other humans, spirits, and nature.

Power of Truthful Speech

Foremost amongst these powers and repeated in several different forms within *The Negative Confession* is the power of truthful speech. The power of truth is more closely connected to living in harmony with Maat than any other thing.

To comprehend the central significance of truthful speech to the Egyptians, it is worthwhile to recall that one of the primary means by which existence is brought into being is through sound—the utterance of the god's own name brought forth in rapture. One consciously directed word has the power to impregnate the cosmos. Thus one's tongue, lips, and teeth form part of a dynamic vessel of creation capable of uttering new forms into being when spoken with the full force of one's heart. In this view, untruthful speech becomes a violation of the primary means of creation manifesting.

Imagine the result if all the world's leaders consistently spoke that which is true into being. Imagine the relations that would exist between individuals if each person spoke that which is true. Consider the vast freedom if each one of us was truthful to ourselves.

Through a personal application of this power, immense energy is unleashed. If one speaks the truth of the heart, each person is truly free. Speaking truth ensures that balance is maintained, for in this act no energy is held back; there is no need to hide, no fear of discovery. Untruth breeds untruth until a maze of deceit exists. When truth is consistently spoken, a high level of personal honour exists. Even when speaking truth may bring one into disagreement with others, this is of no consequence in comparison to the imbalance that is wrought through withholding truth.

For this very great reason, Maat is enthroned in an inviolable domain known as "The Seat of Truth," an otherworldly palace that each one must pass through on his or her way to rebirth. It is in this place, also known as the "Judgement Hall," or the *Hall of the Double Maat*, that the famous "Weighing of the Heart" ceremony takes place and before which *The Negative Confession* is sworn. In observing the moral precept to uphold Maat through speaking truth, an individual lightens his or her heart.

Power of Doing That Which Is Right

Only each person knows if he or she is truly doing that which is right—*for him or her.* This point is made at the very outset of this discussion to avoid any tendency to consider *The Negative Confession* as a set of absolute "rules" by which to live, or worse, to judge another. It is neither of these things.

As a philosophical statement inspiring deep self-evaluation and ongoing regard for the world in which we exist, *The Negative Confession* provides a worthy scale by which we may rebalance or refocus our perspectives on living. The declarations also reflect an ideal of life in balance to which we may aspire.

The composite version of the text quoted at the outset of this chapter (*Theban Recension, Papyrus of Nu*) includes an older form of this declaration from the *Papyrus of Nu* than the usually known version from the *Papyrus of Ani*. This is significant because the older the version, the closer we are brought to the earliest philosophies of the Egyptians—closer to the First Time than later versions and, hence, closer to the primordial thoughtforms of the neterw. Though there are countless other versions, each differing in emphasis due to the unique perspective of scribal hand, the core similarity of vision shared between papyri of different generations and temple regions is that each is imbued with an absolute personal regard for sustaining all aspects of life in balance as part of *an individual's sacred obligation to life.*

It is to be kept in mind that an individual did not swear this declaration until after death. The continuity of existence beyond death was central to the entire ancient Egyptian way of life and thinking, and is reaffirmed throughout the temple traditions.

The future vision of the Egyptians was to be able to swear this declaration and to be acknowledged as *Maat Herw*, a "Justified One," "True of Voice." This firmly placed the responsibility upon each individual during life to do that which was right.

Within *The Negative Confession* there are clear guidelines as to those areas which require conscious consideration during life and also what will bring an individual out of harmony with Maat. This includes disregard of truth, wilful desecration of the sacred, and ignoring the rights of other beings.

The significant regard for the rights and habitats of animals and for the elemental realms of water and fire spoken in *The Negative Confession* surprisingly reveals the ancient Egyptians as visionary ancestors of today's environmental and conservation movements.

Through stating that an individual had "not taken milk from the mouths of children," the rights of the young are also acknowledged to be an expression of Maat. In a later version of this declaration Ani swears: "I have not snatched away the bread of the child."[14] This declaration on behalf of the rights of children predates by almost four thousand years the reiteration of children's rights by the United Nations in the late twentieth century, after centuries of childhood labour and oppression throughout the world—still ongoing in impoverished regions.

It is significant that for the many thousands of years during which Maat was upheld by the ancient Egyptians that the highest level of cultural expression, artistic and religious inspiration, and environmental sustainability resulted.

In the twentieth century, the modern Egyptians learned the disorder which resulted from ignoring the wisdom of their ancestors in environmental matters. In disregarding the principle to "not stop water when it should flow" and to "not (build) a dam on flowing water" and following the "successful" construction of the Aswan dam in the mid-twentieth century, for the first time in Egyptian history the Nile Valley now requires artificial fertilisation.

Though water is now on tap all year around, the vital annual flooding of the Nile, which since time immemorial brought not only water but life-giving fertile silt flooding onto the river banks, now no longer occurs. As the land is no longer fertilised by the gods, imbalance has resulted. The Nile is now polluted, dangerous to drink or to swim in. The ancient Egyptians would weep into the river, seeing their beloved Osiris unable to consummate the annual sacred marriage. Thus is Isis truly widowed in that land.

But of course the Ancient Ones do see . . . and do weep. The power of the ancestors to express dissatisfaction with their own kind undoing Maat is not to be underestimated.

Power of Being Honourable in Dealings with Others

Personal honour is evoked through upholding Maat.

Envision a future where people dealt honourably with each other, speaking truth, rather than from a perspective of need or greed. This is a vision of society unmasked.

The development of honourable personal ethics based upon a magickal philosophy which actively works with and reveres nature is offered as a viable means to transcend the limitation of commonplace thought and marketplace trends.

Through consideration of magickal wisdoms which have stood the test of countless generations of practitioners, adapting to the needs of each time and place, an individual gradually learns how to become empowered. In this vision empowerment is cognate with honour—with Maat.

Having considered the central power which is Maat, it becomes apparent that an honourable life is a life in harmony with those principles and powers which sustain existence throughout all its manifestations. Embracing Maat leads to an opportunity to gradually embody Her.

Once limiting human tendencies are transcended, particularly in relation to speaking truth, doing that which is right, and accepting personal responsibility for our actions, empowerment begins.

Power of Preservation of Life (Human, Animal, Plant)

The unique gift accorded to humans is freedom of choice in all the details of our lives. Unlike other species, our diet may comprise an endless variety of foods, prepared in infinite ways; our habitat and lifestyle is for us to select and change as we please. With such freedom comes the absolute responsibility to use this power in ways that do not infringe upon the freedom of other beings to live.

In addition to a clear declaration that an individual had "not killed, or commanded to kill" those of their own kind, the rights of other humans, animals, and natural surroundings were to be upheld without interference.

As life is preserved, a paradox presents itself: to sustain human life, we each daily take life. This is a sobering realisation.

For whether carnivore, vegetarian, or vegan—with those extremely rare exceptions of fruitarians who eat only fruit (thus not taking the life of the tree which grew it), every meal we consume has undeniably involved the taking of life. Even a diet which consisted only of wild-crafted seeds and nuts would take life—for the full life of the plant resides in the seed. In consuming those nuts and seeds we take the future life of plant or tree to sustain our own. Once this is recognised, personal responsibility for the taking of life must be embraced. This realisation may prove a shock to some readers, especially those who may have previously considered certain types of diet as being noninjurious to life. However it is clear why there is no space for any false assertions in this matter. The arguments between those of differing dietary choices are often seen to be founded upon a subjective vision of what denotes life and respect for life upon this planet. While it is to be noted that whilst a vegetarian or vegan lifestyle may undeniably minimise or eliminate the amount of certain resources consumed, the plant kingdom is a living system filled with ancient beings.

To the ancient Egyptians, *Asar* (Osiris is the Greek form of his name) was the life force of nature, a green-faced, ever-youthful god embodied in plants. Significantly, He was also incarnate in a sacred bull, the Apis, in the river Nile and also the Moon. As bull is sustained upon the grass and grain grown from the fertile earth, we learn the lore that Asar is both sustainer and sustenance.

As a form of the green-faced god, that salad bowl had as much right to live as the fillet of beef or chicken thigh. To posit the life of fish, chicken, or cow as of "greater worth" than the life of lettuce or carrot derides the life of the kingdom of plants to a subservient level, when it is in reality another and equally potent living manifestation of the neterw.

Though human emotions may more easily bond with fish or bird or majestic old-growth forest than with relatively small and fast-growing plants such as grass or corn, for the Pagan or magickal practitioner seeking a sustainable vision of the future, all such divisions may ultimately be recognised as artificial and subjective.

Once life is acknowledged wherever it exists and in whatever form, the onus is upon each person to develop an ethical strategy of how to sustain their existence. As the taking of life in order to eat has been demonstrated to be unavoidable for the majority of humans, no matter which personal diet is followed, how do we attain balance in this matter?

An attitude of reverence towards life accepts responsibility when life must be taken in order to sustain existence—whether it be the life of plant or animal.

A need for an awareness of the rights and lives of plants may be usefully acquired by all who eat. This is in addition to the widely known and unquestioned rights of animals, well recognised today around the world through animal activist campaigns and animal care organisations.

In order to develop a sustainable future, rather than singling out any particular dietary or lifestyle choice, there may well be the need for an intelligent and magickally aware debate of how to re-sacralise the whole process of obtaining both plants and animals for food.

The need for people to individually grow more of their own foods or to raise and kill their own animals would surely alleviate some of the unsustainability of current farming and marketplace methods. Sourcing foods in the wild, where plants or animals have lived a free life within an ideal habitat, presents another approach.

An individual may enter into a sacred agreement with earth or with individual animal or plant species to protect natural habitats or raise or replant their kind in return for the gift of food.

The magickal technique of not harvesting a whole plant (i.e., not killing the plant) and giving thanks and blessing to the plant for what is reaped may be usefully applied to the reaping of plants for food. Work may be undertaken in a voluntary capacity on replanting projects, or community gardens, or wildlife projects.

Yet even with the utmost respect and having avoided the taking of life without due regard, it is apparent that, as noted above, each lettuce or carrot consumed involves the killing of what was a whole and unique living being: in Egyptian terms, a direct manifestation of Asar.

Because of the implications within the Egyptian tradition, it is of concern that nothing is ever spoken or written in the context of activist campaigns regarding the rights of plants that are used as primary foodsources by humans. Perhaps this is considered unimportant on a global scale compared to campaigns which generally focus upon obtaining chemical-free foods for humans to eat. Yet the thinking practitioner questions this silence upon the rights of the plants to live, in comparison to the loud voice advocated in animal activism. People seem to assume that it is acceptable to kill and consume vast quantities of plant life, but not animals. As both are Asar, this is a disturbing and imbalanced view of life.

Nor is the subject of how to ethically obtain animals for food ever raised publicly within a Pagan or magickal sphere. Whilst this may undeniably be due to a valid concern for the potential of such discussion to be distorted, as there are potentially as many meat-eaters as vegetarians and vegans who exist within these communities, it would seem essential for the subject to be raised.

There is an absolute need for any future vision to include an intelligent approach to the subject of all food—whether plant or animal sources.

In this regard it is a point worthy of consideration that two of the monotheistic religions of the world, Judaism and Islam, both have maintained a sacred approach to the process of the preparation of all foods, including animals (kosher and halal foods), since ancient times. Other indigenous traditions likewise have such an awareness.

Yet in a Western context this is an area yet to be publicly raised as an issue of sustainable living. Assuming that everyone will one day be vegetarian, or vegan, while perhaps an appealing ideal, is an unrealistic vision in the light of human history. A sustainable vision of the future of necessity must include the re-sacralising of obtaining all foods.

On behalf of the animals who die each year to enable humans to live, I make this plea: that not only the whole process of raising livestock, but also the manner in which animals are killed for food, be carefully reconsidered.

To intelligently deal with this, a future vision will need to address a range of approaches. For carnivores, these could include consciously reducing or limiting the amount and type of meat/animal products consumed, or hunting or raising their own animals for consumption.

Through the sourcing of foods in the wild, an individual enters into nature's realm—the playing field is rebalanced between human and animal. A person coming face to face with the animal they seek to eat—whether hand-raised or within its own terrain or elemental realm—will experience something profoundly different from purchasing their meat in individually prewrapped portions. If a person would be unwilling to confront their food "on the hoof" and take responsibility for the death-stroke, what right do they possess to claim the life of any animal slaughtered by some unknown hand to sustain their own?

Undoubtedly, in order to re-sacralise the process of obtaining all foods, there will one day be the need to address the training of sacred practitioners capable of humanely taking the life of an animal. Such people would be trained to honour the life force of the animals that they kill for food, to make appropriate offerings to the spirits of the animals and to the earth which raised them, and to ensure that no god or goddess associated with such animals are transgressed by their slaughter. The need for this may arise within our lifetime, or in some future generation. However, there is the recognition now of the need to resacralise the whole domain of utilising nature for food. Yet, to implement this will ultimately require a specialised level of knowledge and technical skill that would need to be practical, legal, and ethical to effectively function as an ongoing food supply.

While this may not be to every person's appetite, it is a suggestion that would undoubtedly reinstate animals in their life and death to a more honoured domain than the current system of commercial fishing, factory farming, and abattoir. It also needs to be noted that even animals currently raised under the free-range, organic, or grain-fed style of farming are still slaughtered in abattoir settings: their deaths are far from the ideal marketed by their "free-range" style of living.

As a valid and workable paradigm of sustainability, the ancient Egyptian temples provide a comprehensive model to explore. Each temple was a self-sufficient complex, some as large as a city. A range of workers were housed adjacent to the sanctuary buildings: brewers and bakers, a butchery, artisans, and priestly quarters. Each temple possessed herds of cattle, pens filled with geese and ducks, and fields of crops under cultivation.

Everything required to sustain life was part of the temple. Each occupation was considered sacred and under the direct patronage of one of the great gods or goddesses. Thus, brewers of beer were beneath the auspices of the Goddesses Menquet and Tjenmyt,[15] with beer also holding especial significance to Het-her (Gk. Hathor) and Sekhmet.

Artisans served Ptah. Tenders of geese held the pens of the God Ra, also Khnum. All cattle were revered as being sacred to Mehurit, Hether, or Asar.

In returning to a philosophy of no separation between "sacred" and "secular" aspects of life, every aspect of living holds the potential to be reintegrated into a whole expression of life in balance. Thus, the vision to become as self-sufficient as possible presents itself as one practical means of establishing a sustainable future. A pooling of talents and skills, as in the ancient temples, could potentially enable Pagans or magickal practitioners within a close range of each other to reestablish self-sufficient sacred communities. This is something that some may have already done, have begun to do, or envision doing in the future. Those dwelling in urban environments may also work at sustainable living through accessible and effective measures such as installing solar water heaters, a rainwater tank for drinking, and a small vegetable and herb garden. In growing, raising, and perhaps even accepting responsibility for killing food, injury to nature may be minimised and healing work undertaken. Through resacralising all aspects of life, magick is experienced in every moment.

It is worthy of consideration that "mad cow disease," which resulted in the destruction of so many animals, and illness and death to humans, was brought about through the violation of the ancient Egyptian principle regarding not feeding an animal of the same species to one of its kind. The affirmation that an individual has "not caught fish with bait made of the bodies of the same kind of fish" speaks of the ancient's clear consideration of the wider implications of one's actions upon life.

Vegetarians and vegans will argue that everyone could simply stop eating meat. Carnivores will equally loudly state that vegetarians and vegans could simply start eating meat. Both present unworkable propositions, and implicit in such statements is a denial of the validity of other people's rights to exercise free choice. It is apparent that these arguments also fail to address the fact that a large proportion of mankind (who can afford it) will continue to eat meat regardless of ethical considerations.

For the Pagan or magickal practitioner who eats meat because it is right for them, and who take into account personal, or, if applicable, magickal prohibitions regarding certain foods, it is apparent that a different approach is required. Accepting responsibility for taking the lives of animals as well as plants for food will lead to a personal and ethical consideration of how to avoid causing suffering to the animals and how to give something back to nature. Meat has been consumed as a central part of the diet for mankind's entire history along with plants, and both have been offered in thanksgiving. The statement, "I have not withheld cattle from the god's offerings" reaffirms that taking the life of an animal for food comes within the domain of the sacred and may carefully be reconsidered in our time with respect to any vision of a sustainable future food supply.

A key to this issue may be that the ongoing separation of "sacred" and "everyday" aspects of life and death has distorted the relationship of mankind to its world over time. To fully incorporate a recognition of the sacred, any future vision must include the resacralising of the domain of death, whether human or animal, not only the sphere of life. While it may be unfeasible, or undesirable, for an individual to move to the country and grow and kill their own food, perhaps the cooperative approach to food production prevalent within the organic and biodynamic farming sectors will become more widespread with regard to animals.

What is offered here is the reminder from the wisdom of our magickal predecessors to honour all life as sacred. That plants are a lifeform of as much, or perhaps even greater, value to earth than either animal or human may usefully be incorporated when developing a personal philosophy. That the ancient Egyptians both ate and offered a wide variety of meats and plants to the gods is significant when the identity of the gods and goddesses of these same plants and animals is consciously considered.

As all living things are equally sacred in formulating a personal ethic, an individual's guardians and personal power allies will guide what is right for them. The rights of each person to make their own decisions are inviolable, for *The Negative Confession* is ultimately a personal declaration to the gods.

Power of Maintaining the Sacred in Our Lives

Through celebration and thanksgiving, through offerings by day and night, through honouring one's ancestors and working in harmony with times and seasons we are able to sustain a sacred way of living anywhere, whether our resources are large or small. The personal responsibility to discover and maintain the sacred is the essence of a timeless quest. While formal training in initiatory traditions may guide one within, the place of truth is ultimately also the place of the heart.

The experience of the sacred is profoundly connected to love. Magick is ultimately the art of living consciously, connected to all life. In this enraptured state, every breeze, moonrise, sunrise, or star rise, every blade of grass which grows and falls, every birth and death upon earth echoes within our cells. This passionate connection with life enables practitioners to grow, to change, and, with this, to learn how to further transform their worlds, utilising their connection to life with willed intent. This is a heightened sensory world, as painful as it is pleasure-filled.

In the twenty-first century, those who have accepted the responsibility of their consciousness may need to harness greater inner reserves in order to effect this transformation as the very sources of energy in the natural world are denuded and devitalised of power. This suggests a future vision of aspects of sacred work. It may now and in the future no longer be sufficient to celebrate times and seasons; there

may be the need to ensure that such times and seasons and elements
of life are maintained or restored. In this, the presentation of offerings
becomes a vital exchange.

Power of Permitting Life to Exist as It Is Without Interference

In this regard the scientific intervention in species (transgenics) and
the manipulation of genetic codes are seen to be an aberration and
misuse of power with undeniable repercussions for humanity laying
in wait. Not only do animals have the right to exist as they are without violation—each human being also has this right.

Power to Dwell in Peace with One's Gods, Other Humans, Spirits, and Nature

"I have not lessened the food-offering in the temples, I have not destroyed the loaves of the gods, I have not taken away the food of the
spirits"—so an individual declares in *The Negative Confession*.

Through maintaining the sacred, the power to dwell in peace
with one's gods and spirits is obtained. Further, as the understanding
of the presence and identity of the gods within nature and cosmos is
gained, so too is the ability to live in peace with nature—they are
inseparable. To dwell in peace with the realm of invisibles depends
upon being able to dwell in peace with the realm of visibles, including other humans. To lead a full and balanced life requires activation
of both realms.

This involves the recognition of the interconnection of life forms—
the interconnection of realms of spirits/humans, the interdependence
of living natural systems, and that coexistence is the birthright of all
species upon earth. Through being attuned to the spirits of time and
place, including past and present times and places, a potent means to
learn how to access future wisdom is granted.

To dwell in peace with other beings raises issues of domination/
suppression and wealth at the cost of others/nature. To cause an-

other to live in imbalance denies all the right to experience inner and outer peace.

From a consideration of *The Negative Confession,* the sustainability of future life emerges as attainable on an individual level if predicated upon an ongoing reevaluation and implementation of ancestral wisdoms. This is a grassroots vision of personal responsibility that requires nothing outside of the individual to implement.

Through seeking out what worked before and what continues to be of need now, we learn how to work in harmony with Maat in order to prevent or replace what has been lost. Transforming and empowering, this future vision has the potential to extend in time and place wherever the name of Maat is heard.

Natural Philosophy in Action

Magickal ecology, or ekology, utilises the conscious connection to life that an initiate possesses in combination with an awareness of the current scientific, environmental, and ethical issues surrounding any work with the kingdoms of nature. It is a philosophy concerned with life— in particular, the magickal use of anything within the environment, or with which an individual may enter into a relationship. This includes everything within the natural world with which our senses interact on earth, beyond earth into the cosmos, and within to the inner-plane realms.

Magickal ecology is concerned with the study of living things now, in particular, the ongoing effects that developments in science are having and will potentially have in the future upon magickal work in the twenty-first century. Due to this, magickal ecology differs in objective with mainstream environmental movements, though sharing the same core concerns for the welfare of all natural systems.

Though seemingly unrelated, any magickal work in the twenty-first century that draws from or works with the elemental realms,

the kingdoms of mineral, plant, animal, or human, elemental manifestations, or ancestral issues is now and will continue to be directly
affected by scientific manipulation of life and environmental degradation in ways unprecedented.

Where once it was reliable to call upon the powers of bull and
cow as a source of strength and fertility, now such a call may be rendered into something completely different through transgenics. As
animal genes are increasingly spliced into the plant kingdom, a call to
the power of a plant may end up becoming entwined with an unrelated or antipathetic force of a completely different species.

Many people may be unaware that vegetarian foods are genetically modified with animal genes to enhance growth. Though the
potential consequences of this may not be as apparent at first as that
giant tomato, or strawberry fused with pig genes, nor of any concern outside the Pagan and magickal communities, contemporary
practitioners must be alert to the implications of scientific interference with nature upon magickal work. It is apparent that according
to the Hermetic axiom of absolute correspondence—As Above, So
Below—over time there will undeniably be a reciprocal change in
the characteristics of magickal forces embodied within, or personi-
fied by, aspects of nature that undergo alteration.

Thus, care needs to be exercised in the current work with nature,
for reasons unknown to our magickal predecessors. Because of this,
the approach of magickal ecology suggests fully taking into account
what is happening in science as a necessary adjunct to application of
traditional magickal knowledge.

Magickal ecology also acknowledges that there is the potential
for a reciprocal exchange back into nature. Through infusing all life
with the wisdom of the ancients and using the initiates' conscious
connections to living forces, a powerful antivenom capable of healing through the assertion of the right of each being and habitat to
exist as is may be unleashed.

To avoid working with scientifically tampered nature—and this will become increasingly difficult in the years and decades that follow—one suggestion is to begin to replace those animals and plants known to currently be the subject of transgenics and genetic manipulation which have traditional associations with gods and goddesses with older, primordial, and nondomesticated forms.

Return to the Wild

The oldest gods and goddesses exist in wild forms. It was not until humans settled and cultivated one area continuously, generation after generation, that aspects of the wild were gradually domesticated for the benefit of humans. Thus everything was originally untamed and untainted. To counteract the manipulation of living things, a return to the wild and primordial forms of gods and goddesses reasserts itself as offering a valid and potent means to maintain balance in magickal work with nature. Magickal ecology acknowledges that any species traditionally honoured within magickal work which is currently under scientific manipulation is already correspondingly changing in its magickal force. Pause to consider the implications of this for the future.

The practitioner, then, has two viable options: continue to work with the plant or animal to petition and aid healing of its kind, or cease to work with that form altogether and investigate whether there is a corresponding wild plant or animal associated with the work.

Within the Egyptian traditions, a large number of primordial wild forms of neterw are fortuitously preserved—both in text and image. Domesticated animals and plants of sacred lore within ancient Egypt that have been or still are being subjected to transgenics and genetic manipulation include cattle, sheep, and grains (especially corn). These three examples are offered as extremely well-known neterw from the Dynastic (i.e., settled) period of Egyptian history onwards. They are also examples known and of sacred significance to other traditions.

Examples of Replacing Domesticates with Wild Species

Neter	Domesticate	Wild Form
Amun	Ram	Invisible rushing air
Hathor	Cow	Hippopotamus (Taurt); wild fig
Asar	Bull	The green life force in all nature
	Corn	River flood waters that carry fertile silt onto the land (note: both the river Nile and the Moon are ascribed as godforms within Egyptian lore)

This need for a change in form and elemental shift appears to have been provisioned by the neterw in a future time of imbalance:

O Thoth, what is this that has happened through the children of Nut? That have done violence, they have created an uproar, they have done wrong, they have created rebellion, they have made slaughter, they have created imprisonment! They have made that which is great small in all that I have done. Show greatness, Thoth! So said Atum . . .

(The Justified One speaks) I am your palette Thoth, I have brought up your water pot, I do not belong to those who have done secret wrong, wrong will not be done to me.

(Atum speaks) You will be for millions (of years), a lifetime of millions (of years).
. . . This land will go into the primeval waters, into the flood as its original state.
I will remain, together with Osiris, having made my transformation into other snakes which people do not know and gods have not seen.[16]

In disclosing the future intent of the neterw to return to primordial forms which are unknown, Atum reveals the precarious position in which mankind places itself by creating imbalance in nature.

Inherent within this disclosure is the recognition that in failing to treat with honour those forms of the neterw that have consented to dwell beside mankind for thousands of years, providing inspiration, sustenance, and service, the neterw will choose new forms that will be unknown and inaccessible.

The reference to "this land will go into the primeval waters . . . as its original state" bespeaks a future cyclical period of total renewal. Such a renewal could take place either esoterically or exoterically and accords with the ancient Egyptian seasonal cycle *akhe*, an annual period during which the Nile would completely flood the Delta and Valley, renewing the fertility and creative potency of the land. To the Egyptians, the image of the primordial flood waters was synonymous with restoration and return to the First Time, in which all creative potential is contained. Such a "flood" could take place on the inner or outer planes, renewing the fertile matrix of the neterw and hence also the living practise of Egyptian magick.

If we demonstrate and actively care for the forms and habitats in which neterw dwell, Atum and other neterw may consent to remain in wild forms that can be known.

Through careful research, a range of wild animal, plant, and environmental/elemental forms of the neterw can be located and correspondences intelligently utilised—keeping in mind that these forms remain untamed and thus require an especial respect when entering or seeking to access their domain. This technique may usefully be applied to other gods and goddesses.

The power of the visionary to see new ways to sustain future life has already been proven from the example of *The Negative Confession*. The stability of life characteristic of ancient Egypt inspires renewed consideration today.

Equilibrium

The future vision of the need for an integrated life emerges from ancient Egypt. In this vision, all realms of life are accorded their own unique status. Each being receives sustenance from earth according to its needs. Each person accepts responsibility for their actions and the consequences of their actions upon other lifeforms. Speaking of truth is characteristic of this visionary age, where people do not cheat each other or the earth. Preservation of Maat is essential to attain a sustainable future.

The absolute inseparability of Maat and the world in which we dwell is expressed within *The Negative Confession* in a thought-provoking way. As Maat has ever held a central role in all matters of creation and re-creation, there is an urgent need to ensure that the responsibility to preserve equilibrium is accepted by each one of us in this time. In considering implementing an approach such as ekology, an individual recognises the need to reconnect life to its timeless sources as a means to maintain the future ecology of magick.

By whatever name or form Maat is known within various traditions, may each individual deeply consider how his or her life and work may uphold the balance. There is an urgent need for the re-sacralising of the domain of decision-making with regard to earth. There is a need for those in power whose decisions affect multitudes to acknowledge the kinship of all life—now proven beyond a doubt through recent scientific examinations of the genetic codes of various species.

As we are not apart from earth and other beings, our decisions inevitably affect others, whether for better or worse. The responsibility for sustaining life is held by each generation. The future will exist because we each actively participate in its creation. In this recognition lies the powerful future vision entrusted within *The Negative Confession*.

Notes

1. Ockinga, *A Concise Grammar of Middle Egyptian*, 146. Translation of the word *Isfet* as "sin, disorder." "I have done no evil" (Faulkner); cf. "I have not wrought evil" (Budge)—in this translation, Budge used "evil" for the word phrase *bw bin,* which means "bad" and "misery" (Gardiner).

   I have rendered the phrase as "I have not wrought disorder" due to the stereotypical connotations of the word "sin" or "evil," which fall far short of the ancient Egyptian conception of Isfet. "Disorder" provides an exact insight into the nature of what the Egyptians were meaning. In Egyptian philosophy, Isfet is the opposite principle to Maat. In the Papyrus of Ani version of *The Negative Confession*, the word "Isfet" is clearly inscribed within the text (Faulkner, 1994, Plate 31, left register line 1) and there is simply translated, "I have not done wrong."

2. Budge, *The Book of the Dead.* Rendering used here for "calumniated" (Faulkner).

3. "I have not copulated" (Faulkner) is a difficult rendering for those unfamiliar with the Egyptian temples, as the Egyptians were not a celibate people. Budge offers, "I have not had intercourse with men, I have not masturbated in the sanctuaries of the god of my city."

   Translations such as these, when encountered in versions of *The Negative Confession,* should not be interpreted as a general statement against forms of sexuality.

   In this regard, the ancient Egyptian views may at times appear to be contradictory—however, it must be kept in mind that Egyptian temples never attempted a syncretic philosophy, and thousands of years and hundreds, perhaps thousands, of temples continually developed older precepts in distinct ways within an overall tradition throughout time.

   Given the precedence of ancient Egyptian creation legends of Khephra and Atum—both androgynous neterw who create via onanism—leads to the need to carefully consider this declaration in the broader context of ancient Egyptian religion (Ford, 2001).

   In this context, the statement accords with certain ancient Egyptian rules of purity regarding sexual continence of priests prior to entering the temples during their roster. This also applied to others making offerings to the gods.

It implies that an individual entering into the presence of ritual and hence the neterw is required to uphold a standard of conduct. To convey this, I have rendered the declaration into a form equally applicable to men and women—following the ancient precedent of revitalising texts in use—with the expression "I have not conducted myself improperly in the presence of the gods."

4. "I have not misbehaved" (Faulkner) is a very generalised translation. I have rendered this statement, "I have not behaved in a harmful manner," to convey a more specific meaning.

5. An "aroura" was an ancient Egyptian measurement used in regards to land, similar to the way we use the word "acre," though of different dimension.

6. The Budge rendering of this line is used here, as it evocatively expresses the sentiment, "I have not trapped the birds in the preserves of the gods."

7. "I have not caught fish of their marshlands" (Faulkner).

8. The compact Budge rendering is used here for the Faulkner, "I have not diverted water at its season." Both clearly express what is intended.

9. "I have not quenched the fire when it is burning" (Faulkner). The Budge version is used here, as it also conveys the Egyptian appreciation that each thing has its own time to exist.

10. Composite translation prepared from Faulkner & Goelet, *The Egyptian Book of the Dead*, 115. Theban Recension chapter 125, "What should be said when arriving at this Hall of Justice . . ." Lines footnoted 1–7 derive from the older *Papyrus of Nu*, British Museum #10477, sheet 22, as translated in Budge, *The Book of the Dead*, 572–576. Lines footnoted 1, 3, and 4 are based upon an additional reevaluation and interpretation of the hieroglyphic texts rendered into a contemporary form by the present author (Ford, 2002) and do not reflect upon the distinguished critical translations cited above.

11. Faulkner and Goelet, *The Egyptian Book of the Dead*, 14.

12. *The Nature of Things*, David Suzuki, Canadian Broadcasting Corporation: November 2002, documentary series.

13. Budge, *The Book of the Dead*, 582, vs. 41.

14. Ibid, Chapter XLII, "Deification of the Members," 597–604.

15. Faulkner and Goelet, *The Egyptian Book of the Dead*, 174–175.

16. Chapter 175, Book of the Dead, translation by Dr. Boyo Ockinga (Australia: Macquarie University, 1998).

Bibliography

Budge, E. A. Wallis. *The Book of the Dead*. New Jersey: University Books, Inc., 1984.

Faulkner, Raymond, and Goelet, Ogden. *The Egyptian Book of the Dead*. San Francisco: Chronicle Books, 1994.

Ford, Akkadia. *The Powers That Seek*. UK: Capall Bann Publishing, 2001.

———. "The Staples of Life: Bread and Beer" in *Egyptian Art Principles and Themes in Wall Scenes*. Prism Archaeological Series 6, edited by Leonie Donovan & Kim McCorquodale. Cairo: Ministry of Culture, 2000.

———. *Egyptian Animals—Guardians & Gateways of the Gods*. UK: Capall Bann Publishing, 2005.

Gardiner, Sir Alan. *Egyptian Grammar*. Oxford: Griffith Institute, Ashmolean Museum, 1994.

Ockinga, Boyo G. *A Concise Grammar of Middle Egyptian*. Mainz am Rhein: Verlag Philipp von Zabern, 1998.

"Of Worms, Snakes, and Dragons"

Can Magic Lead to an Ecological Worldview?

DR. SUSAN GREENWOOD

These are times of increasing environmental awareness, and we are desperately in need of ways of seeing the world that will help us relate to nature. Pagans say that they see nature as sacred, and Paganism is often said to be an environmental spirituality, but do Pagan practices actually lead to an ecological approach to life? Do we focus too much on human relationships—our power, identity, and what we need—at the expense of other beings in nature?

When I first got involved in Paganism at an Autumn Equinox ritual in 1984, it was like "coming home," a feeling that many have when they assume that they are with like-minded people. I thought Paganism was about being able to relate magically to nature—both within the self and with the outer natural world—but as I became more involved I realized that things were inevitably more complicated than I had initially (rather naively) thought.

The well-known psychologist and Pagan Margot Adler in *Drawing Down the Moon* (1986), a study of Paganism in America, explained that she came into Paganism (she calls it Neo-Paganism) from a search for a "celebratory, ecological nature religion that would appease my hunger for the beauty of ancient myths and visions." Adler believed that Paganism could heal the breach between the spiritual and the material; she saw in Paganism a philosophy that would join ancient and modern values in a religious way of life that allowed a regaining of kinship with nature. Adler tended towards viewing the Craft as "ecological religion" and assumed that a religion that venerated nature would consider the protection of the earth and restoring the balance of nature as paramount.[1] My own assumptions were similar to Adler's when I first got involved in Paganism in the mid-1980s. I thought that people would automatically be interested in the natural world; however, I found from my anthropological research among London Pagans in the early to middle 1990s that there was more emphasis on ritual and psychospiritual "internal" nature as personal experience rather than a connection to, or even an interest in, the environment. Adler found that there was a split between Pagans with ecological principles who called for a change in lifestyle and those who had a religious vision and thought that change would evolve by itself. It was these observations that led me to conduct further research on nature religion.

This chapter recounts a journey through my own experience of Paganism since the 1980s. My relationship with Paganism has been one of questioning, using my own feelings as well as through more "distanced" academic research. Why look to the past when we need a vision for the future? We need to learn from the past—both in terms of our own experience and as a more generalized cultural awareness—and to look at issues that will affect the future; past, present, and future are but different points in the spiral of time. My aim in this chapter is to look at some of the issues that I've seen to be important, especially the use of magic in terms of an expanded awareness. I shall suggest that magic has the potential to help us make meaningful connections to the natural world and gain a beneficial ecological perspective on life that, hopefully, has wider implications.

An Autumn Equinox Ritual

It was the evening of my daughter Lauren's fifth birthday party, September 22, 1984. There had been all the usual birthday festivities—the party, lots of children noisily playing games in the garden, the birthday cake, ice cream—everything that spoke to me of an ordinary, everyday special event. The sounds of laughing and shouting still ringing in my ears, and trying to ignore the creeping exhaustion from the hard work of preparing and organizing the event, my mind turned to the planned witchcraft ritual that was to be performed in London. The ritual was to celebrate the Autumn Equinox, a time when light and dark are in balance, as well as a significant part of many modern witches' "wheel of the year" celebrations; it was to be held in a backroom at a women's café called Tabbies in Balham. I had already attended a talk there on "The Goddess," given by Shan Jayran, one of the co-owners of the place.

The Autumn Equinox ritual was my first introduction to what I afterwards learnt was "feminist witchcraft." There were about twenty women present, and as we worked through the stages of the ritual—opening the circle; invoking the four quarters of north, east, south, and west; celebrating the time of the year and what it meant to us; and finally closing the circle, after passing around (and around) a large cauldron of wine so that we would "never thirst"—I felt as though I was reconnecting with something very deep inside me. This "something" was my connection with nature. Somehow I had become disconnected. To explain this disconnection—this separation—I will need to return to my childhood.

I grew up in Surrey, on the borders of south London. I was an only child and spent a lot of time in solitary play at the wild and overgrown end of our small garden. I had a brick-framed sand pit screened from the house by a rose trellis; being open and uncovered all year, it became a locus for all sorts of wildlife: from millipedes and woodlice to wriggly ginger wireworms, but most especially for earthworms. The worms fascinated me: how they could change shape by contracting and then extending their bodies, and how they gradually brought the sand and the earth in the sand pit together to form a new combination. When I was at the end of the garden, away from the house and all the doings of people, I felt connected to nature in such a way that I felt closely linked, in an animistic sense, to the animals in the sand pit and also to the plants around.

Animism is a view shared by many non-Western peoples and is a way of seeing the world, or certain aspects of it which we might consider to be inanimate, as alive. Perhaps many children think in animistic ways when they talk to soft toys, such as teddy bears. It is a way of thinking that we in the West learn to grow out of. At some point, it is considered "childish," and other, more rational thinking is encouraged. The biologist and naturalist Rachel Carson, whose book *Silent Spring* (1962) helped to start the modern environmental movement, wrote that a child's world is fresh, new, and beautiful, "full of wonder and excitement." She also said, "It is our misfortune that for most of us that clear-eyed vision, that true instinct for what is beautiful and awe-inspiring, is dimmed and even lost before we reach adulthood."[2]

As a child I found nature both beautiful and awe-inspiring. I was curious about how different trees, like horse chestnut, formed buds that then unfolded into leaves. I took jam jars of buds up into my bedroom to observe; I planted apple pips and peach and apricot stones and watched them grow and sprout leaves. I also kept grass snakes and was captivated by their abilities to slide across the ground and swim through water. As I learnt more about nature, it induced in me feelings of being linked to something greater; this took me deeper into another part of myself that is often termed "mysticism," a feeling of being linked to everything else in the cosmos.

The nineteenth-century nature mystic Richard Jefferies starts his autobiography, *The Story of My Heart* (1883), by saying that in the glow of his youth there were times when he felt the necessity of a strong inspiration of "soul-thought." Jefferies describes how he used to walk to a hill during such periods of needing soul-thought. At the top of the hill he had forgotten the petty circumstances of existence and felt himself to be himself. It was there that he had deep experiences of nature, feeling himself to be utterly alone with the sun and the earth. Lying down on the grass, he spoke in his soul to the earth, the sun, the air, and the distant sea. He felt as though the earth was speaking to him. Sometimes when lying down on the grass looking up at the sky, gazing at it for a long time until he felt he could see deep into the azure, Jefferies felt his eyes to be full of the colour. He would turn his face into the grass and thyme and become lost and absorbed into the being or existence of the universe: "I felt down deep into the earth under and high above into the sky, and farther still to the sun and stars. Still farther beyond the stars into the hollow of space, and losing thus my separateness of being came to seem like a part of the whole."[3]

When I've had mystical experiences, similar to those of Jefferies, my consciousness expands so I feel myself to be myself—more in touch with the deeper parts of myself—but also, paradoxically, part of everything else, too. As an adolescent, I used to spend days in this state of expanded awareness, listening to music, reading poetry, and thinking and feeling. To this day, I couldn't tell you where I "went," but I was exploring another world that opened up through listening to sounds and feeling the "other side" of words. This world was beyond everyday explanations.

So it was experiences like these—the close contact with other beings like worms and snakes, and the intense mysticism—that drew me into the Autumn Equinox ritual in London on the night of my daughter's fifth birthday. My animistic and nature-mystic sensibilities were aroused and awakened. In the years since "growing up" and having children (my son, Adrian, was two and a half at the time), I suppose I had progressively lost touch with this side of myself. Maybe many people lose their animistic way of seeing the world. The ritual did feel like coming home at the time because of the imagery invoked by the calling in of the elements; it reintroduced me to nature through the elements—the north representing earth; east, air; south, fire; west, water—and also aspects of myself: body, intellect, will, and emotions. Influenced by the political activist and feminist witch Starhawk, someone had put a bloodied sanitary towel in the centre of the circle to show all that had been denigrated by patriarchy—i.e., women's bodies and sexuality—was now to be considered sacred.

The Otherworld

After the Autumn Equinox ritual and subsequent reading of Starhawk's *Dreaming the Dark* (1982), I learnt new ways of interpreting my childhood experience and how I had come to feel about myself and my place in the world in terms of magic. I realized that I had always "known" about magic. I just didn't have a word for it. It was this feeling of unspoken communication—an awareness of something deeper, something "hidden" that was caught out of the corner of an eye, a strange consciousness of alternative worlds—that seemed to be shared amongst Pagans that initially made me feel that I'd come home.

Sometimes the feeling of being connected to something larger or deeper is referred to as "the otherworld." It's not an otherworld in the sense of being "other" to the everyday, but it does concern an awareness—an expanded consciousness—that includes sensitivity to other experiences and the connections between things. An email correspondence with a friend in Australia in 1998 provoked me to reflect on how I saw the otherworld, that place of deeper awareness:

> The otherworld is a great surge of energy, of joy, that starts deep down inside and then gradually takes me over until I feel connected to the flow of life. It is a place where special connections with spirit animals, spirit beings, places and people are especially important.
>
> The otherworld is not "mystical" in the sense of being out of touch with the ordinary world because I can take great joy in "rationally" studying the detail and colour of a chiffchaff [a bird] (for example), listening to its call, watching its movement as it flits among the branches of a silver birch tree. Everything becomes intensified and I feel more alive—really alive. It reminds me of the well-known Inuit shaman's song:
>
> > The great sea
> > Has set me adrift,
> > It moves me as a weed in a great river,
> > Earth and the great weather
> > Move me,
> > Have carried me away
> > And move my inward parts with joy.[4]

Perhaps it is this spirit or energy—it doesn't matter what it's called—that connects with the corresponding spirit or energy within other beings. The otherworld is a place of communication and many alternative possibilities. It is a place of magic. Margot Adler defines magic as a convenient word for a whole collection of techniques that involve the mind. These techniques involve the mobilization of confidence, will, emotion, and imagination, particularly the ability to visualize.[5] All of these are important in developing a "magical consciousness."

Recently, I've been working with a shaman called Jo Crow on a research project; we've had conversations in which she has told me that she sees magic as a deeper state of awareness. Magic, according to Jo, is almost like going into a "three-dimensional picture to investigate and play, to swim in the water of possibilities." This awareness may involve random creative possibilities of free association that may enable communication with other beings. It is important, she says, to let go of boundaries, of categorization and preconceptions from a more everyday awareness; it is necessary to relax the logical mind and trust to not knowing. The minute you try to understand it logically, "like a slippery fish or a bar of soap, it's gone."[6]

The language of this deeper state of awareness is symbolic and mythological; psychological connections or associations are made between things that in the everyday world would have no relationship. This is what the early anthropologist James Frazer called "sympathetic magic."[7] Symbols have what another anthropologist named Victor Turner described as "multivocality": they speak on many different levels. They have personal meanings, but they also have shared social and cultural associations, too.[8] How do symbols work in an individual psychological state? I'll give an example from my own experience that demonstrates how sympathetic magic—the psychological association of ideas—is deeply personal and formed through the process of growing up.

My early experience of the worms in the sand pit has shaped my consciousness—both in empirical terms by my curiosity about what worms did, and also in my imagination.[9] Charles Darwin, in *The*

Formation of Vegetable Mould through the Action of Worms, with Observations on their Habits (1881), changed many people's perceptions of these seemingly lowly creatures. Darwin thought that we are a part of nature; no longer can we assume that we are separate from other forms of life, as perhaps we have been led to believe by certain religious ideologies that claim that humans are special in the eyes of God. We are more like worms than we might think, and we're not superior to other animals. As Darwin noted, worms are better at tilling the soil than us; they swallow the earth, ejecting what they do not need for nutriment in a fine tilth that can't be matched by human ploughing. The message is that we can learn from nature; if we look deeper we can see that underneath the earth is a hidden process, and we are a part of that process.[10] The process has many dimensions and has been described in evolutionary and ecological terms; it has also been likened to Taoism or the Anglo-Saxon notion of "wyrd" (of which more later).

Worms are symbolically associated with both snakes and dragons. In the magical, deeper state of awareness, all the necessary boundaries and categorizations that we impose in nonmagical reality in order to communicate in the everyday world disappear, and then all sorts of possibilities entwine and slither into the imagination. Magical consciousness is deep and infinite; it is a source of untold creativity that leads to all manner of alternative modes of communication with otherworldly beings. Worms, snakes, and dragons all share long gracile bodies and abilities of transformation: worms transform the earth; snakes shed their skins, representing sexuality and cosmic renewal; and dragons are symbolic of creative and destructive energy associated with water and the earth.[11]

In a culturally hierarchical sense, worms may symbolize the lowliest of the low. For me, they have represented bad feelings about how I have sometimes felt about myself; the sorts of things that women frequently feel in a patriarchal society, such as being seen as inferior to men and associated with nature in a negative way. Starhawk says that due to what she calls "estrangement"—a cultural consciousness that cuts us off from nature, other human beings, and parts of our selves— we live within manipulating and dominating power relationships that are oppressive to men and women.[12] She defines three types of power: "power-over," "power-from-within," and "power-with." Each speaks its own language and has its own mythologies, and she enjoins the use of power-from-within and power-with to overcome power-over, the language of estrangement. Needing to start within the self, the "technology of power-from-within" is magic, the art of changing consciousness at will.[13] Magic works through symbols and the active imagination and is primarily a form of expanded consciousness.

A symbolic language can help transform consciousness—in Starhawk's words, from "power-over" to "power-with"—by letting significant symbols or images speak, maybe over a period of time. For me, snakes, with their worm/dragon aspects, came to be "power animals" or familiar spirits that represented my being in touch with a deep part of myself; some people may call this "soul." As a child I enjoyed feeling the smooth, scaly green-brown bodies of my grass snakes glide over me; I had unconsciously connected with these creatures. The snakes were a powerful symbolic trigger for me.

Symbols are thus very personal, as well as being social and cultural. They also have unconscious aspects. The psychologist Carl Jung thought that we share a collective unconscious at the deepest levels of our brain physiology that has formed through the development of the human species. Within this collective unconscious are archetypes that predispose us to think in certain ways according to patterns in the psyche. Snakes are one example of archetypal animals; they may, according to Jung, find expression in myths and dreams.[14]

I had a powerful dream on the night of January 28, 1991; I later saw it as an initiation. In the dream, a friend handed me a basket that another friend had given her. I took the basket and removed the embroidered, flowery lid; a white snake rapidly unwound itself from inside the basket and sprang out upon me. It fastened its fangs into my arm. I awoke feeling that it was a very profound experience. Some dreams you just *know* are different from the ordinary, run-of-the-mill, everyday ones. Several years later—six years, to be precise—I was able to interpret this dream as the beginning of my awareness of my true self—my sense of self that was connected to the wider web of existence. The snake had come to me as part of my initiation into another mode of consciousness. It would disappear and resurface at intervals in my awareness, but I always knew it was special. It connected me to another rhythm of life.

Psychologist Joseph Henderson and anthropologist Maud Oakes see snakes as symbols of rebirth following death. Taking a Jungian approach, they say that the unconscious contains archetypal rhythms of change, reflected in death and rebirth themes that follow the yearly vegetation cycle of nature; these archetypal themes are a touchstone for understanding certain important psychological experiences. Joseph Henderson had a patient who had a dream in which she was threatened by a white cobra. Henderson says that the bite of a poisonous snake is frequently a symbol for fear of death and/or insanity, and that snakes represent death and the souls of the dead. However, the dead are only dead in this life. They live a heightened life in the otherworld as ghosts or ancestors; they are harbingers of life that springs anew from the original source of all things. The colour white is significant, and represents the spirit of paradox: white is to black as life is to death, and death is life renewed.[15] This is the cyclic rhythm that underpins magical patterns of being.

Questions, Questions, Questions

I started my formal academic career in 1985, a year after the first Autumn Equinox witchcraft ritual, when I registered to do a degree in anthropology and sociology at Goldsmiths College, University of London. My academic exploration eventually turned into PhD research on magic and was published in 2000 as *Magic, Witchcraft and the Otherworld: An Anthropology.*[16] In this work I tried to communicate between the world of academia and the Pagan counterculture; my aim was to give some idea of the importance of the otherworld in Paganism. I've tried to view Paganism from the inside and also from the outside, as well as attempted to combine science and magic, both of which are slippery terms that have changed over time. Generally speaking, science today uses rationality, observation, and logical thinking, while magic employs more analogical thought, working primarily though intuition, mythology, symbols, and so on.[17] Richard Jefferies combined his nature mysticism with detailed "scientific" observations of nature and country life,[18] and Margot Adler became involved in Paganism as a way of bringing together the different approaches of science and magic in a celebratory ecological nature religion.[19] Combining both was, and still is, my approach, too.

I looked at three main areas in my initial research: magical identity, sexuality, and morality. Starhawk's concepts of "power-from-within" and "power-over" made me question how women and men come to practice magic. Were there differences in magicians' intent and focus according to their gender? Did women and men have different experiences? I explored how girls might have fluid ego boundaries while boys might have a more clear sense of self. This certainly seemed to be the case when I compared feminist witchcraft (a more "feminine" approach) with Aleister Crowley's particular brand of magic called "Thelema" (the Greek for "will"), a very individualistic, "masculine" interpretation of the magical will based on the philosopher Nietzsche's view that the will was an inner cosmological force striving for power. This raised what I thought were important issues about power. How does magical power affect our identity, our sexuality, our deepest experiences, how do we see ourselves in relation to the otherworld, and how are we seen? Questions, questions, questions. I have frequently been accused of asking too many!

My research fieldwork was based on what anthropologists call "participant observation." I participated in many rituals with many different people among varying Pagan groups. I came across interesting people, had good experiences, and also had some negative ones. On a couple of occasions, I was really scared by how some people conducted rituals. Magic is often termed a psychospiritual path of self-discovery, but sometimes, because of what has happened to us in our past, we may behave in ways that make us feel magically powerful at the expense of others. We might decide to use a magical charisma that often develops during ritual for our own ends to make us feel better about ourselves rather than using the energy in a more "honourable" way. We might manipulate others using this power from a place of insecurity rather than a place of being in accord with our true self, that part which is connected to the web of existence. Morality is pretty much seen as an individual thing in contemporary Paganism—"And it harm none, do as you will." This can be interpreted in all manner of ways. How do we work out the implications of our actions? How can we be sure we're not harming anyone or any being when we look beyond our own self-interests at the broader picture? Are we more interested in impressing people with our ability to harness "dark forces"? These are very difficult questions.

I also researched myself—I was a "guinea pig" in my own research project. It was a time when I explored deeper aspects of my consciousness in trying to work out what magic actually was. I've found that magic involves looking deeply into the self and facing the subconscious and unconscious. We might be too scared to really see what is shown, or we might decide to take action in dealing with what we see. Shaman Gordon MacLellan sees the otherworld as a "three-dimensional mirror" that reflects back what we bring to it; whatever is hidden will ". . . sooner or later, come walking through the woods towards us."[20] Sometimes it takes us to the borders of "madness"; we have to be able to deal with working in different streams of consciousness. We need to be strong within ourselves—to feel "power within"—to have control or volition of what we are doing, even as we, paradoxically, go with the process of tuning into the wider whole, the wider magical consciousness. We have to be able to "ride the dragon" of all the powerful spirits or energies that arise from consciously entering this world. To me, this is the basis of the practice of magic; it is the core of true knowledge about using magical consciousness as a creative and spiritual aspect of mind.

My research in *Magic, Witchcraft and the Otherworld* was primarily about the relationships that high magicians and witches had to the otherworld. It did not look at the otherworld in terms of either individual consciousness or wider philosophical and ecological terms. My next academic writing project was to explore the wider dimension in terms of magical consciousness and nature, published as *The Nature of Magic: An Anthropology of Consciousness* (Berg, 2005). My main question here was about how some Pagans see nature, and about how some reconnect with nature. Do we see nature in an ecological or environmental way, or do we focus on ourselves in a manner that anthropologists call "anthropocentric," in other words, by being human-centred? Do we perform rituals to make *us* feel good? (No bad reason in itself, but is this the *only* reason?) Do we stop to think about other beings in nature? Do we just see nature as a beautiful backdrop for our rituals?

Reconnection with Nature

What have I learnt from my research experience? Firstly, that there are many more questions than answers; and secondly, that if Paganism is to be considered a nature religion—Paganism is promoted by many Pagans as being an environmentally aware religion—then we need to look to nature to find some of the answers to the questions that need asking. I think that we should make sure that we practise our spirituality—our nature religion—in terms of being *within* rather than apart from nature. It was Darwin who restored the idea that human beings are part of a totality, that we are a part of nature,[21] but it was Jung who attempted to link spirituality with nature in the collective unconscious—the collective unconscious *is* nature,[22] in the sense that we are a part of nature.[23]

"Ecology," a term coined in 1870 by Ernst Haeckel, comes from the Greek *oikos*, meaning "house" or "home," and implying, according to anthropologist Brian Morris, that the natural world is a place in which to live.[24] How can we live spiritually in nature? Many religions, as well as the dominant scientific paradigm (which is not the only way to see science), have set humanity apart from nature; perhaps we are all disconnected in some ways. Part of the problem that we face in gaining a holistic view is our more recent cultural history. Even if we're not Christians ourselves, we live in a multicultural but Christianised society that takes many of its dominant views—such as on morality (good and evil) and on the environment—from its Christian past. We may have been brought up as Christians.

Does this mean that we seek out a more Paganized female version of the Judeo-Christian God in the Goddess, because this is unconsciously familiar? Does it also set us apart from the natural world? Do we only see things from our point of view? Some of the problems of anthropocentrism—seeing everything from a human standpoint—lie in our use of deities. Do we pay too much attention to gods and goddesses, rather than other beings in nature? Does that mean that if we're thinking in spiritual ecological terms we can't work with god-desses and gods?

I think we can, but we do have to be aware of what we're doing and not slip into the worship of *the* Goddess as a deity that stands for everything at the expense of other beings. Egyptian and Greek gods were a part of nature. Egyptian deities, in particular, were often por-trayed in theriomorphic—a combination of human and animal—form; this emphasized the connection rather than the separation be-tween human beings and other animals. Ancient mythologies telling of the deeds of gods and goddesses form a symbolic language of the otherworld, which is part of this world; they don't set the deities apart. During my initial anthropological fieldwork in London, I had a dismemberment experience during a shamanic workshop in which I transformed into a snowy owl.[25] This owl (as well as other owls) has since become what some people call a spirit teacher; I prefer the term "friend." On one occasion recently, my owl spirit came to me and ex-plained (wordlessly) that in order for me to learn what she was going to teach me she needed to take a specific goddess form. Sometimes it is necessary for us to find out about very human matters; some-times—but not always—the human form is the most appropriate "ve-hicle" for this knowledge. Boundaries are not absolute in magical space; they can shift and change, as we can shift and change.

A magical consciousness incorporates all aspects of life; it is a place of infinite possibilities that expands the imagination into many different areas that we have tended to see as separate. Therefore, it is perfectly possible to explore the sounds and silences of music, the myriad colours of a bird's wing, a pattern of thoughts—contrary to a lot of what is said, we can use rationality in this space, too—as well as mythologies in which the activities of gods and goddesses give us deep insight into the nature of our own being, as well as the human condition. What is important, in my view, is that we are continually aware of the greater whole as well as the minute detail. We need to be able to move with ease between the different strands, or fibres, of consciousness. This is the essential skill of a practitioner of magic. Seeing the whole may concern a shift from seeing deity as all-powerful and external or transcendent to the world. The gods are part of the whole, not *the* whole. *We* are not the whole.

A central tenet of the Western Mystery tradition is seeing the human being as microcosm is to macrocosm, meaning that the person (as microcosm) is not only the centre of the macrocosm, or cosmos, but contains the macrocosm within. This is anthropocentric or human-centred to the extreme. Far better, in my view, to see nature as a dimension of ourselves; as Paul Shephard has pointed out:

> . . . ecological thinking requires a kind of vision across boundaries. The epidermis of the skin is ecologically like a pond surface or a forest soil, not a shell so much as a delicate interpenetration. It reveals the self ennobled and extended rather than threatened as part of the landscape and ecosystem because the beauty and complexity of nature are continuous with ourselves.[26]

Nature is a part of us. We are nature and we are shaped by our environments.

In the popular imagination, Paganism in Britain is associated with well-known places such as Stonehenge during the Summer Solstice. Places may become deeply symbolic as "gateways" to a wider magical awareness. Neuroscientist Gerald Edelman has observed that consciousness is shaped through social and environmental interaction;[27] as we grow up we interact with our environments in an active way. Deep feelings may be evoked from contact with place, as I've already mentioned in the nature mystic Richard Jefferies's soul-thought, as well as talking about my sand pit at the bottom of the garden. Poet and scholar Kathleen Raine says that when people look at familiar hills and islands they see the landscape of their imagination as well as the countryside; they inhabit the place both inwardly and outwardly.[28]

Place and mind are intimately connected, and we gain meanings from a sense of place. This might mean well-known sacred sites like the grandeur of the beautiful countryside of western Scotland, but it also includes ordinary, everyday places such as my childhood garden.

Trees can be gateways to different worlds; they have important symbolic meanings in many shamanic worldviews, often forming the basis of otherworldly geographies and cosmologies. When I was a child, I was particularly captivated by Enid Blyton's *The Magic Faraway Tree,* a story about a tree that had magical people and beings living among its boughs; the tree also had exciting and scary different worlds that arrived at the top of its branches, such as the "land of topsy turvy," where everything was upside down. The Faraway Tree was, in many respects, like the Nordic cosmic tree Yggdrasil. It's likely that we all have our own significant special places that we inhabit inwardly and outwardly—we imagine them as we live in them—but how often do we let the place speak to us? And do we hear what it says?

One of my special places is a small copse in a park near where I used to live; it has all manner of personal associations for me. These developed after working with Jasper Lee, a Gypsy shaman (*chovihano*) and Lizzie Gotts-Lee, his partner and herbalist assistant (*patrinyengri*). I was having difficulties in contacting my ancestors. Mainly through family relationships but also through my anthropological training, I didn't want to associate with my European imperialistic past. Jasper and Lizzie helped me to connect to my ancestors through a healing ritual and some practical advice concerning Romany attitudes towards death.[29] After this, I got talking to an old—probably 150-200 year-old—beech tree which was showing the ravages of age. Parts of it were covered by fungus, and its boughs were starting to break off. This tree has been my teacher since 1998, and it has told me, amongst other things, that in the middle of life we are in the process of death. I regularly visited it when I lived close by; now I visit it in my imagination when I want to deepen my awareness, to expand my consciousness. The beech tree is a place where it's possible to have communications with various otherworldly beings, such as ancestors. Sometimes I'm taken to the top, among the canopy of its branches, to bring a different perspective on a question that I might be asking. Sometimes it asks things of me. Trees can help us journey to other places to find connection with nature; and we do need to find ways of connecting with nature.

According to scientist and environmentalist David Suzuki, our problem is the way that we see our relationship with the rest of nature. Suzuki quotes biologist E. O. Wilson, who proposes that we foster *biophilia*, a love of life. Wilson once told Suzuki that it was important for us to rediscover our kin with other animals and plants; we are related to them through our DNA and through evolution, and "[t]o know our kin is to come to love and cherish them."[30] Suzuki searched for different ways of relating to the planet, and he has pointed out the relevance of aboriginal peoples' knowledge and worldviews. Suzuki talks about an Australian aboriginal community called Yarralin, located in the valley of the Victoria River in the Northern Territory. The Dreaming, the mythical time of creation, is etched into the living landscape like a sacred geography. They note how the "sprawling sand-strewn deserts, the tree-pocked savannah grasslands (yellowed under a scorching tropical sun), and the scrub woodlands that cover the Victoria River valley are no mere landscape." This "orderly mosaic" is a sacred map, a living record of the primordial origins of the earth and all its life-forms, known simply as the Dreaming, or Dreamtime:

> In the Dreaming—that timeless epoch of creativity that gave form to the diversity of life, set in motion nature's cycles, and left its enduring imprint upon the earth's crust—all species, including kindred humans, were subtly entwined within a transcendent web of meaning that renders eternally sacred the processes, places, and personages of the natural world.[31]

The Dreaming connects all into a sacred web of meanings of nature. As a worldview it has much to teach us, although we need to be aware of how despicably Europeans have treated aboriginal peoples in the past, taking their lands and forcibly breaking their connection to their sacred heritage. We mustn't make the same mistakes again by taking and using their spirituality for our own ends—we can learn (with respect) and then develop our own ways of relating to the land in which we live.

If we're looking to nature, we can gain inspiration from the Chinese philosophy of Taoism. The search for the Tao, the Way of Nature, according to Chinese scholar Martin Palmer, takes you to "the edge of reality and beyond"; it underlies the change and transformation of all beings, the "spontaneous process regulating the natural cycle of the universe."[32] Taoism is said to have three founder-teachers, one of whom was Chuang Tzu, who said:

> The sage finds his place as a quail settles,
> or as a fledgling is fed
> and as a bird flying leaves no mark of its passage.
> If the whole world has the Tao,
> he is part of that well-being.
> When the whole world has lost the Tao,
> he develops Virtue and avoids involvement.
> After a thousand years, wearied by the world,
> he departs and rises to be with the immortals,
> soaring up upon the white clouds,
> arriving at the Supreme One's abode.[33]

In Taoism, our place is within nature, and Taoism, the "way of nature," involves becoming part of nature, not being separated from the world in a mystical union with God, as many mainstream religions teach.

We have much to learn from non-Western indigenous worldviews and spiritual philosophies, but we also need to look to our own European roots to find out about Western holistic, nature-based ways of seeing the world. Psychologist Brian Bates writes, in the preface to his "psychological archaeology" *The Way of Wyrd,* that the Anglo-Saxons during the first millennium saw wyrd as a way of seeing the world whereby everything was connected by an all-reaching system of fibres similar to a three-dimensional spider's web; any event, anywhere, resulted in reverberations and repercussions throughout the web. For Bates, this web of fibres offers an ecological model which "encompasses individual life events as well as general physical and biological phenomena, non-material as well as material events, and challenges the very cause and effect chains upon which our ecological theories depend."[34]

Physicist Fritjof Capra, author of *The Web of Life* (1996), also sees ecological awareness as all encompassing; it is spiritual in its deepest essence. He has called for a new scientific understanding of life to include a spiritual mode of consciousness at all levels of living systems—from organisms and social systems to ecosystems:

> When the concept of the human spirit is understood as the mode of consciousness in which the individual feels a sense of belonging, of connectedness, to the cosmos as a whole, it becomes clear that ecological awareness is spiritual in its deepest essence.[35]

What is a spiritual ecological awareness? Brian Bates says that we need to reconsider the psychological relationship we have with the environment so we can heal the wounds we have wrought on ourselves and the land; we need to establish a sacred grounding for the development of a deep ecology of place. Wyrd allows a person to place themselves spiritually in harmony with the environment,[36] and Bates' work shows how we can "encounter deep, timeless elements of our psyche."[37] We can learn from the essence of the deeper aspects of the relationship between people and nature.[38] The wyrd worldview encompasses an image of interconnectedness, an ecological, holistic vision[39] that has relevance for us today.

Psychologist Theodore Roszak, drawing on Jung, argues that the psychological dimension to the ecological problem must be addressed to connect mind to the world. He says that we must discover our ecological intelligence; this is located in the deepest part of the collective unconscious, and is the source from which culture unfolds as a reflection of nature's mind. We need to awaken our sense of relating to the environment—what he calls our "environmental reciprocity"—through what lies within ourselves. Roszak's ecological psychology seeks to recover a child's enchanted sense of the world: an innate animism.[40]

A Vision for the Future

How can we reconnect? Maybe we need to rediscover, or discover for the first time, a childlike sense of wonder at the world. To quote Rachel Carson again, as she ponders the value of preserving a childlike sense of awe of nature's capacity to take a person beyond the boundaries of human existence:

> I am sure there is something much deeper, something lasting and significant. Those who dwell, as scientists or laymen, among the beauties and mysteries of the earth are never alone or weary of life. Whatever the vexations or concerns of their personal lives, their thoughts can find paths that lead to inner contentment and to renewed excitement in living. Those who contemplate the beauty of the earth find reserves of strength that will endure as long as life lasts. There is symbolic as well as actual beauty in the migration of the birds, the ebb and flow of the tides, the folded bud ready for the spring. There is something infinitely healing in the repeated refrains of nature—the assurance that dawn comes after night, and spring after the winter.[41]

Personally, I think that this is the basis of nature religion. There is beauty and mystery in the earth, an inner contentment combined with excitement for life and strength. In nature there is symbolic as well as actual beauty; there is healing in the natural cycles. If we can regain, or find out in new ways, how it's possible to think as a child—with senses fresh and curious—we are in a position to relate with enthusiasm and passion to the world around us. Much is written on the power of ritual: the right way of doing things, the right "tradition." How much of this really matters beyond the bounds of our own quest for identity, security, and power? Perhaps we lose the simplicity of magic. It was Jung who wrote in a letter to a colleague who was in psychological crisis, and who had been studying Sanskrit and Indian philosophy, "You must go in quest of yourself, and you will find yourself again only in the simple and forgotten things."[42] Perhaps we as Pagans have lost the simple and forgotten things, the simplicity and joy of nature.

Practically, how can we find this? One way is to view the other-world as a place peopled with beings very much like everyday reality. When we expand our consciousness through trance—which might be through ritual, drumming, meditation, or any other means—we gain access to magical reality. In this reality we can make friends and acquaintances in nature, in pretty much the same way that we do in everyday nonmagical reality. Try talking to a stone, or a tree, or whatever calls to you. Some of these friends might become "spirit helpers" or teachers; you can visit them to have a chat or sort out a problem, just as you might do in the everyday world. It's also a time to find out more about *them*—as in any relationship, it's a two-way affair. It's very ordinary, really! It's also very simple, but the simple is also completely profound. Therein lies the paradox.

In essence, magic is about relating and relationships. Not the every-day relationships of the consumerist world, but the relationships that begin from a place of deep connection inside—the relationships that are built on intuition, communication, and love. These relationships cross ordinary social and cultural boundaries and include all manner of human and nonhuman beings. It takes courage to shift awareness to listen to what they have to say; it changes how we see ourselves, our place in the world, our values. It takes courage to stop trying to control our lives to go with the wider patterns—to become the Fool and step off the edge of the cliff, into the abyss.

In a sense, my journey that I've recounted here is anyone's and everyone's journey. It's a story of reconnecting with nature. It could be seen in terms of "soul retrieval"—a voyage of discovery, if you like, into recovering lost aspects of the spiritual parts of the self. It is a search for the "true self," that deep part within ourselves that connects to the wider whole; the place where we face ourselves when we look in the mirror and see what's really there—not what we would like to see, or what we fantasize about, or a self that we might project onto others. This journey is a story of communication with nature—both within the self and with the natural world—through the creation of meaningful connections, and of finding a language to discover what often turn out to be profound understandings "encoded" in significant symbols. For me, one way that this came about was through the shifting forms of worms, snakes, and dragons, and of relating to special places—ordinary, everyday places. They don't have to be "special," in the way that Stonehenge, for example, is special—the ordinary *is* special. My journey is an ordinary journey, but in magic the ordinary is always special.

Above all, we must always remember that we are a part of nature; therefore our spiritual practices should be rooted in nature. We need to see ourselves as a part of nature through worldviews that encourage this, such as wyrd, and to look to nature for harmonious ways of living our lives, as well as for answers to questions that we might be asking. Perhaps we are already doing this in terms of exploring our inner selves; magic is a psychospiritual path after all. However, we also need to look to the wider picture, the web of existence. It has much to teach us about ourselves if we are willing to look. In this way, I think it is possible that magic can help us develop a more ecological worldview, one that may help us to honour, rather than dishonour, our environments and ourselves.

Notes

1. Margot Adler, *Drawing Down the Moon: Witches, Druids, Goddess-Worshippers, and other Pagans in America Today* (Boston: Beacon Press, 1986), 374–403.

2. Rachel Carson, *The Sense of Wonder* (1956), reprinted in *This Sacred Earth: Religion, Nature, Environment,* ed. R. Gottlieb (New York: Routledge, 1996), 23.

3. R. Jefferies, *The Story of My Heart* (1883) (London: Macmillan, 1968:1), 6–7.

4. Danish explorer and ethnologist Knud Rasmussen recorded this song of an Inuit shaman called Uvavnuk. She was struck by a meteor in the form of a ball of fire; as the fire entered her body, she felt lit up from within by a glowing half-human and half-polar bear spirit. For a while she lost consciousness, but when she recovered she was intoxicated with joy. P. Vitebsky, *The Shaman* (New York: Little, Brown & Co., 1995), 60, 167. See also B. Bates, *The Wisdom of the Wyrd* (UK: Rider & Co., 1996), 161.

5. Adler, *Drawing Down the Moon,* 8.

6. Conversation with Jo Crow, March 7, 2003.

7. J. Frazer, *The Golden Bough, A Study in Magic and Religion* (New York: MacMillan, 1921).

8. See V. Turner, *The Forest of Symbols: Aspects of Ndembu Ritual* (1967) (London: Cornell University Press, 1972), 50–58.

9. For some interesting discussions of how children think, see K. S. Rosengren, C. N. Johnson, and P. L. Harris, eds., *Imagining the Impossible: Magical, Scientific, and Religious Thinking in Children* (Cambridge: Cambridge University Press, 2000).

10. See A. Phillips, *Darwin's Worms: On Life Stories and Death Stories* (New York: Basic Books, 1999).

11. For a materialistic evolutionary perspective on dragons see D. E. Jones, *An Instinct for Dragons* (London: Routledge, 2000).

12. Starhawk, *Dreaming the Dark: Magic, Sex and Politics* (Boston: Beacon, 1982), 5.

13. Starhawk, *Truth or Dare: Encounters with Power, Authority and Mystery* (San Francisco: Harper & Row, 1990), 14–15.

14. See C. G. Jung, *Man and His Symbols* (1964) (London: Pan, 1978), and A. Stevens, *On Jung* (London: Penguin, 1991), 39.

15. J. L. Henderson & M. Oakes, *The Wisdom of the Serpent: The Myths of Death, Rebirth, and Resurrection* (1963) (Princeton: Princeton University Press, 1990), 13,17, 32–34.

16. Oxford: Berg, 2000.

17. See in particular G. Samuel, *Mind, Body and Culture* (Cambridge: Cambridge University Press, 1990). This is a complex text, especially for nonanthropologists, but it rewards patient study, especially for its insights into shamanism.

18. According to B. Morris in *Deep Ecology and Anarchism* (London: Free Press, 1996), 34.

19. Adler, *Drawing Down the Moon*, 374, 399.

20. See G. MacLellan, *Shamanism* (London: Piatkus,1999), 55.

21. Morris, *Deep Ecology and Anarchism*, 36.

22. See M. Sabini, ed., *The Earth Has a Soul: The Nature Writings of C. G. Jung* (California: North Atlantic Books, 2002).

23. Jung's view of the evolution of human consciousness was very different from the idea of spiritual evolution promoted by those such as Madame Blavatsky and Dion Fortune as a counter to Darwin's material evolution.

24. Morris, *Deep Ecology and Anarchism*, 41–42.

25. This is described in detail in my book, *The Nature of Magic: An Anthropology of Consciousness*.

26. P. Shephard, "Ecology and Man—A Viewpoint" in *The Subversive Science,* eds. P. Shephard and D. McKinley (Boston: Houghton Mifflin, 1962). Quoted in "Spiritual Deep Ecol-

ogy and the Left: An Attempt at Reconciliation" in *This Sacred Earth,* ed. R. Gottlieb (New York: Routledge, 1996), 518.

27. See Gerald M. Edelman, *Bright Air, Brilliant Fire* (London: Penguin, 1992).

28. This quote by Kathleen Raine comes from "Outer World as Inner World" in *The Green Fuse,* ed. J. Button (Quartet, 1990). It is reproduced in *Re-Visioning the Earth: A Guide to Opening the Healing Channels Between Mind and Nature,* P. Devereux (New York: Fireside Books, 1996), 86.

29. For a full account of this ritual, as well as my other fieldwork with Jasper and Lizzie, see my *The Nature of Magic: An Anthropology of Consciousness.*

30. D. Suzuki and P. Knudtson, *Wisdom of the Elders: Sacred Native Stories of Nature* (New York: Bantam Books, 1992), xxx.

31. Ibid., 45–46.

32. According to K. Schipper in *The Taoist Body* (1982), trans. K. C. Duval (Berkeley: University of California Press, 1993), 3.

33. M. Palmer, *The Book of Chuang Tzu* (London: Penguin, Arkana, 1996), 96.

34. Bates, *The Wisdom of the Wyrd,* 12.

35. F. Capra, *The Web of Life: A New Scientific Understanding of Living Systems* (New York: Anchor Books, 1996), 7.

36. Bates, *The Wisdom of the Wyrd.*

37. Bates, *The Real Middle-Earth* (London: Sidgwick & Jackson, 2002), 254.

38. Bates, *The Wisdom of the Wyrd,* 25.

39. Bates, *The Wisdom of the Wyrd,* 259.

40. T. Roszak, *The Voice of the Earth: An Exploration of Ecopsychology* (New York: Simon & Schuster, 2001), 304, 311, 320–321.

41. R. Carson, *The Sense of Wonder,* reprinted in *This Sacred Earth: Religion, Nature, Environment,* 24.

42. C. Jung, *Letters I & II,* ed. G. Adler (Princeton: Princeton University Press, 1975), 479.

Towards a Sacred Dance of the Sexes

An Integrative Perspective

MARINA SALA

Our societal structures and relationship to environment have been built upon an ethos of domination and control, which continues to prevail in our lives. Many human relationships are also marred by the fear from which this ethos stems, further separating us from the true notion of pleasure and enjoyment without guilt. If we continue to operate from this paradigm, we will only persist in rendering our gender relations in such a way as to perpetuate conflict and distance ourselves from the pleasure we seek.

Our disagreement is over the parameters of gender identity, which are defined through old attitudes that prevent our full self-expression. While this chapter seeks to demonstrate the illusion of a conflict between the genders, its primary focus is on pleasure and respect. This refers to *all* human relations irrespective of sexual orientation and the existence of sex as the basis for interaction. I propose that it is our perceived separation from the earth and each other that impedes us from experiencing the true notion of pleasure and the movement towards a mutual dance.

By revising our paradigm and our ethics, we can establish a relationship that is mutually beneficial and equally honouring, in which pleasure is the focus. Moreover, through ritual and ceremony we can reinstate celebration into our lives and once again make sacred our relationship to the earth and to our bodies.

For centuries, human beings have sought to dominate the earth and each other, but we have instead found ourselves caught up in a societal addiction to pain and fear. In our belief that everything is separate, we have lost our connection to our environment and have instead sought only to control it.

Ironically, all we have succeeded in achieving is disconnection from the sacredness of life and the celebration of pleasure. As we have come to perceive all that is natural as being "unnatural," we have lost the true meaning of pleasure and blocked our flow of ecstasy in the process. Furthermore, in so doing we have stopped seeing our human traits reflected in the natural world, including our innate desire for that ecstasy and its celebration.

The current state of gender relations in which the sexes continue to regard each other as being in conflict proves that we are still defining pleasure in terms of domination and control. Through our adherence to this paradigm we are simply perpetuating the misperception of the existence of a "battle." What we are instead seeking is the freedom of expression of our true and complete identities, in which all of our traits are valued. One way in which we can attain this is by reconnecting to and understanding suppressed archetypes.

Until now, the dominant archetype in history has been that of the warrior, whose negative traits of bravado and an unquenchable thirst for control predominates. Although the warrior in itself is a valuable archetype to have, on its own it can lead to an imbalance in attitudes and actions. While there is a marked absence of the traditional warrior in today's societies, we still mirror aspects of the archetype of Ares as the ultimate fighter.[1] In the pursuit of hegemonic rule, his instinctual use of aggression and battle-thirst is enacted in social and environmental actions. Hence the use of the term "warrior" in this work describes present-day, warlike actions in which ethics and respect are often significantly absent.

Conversely, our mythological hunter relates to his/her environment in a much more respectful way than our present-day hunter, whereby many have rendered the skill a controversial "blood sport." Therefore the term is based on those archetypal qualities seen in Pan and Artemis as sacred hunters, as well as on the behaviour of predators found in the natural world. The use of "the warrior" and "the hunter" hence refer to aspects of mythological archetypes. Moreover, it is not the intention here to focus on emulating the archetypes themselves, but rather to reconnect to their virtues and approaches to life, found to be currently lacking. "The warrior" in this case is seen in terms of rampaging through life without regard, whereas "the hunter/ress" reveres the environment, in both its limitations and plenitude.

In our quest for self-expression, it is the hunter/ress who offers us the greatest rewards. As we connect to the true qualities of this archetype, we can establish a more respectful relationship to the environment and to each other. Indeed, our denial of pleasure and our misunderstanding of strength have suppressed aspects of our true nature, and have limited our self-expression. In our inability to manifest all of our human traits, we have regarded ourselves as being in conflict and have failed to see the commonality of our goals. As we allow the qualities of the hunter/ress to emerge, we obtain the sense of identity we are seeking and open ourselves to greater compassion. Eradicating the misperception of an enemy from our lives allows us to reclaim our joy of pleasure from the clutches of fear and guilt.

Due to the misinterpretation and misrepresentation of the two archetypes (warrior and hunter), aspects of our human nature are presently out of synch at both the collective and individual levels. Gender identity and group definition have today become an issue, as a result of the state of malaise that this imbalance has produced. Rather than seeing the indivisibility of our human qualities, the genders are today staking claims over which of these most belongs to which sex. Looking at these two archetypes from a different perspective, we can reopen a conscious connection to the earth and nature from which they stem, and cease to find ourselves at loggerheads over our claims.

Indeed, what we have historically failed to realize is that the difficulty in gender relations is nothing more than a red herring, and a by-product of the guilt and fear that have encompassed our lives.

The issue is in fact the totality of the identity of man and woman, in which the desire for pleasure and the pleasure in desire are integral to our human nature. By denying sexual ecstasy and longing, we have sustained a conflict-torn society. We have created a culture in which control and subjugation, rather than honour and respect, have become the central pillars. As we continue to denigrate each other, we have also lost the ability to understand and respect our bodies as the vessels for ecstasy and ceremony that they are.

Today's open attitudes towards the Old Ways are providing an opportunity for us all to reconnect to the earth and her cycles in a way in which we can celebrate and honour all of our human traits, including our passion for life and pleasure.

This chapter looks at methods by which we can renew our relationship to the earth and her celebration and begin to free a deeper identity. In order to do this, we first need to retrace our steps back to the point where the intimacy and vibrancy of our connection to the environment began to diminish. From this place, we can reestablish an acceptance of our true nature before guilt and fear took over. Secondly, by addressing the issue of gender identity through our misinterpreted and lost archetypes, we can remove the blocks that impede us from being ourselves. In so doing we can redefine our ethics and human relations, in which honour and mutual respect become the basis of our interactions. Finally, we explore how ritual and celebration can help remove guilt and the concept, or invention, of "sin," enabling us to once again honour the beauty of our bodies' passage through life.

Retracing Our Steps

Since the end of the Neolithic era, we have incrementally separated ourselves from the earth and our quest for pleasure. In this process, we have also lost the teachings of our ancestors, whose fascination and respect for their environment enticed them into a deeper relationship and understanding of it. Through their observations they recognised that nature moved in a pattern of cycles, which were mirrored by their own bodies' rhythms and changes. As life celebrated the transformations of the seasons, our ancestors made celebration a natural part of their lives. They noticed how spring was a time in which nature emerged to re-create itself. Plants once again emerged from the cold winter's frosts, and animals began the regenerative mating season. The equal role between the life-giving feminine and the creative masculine principles in the world around them was reflected in social structures. Through an attitude of respect and appreciation, our ancestors created nomadic agrarian societies, which were reputedly egalitarian and peaceful.[2]

With the rise of territorial conquests, however, things begin to change as the environment was regarded as something to be controlled, and land ownership replaced many a nomadic way of life. Egalitarian societies fell under the domination of the conquerors through the rising paradigm of supremacy and control. While there are numerous theories that explain the reason for this transition, what is important here is that societies did move towards less egalitarian and respectful interactions. Indeed, with the arrival of hierarchical structures, men started to take a dominant position in social and religious life, and began to exert their power over women. With this approach to life and the environment, we begin to see the emergence of societies ruled by god-kings in which women take a secondary role. Reverence for the Earth Mother, once alive in Neolithic times, slowly faded into the background in favour of the Sky Father. While there was a shift in the hierarchy between feminine and masculine principles, pleasure and the celebration of natural cycles remained an integral part of life. (This of course does not justify the loss of women's social equality and status.)

Even as women took a secondary role in the social and religious structure of these societies, their true nature remained represented by the goddesses venerated at this time. For instance, female deities in the Olympian pantheon held a power of their own for which they were revered, emulated, and even feared. Similarly, the relationship between gods and goddesses in mythology was also represented in what is termed the "sacred marriage."[3]

While the slant had markedly changed from the reverence of the earth goddess, understanding of life as a sacred union between masculine and feminine principles persisted. Polytheistic veneration continued to be an intrinsic part of many Western societies until the transition to monotheistic worship in biblical times.

With the rise of a patriarchal monotheistic system, within which we are still by and large operating today, an omnipotent father-god replaced the god-king as well as the lesser gods and goddesses. With this shift we not only lost the divine feminine as a determining principle in creation, but we also began to sever from our consciousness the forces of nature that reflect our own human qualities. Through these changes, we separated ourselves from the celebration of life and pleasure and develop instead a relationship to suffering and guilt. The story of Adam and Eve began to rule our ethics of behaviour in our relationship to the divine, as well as to each other in sexual relations. Indeed, sex and ecstasy, once so much a natural part of life, became defined as profane, as was our human naturalness from which they stem. The qualities of the godhead also became disconnected from any earthly aspect in favour of more celestial ones. The new god lost his sexuality, once so rife in archetypes such as Zeus and Pan, whose virility was revered as part of the creative force. Similarly, a virginal Mary, who was able to bring about life through an immaculate conception, replaced the fecund Goddess as the Mother of all things.

When we emulated and ingratiated ourselves to a new god, we lost our connection to our old deities who once reflected our human nature so well. Through this loss, our relationship to pleasure also suffers. For men the task of emulation was made difficult as their association with the characteristics of the old god, found in ancient and more earth-based theologies, was totally lost. This ancient god, known in different societies by many names such as Pan, Cernunnos, and Osiris, became defamed and driven to the depths of "hell" by the rising monotheism, the Roman Church: his new name was "The Devil." His role as lover, son, and consort to the Goddess was totally abolished, and any reverence of him punishable by death. By castigating his nature and calling it "evil," the male character, too, was stigmatised for not being "holy" enough and similar to that of the acceptable god. This more ancient god provided men (and women) with a connection to the hunt, the playfulness of life, the sacredness of sexual pleasure, and sacred marriage beyond the church. Men subsequently began to struggle with their sense of power, independence, hunting instincts, playfulness, and virility, so that just as Pan had come to be considered the devil, so too did men's natural instincts become "devilish."

For women, the Virgin Mary became the closest approximation to a female deity, whose fecundity was now completely lost through her "immaculate conception" of Jesus. The word "virgin," which originally meant "owned by no man," was also lost in translation and became synonymous with a woman's sexual purity. So, the nurturing, abundant, structuring, powerful, and giving mother goddess was no longer a symbol of woman's strength, but of her unruliness. Self-determination, also once seen in the virgin goddesses, now became an aberrant (a political and doctrinal ploy) rather than a state of being. Indeed, to seek to embody the characteristics of the Goddess was regarded as rising above one's station. The aspects of wisdom as seen in Sophia and the Shekinah, the strength and independence of woman as seen in Artemis and Diana, or her voluptuous and sensuous nature as seen in Venus and Aphrodite were also relegated to the "profane" kingdom of "The Devil."

Such a woman became the revolutionary temptress, the whore, and the corrupter of men. The Magdalene, a great role model for many a self-determining woman, was vilified for her use of sex in sacred ritual.[4] She was called "The Great Whore of Babylon."

Within this new framework, woman's sexual role and body became sullied, as did all ritual of a Pagan and sexual nature. Women's status as the representative of the goddess on earth is now considered obscene. Indeed, prior to this transformation of attitudes, as women's bodies reflected the divine feminine principle, sexual union between man and woman was a way for woman to emulate a goddess, and was enacted with respect, reverence, and joy. Within a patriarchal, father-based, monotheistic framework, however, the divine feminine is pure and virginal, and women are considered by their very nature to be temptresses of desire, which is a sin itself.

This was how, for both men and women, the sacredness of sex and pleasure through ritual became withdrawn from life, and the institutionalisation of guilt entered our social thinking, both in Christianity and in Judaism, the two dominant monotheistic religions of the time. As both sexes lived by the rules of this new framework, they began to view sex in the same sinful way as it was portrayed, losing the connection to the sacred as well as the right to pleasure. Through this chastisement, the celebration of masculinity and femininity through same-sex relations is now suppressed, and regarded as an unnatural perversion. In so doing, part of our human nature became ostracized and judged in its quest for desire and satisfaction.

Hence not only did our connection to sex undergo a drastic change in perspective, but so, too, apparently did our appetites and natural inclinations for union and communion. Similarly, the celebration of our bodies' changes, blood cycles, and puberty became reasons for shame rather than celebration. The virile, pubescent young man or the reproductive young woman began to feel ashamed of the changes in their bodies for fear of succumbing to the "devilish" practices of sex and pleasure. For women in particular, their menstrual blood, once a representation of their power, fecundity, and connection to the feminine principle of creation, is now considered unclean.

When the innate sexual desires are suppressed, however, people are known to seek them in dysfunctional ways, where they manifest in the form of domination, pain, and control. Where the celebration of life and the joy of ecstasy were once venerated, today they are laced with a sense of guilt. As pleasure becomes "sinful," there is a wrestling with conscience to justify it and our lust for life.

Reclaiming the right to pleasure in today's society unfortunately stems from a warped understanding of its true meaning; for after centuries of dominating one another, we seem unable to reconnect to pleasure with a sense of celebration in a way in which it is mutually honouring and respectful. The presence of guilt in our lives drives us to "numb out," to justify our own satisfaction at the expense of another, and to experience it through fear of it being stolen from us. In so doing, we render our social attitudes to sexual relations as a win/lose situation, rather than a mutual enjoyment of the lust that both sexes share.

Guilt has therefore had a catastrophic effect in closing us off to our connection with the sacred in its fecund state as embodied by a goddess. Similarly, this same guilt has severed our association with lost gods, as we have rejected our hunger for life, adventure, and the playfulness of pleasure as embodied by Pan. In our quest for self-expression, our society is today looking to reconnect to those forces that so reflected our nature, as well as to the original meaning of pleasure from which we have been separated.

Towards a New Paradigm: Reintroducing the Hunter

As we reconnect to our understanding of pleasure, so, too, do we reawaken the parts of ourselves that have been disconnected from it—for one cannot occur without the other. In this brief overview of our social history, we have witnessed a change in our relationship to the earth, in which we have come from being aware of our participation with our environment, to becoming (and remaining) intellectually and spiritually aloof from it. In analysing this transition from the point of view of archetypes, we can begin to acknowledge the forces that are present and absent as a result of the above and begin to redress the imbalance.

Looking at our social development, we begin to notice the overwhelming presence of the dysfunctional traits of the warrior in history (and into the present day) and the ever-growing absence of the hunter in his/her more sacred aspects. From a behavioural perspective, we are essentially witnessing the presence of a child and the absence of a responsible adult, for in the warrior we see the capricious child whose environment, in denying him his desires, becomes the adversary. As we continue to witness the warrior's unstoppable tantrums, we note the absence of the conscientious adult who is able to respond to the limitations of his/her environment. The scruples found in the hunter/ress are made evident by his/her ability to take only what is necessary and when conditions allow.

Therefore while we can attribute certain traits of our behaviour to archetypal forces, what we are ultimately realising is the prototype of the hunter/ress's conscientious approach to life. Hence it is not my intention to see how we can best emulate Artemis or Pan in their archetypal qualities, but to learn from their behaviour as hunters instead.

I propose that reincorporating the qualities of the hunter into our lives will have a twofold effect felt in both our gender relations and our environmental ones. Firstly, it will allow both men and women to express their sense of true strength (the pursuit of which is today manifesting itself through attitudes of bravado). In so doing, we can honour the presence of the hunter as a quality in both sexes, thereby allowing the genders to resurrect an archetype lost by both. This subsequently paves the way to greater self-expression in which the flow of respect and pleasure, rather than domination, can be reestablished. Secondly, it will enable us to move away from the ethos of lack and control of our environment, towards that of responsibility, plenitude, and flow.

Gender relations have been in a state of disequilibria since the end of the Neolithic era, and there has been a need to redress the balance ever since.[5] While we have indeed needed to focus our attention on socioeconomic and political equality, today it is also required that we focus on a plight that affects both sexes. As history has shown us, many aspects of our human nature have been denied to us over time, and today our society is manifesting the resulting frustration.

Through our debate over which personal qualities and characteristics each gender most clearly represents, we are today witnessing a quest for complete self-expression. The force that underlies this search is the reconnection to qualities described in archetypes that have been either lost or denied in the course of history.

There is presently a trend in our gender relations towards regarding our differences as being irreconcilable (men are from Mars and women are from Venus), while simultaneously laying claim to the same indivisible qualities in our nature. This only serves to render our quest paradoxical and frustrating.

Today's gender relations have arrived at a point in which men and women are sharing similar tasks once considered sex-specific. Ironically, people continue the ethos of domination by laying sole claim on these traits and abilities. The point we are missing is that while these traits may be inherently different in their manifestation, in themselves they are indivisible, as both males and females of most species share them. While the Horned Gods Herne and Pan are the hunters in the male archetype, Artemis and Diana are the huntresses in the female. Their approach to the hunt and the environment is essentially the same. Similarly, nature itself also demonstrates this parallel in the behaviours found in the animal world. For instance, a lion and a lioness are equally capable of killing any offending attacker who intrudes on the safety of their cubs, irrespective of their "day job" and sex-specific role. Indeed, amongst the lions, the lioness is the primary hunter.

Among humans, this capacity has only been denied by role divisions and expectations, and not by human limitations. In today's society, in which there has been a widening of parameters, men and women have successfully demonstrated the ability to be caretakers and breadwinners with equal fervor. While our everyday lives are exemplifying the same aptitude, popular literature is advocating the opposite, precipitating an unreal conflict over gender roles and identity.

As these roles merge past the point of sex-specific stereotypes, we begin to question the parameters and tenets of gender identity. With this, we are also witnessing trends in which men and women want to demonstrate their strengths and abilities at being able to carry out their "newfound roles," and retain a sense of gender identity. This, today, is manifesting itself as a rising trend in an attitude of bravado, adopted to downplay any insecurities over identity and to exaggerate control. Significantly, it is as equally directed against our existing social structures ("the system") as it is against each other.

As the sexes continue to engage in this game, they reach a point of stalemate and overlook the means by which true potentials can be attained, without the semblance of bravado to carry it through. As men and women reconnect to the hunter within themselves, they learn to tap into that aspect of themselves that acts from capabilities, patience, and respect.

Throughout history, the paradigm of the warrior has shown us that as resources are finite they must be hoarded to ensure our safety. In regarding our natural environment as hostile, we have created the illusion of an enemy which we have sought to dominate in order to control at whatever cost. In noticing that control is futile, this ethos has led us to believe that the forces that are not succumbing to our power simply require stronger measures to ensure compliance. In other words, the hegemony that has been present in our social paradigm has taught us that hoarding is a justifiable reaction to the unruliness of our enemy and our harsh environmental conditions.

The present trend in bravado is simply a continuation of this paradigm in which we persist in regarding one another as the enemy. This approach is outdated insofar as it is evidently futile for the creation of sustainable and mutually beneficial social and environmental relations. Conversely, realigning to the role, activity, and ethos of the hunter in our lives offers us a new framework from which we can establish healthier relationships and interactions.

Observing the hunter's slant on life can help us to understand how necessary changes can be applied. The hunter approaches the prey with patience and discernment. S/he relates to the environment from the perspective of being part of it and takes only what is required to feed his/her hunger. S/he is single-minded in his/her focus, and kills only when all the conditions are favourable. Once again this is as apparent in the natural world as it is in our own (lost) abilities to hunt. A predatory animal will spot its prey and follow it at the expense of all others, attacking only when it is sure that it can kill swiftly and with unfaltering precision. Unlike the warrior, the hunter knows when something is enough, and rather than exploiting the environment, he/she recognizes its limitations and responds accordingly. In his/her response and communion with it, s/he allows the energies to flow during the kill and beyond. In other words, in its precision, the kill does not become a massacre, but stems from necessity.

There is, then, an intrinsic sense of responsibility and focus within the hunter that is absent in the warrior. While the warrior will stop at nothing to obtain his desire, the hunter, by not regarding life as the enemy, carries out the task with respect. As Starhawk explains with regard to earlier hunting societies in her book *The Spiral Dance,* "Animals were never killed needlessly, and no parts of the kill were ever wasted. Life was never taken without recognition and reverence for the spirit of the prey."[6] Many North American indigenous societies like the Koyukon of Alaska also held that the animal must be killed as humanely as possible and treated with the utmost respect.[7]

There is a sense of respect within the hunter that is markedly absent in the warrior. While we have regarded everything in our way as a potential enemy, we have lost the sense of respect both for the environment and for each other. Today's quest for a clearer identity and expression manifests itself in a fight for ownership of indivisible qualities—this has the potential of seeing us falling, yet again, down the same hole. It is neither the opposite sex nor the environment that is the enemy here, but the societal paradigm from which we are currently operating. As long as we continue to cooperate with its tenets, we are responsible for upholding its presence in our society.

As we move closer to reconnecting with the hunter in ourselves and giving him/her expression, we begin to open the channel to a sustainable relationship with the world we live in, and with pleasure. In the case of the environment, we learn to recognise that we are a part of our surroundings and begin to realise its plenitude. As we become aware of our own needs, we learn to take only what is required in a responsible way. In being intrinsically linked to our surroundings, we also acknowledge and accept the uncontrollability of the wild and untamed forces of nature, and so will stop seeking to dominate them. In this recognition we can begin to restructure our personal environment accordingly, allowing for our part in the cycles of life, and to flow in communion with them once again.

As we reconnect to this suppressed archetype and begin to express our true and unsung nature, our relationship to pleasure is also freed. Moreover, as we learn to honour both the differences and the similarities between the sexes, we also seek those aspects of our ethics that are blocking the flow of energy of sex and pleasure. By redefining our ethics in a way in which they are mutually respectful, we allow ourselves the right to enjoy pleasure once again.

Redefining Our Ethics

The introduction of the hunter as a new paradigm of living, of course, does not suggest that we stalk one another and attack and kill rather than communicate! Any paradigm has a spillover effect into all aspects of our lives and our psyches. To help elucidate this, we could visualise a cascading flow of champagne into a pyramidal stack of glasses, each brimming over to feed the next, and the next, and so on. The effects that the hunter brings are far more rewarding than those so far seen by the warrior.

What it offers us is an initial step towards a greater sense of re-sponsibility and connection. As we move away from a predomi-nantly androcentric approach to life and relationships, we begin to see our intrinsic part in the interconnectedness to all things, and be-have accordingly. The hunter as a paradigm liberates our senses of compassion, empathy, and respect, each of which in turn works to-wards the balancing out of the individual's single-minded focus. Moving away from the misperception of conflict towards coopera-tion, we will begin to recognize that the historical wounds brought about by our shared past are similar, if not the same. We also begin to empathise and act compassionately towards one another.

In compassion there is no control; in its deep understanding there is no guilt, no shame, and no power over one another. When we recog-nise that everyone, to a greater or lesser extent, is in the same boat, respect flows more freely. With greater empathy, we can reframe our approach to our human relations. Rather than meeting each other from a position of lack and our need to take, we reframe our position by considering what it is that we can do for our mutual and true needs to be met.

Operating from the hunter's perspective does not imply a transi-tion from warrior to doormat, but rather an understanding of oth-ers' needs as well as our own. Mutual respect of self and other, com-bined with a sense of pleasure rather than pain, becomes the thread with which we weave our new cloth. By coming from a place of compassion in which we nurture others' needs, as well as our own, we allow our quest for pleasure to also stem from this same place. From this standpoint we can then enact our exploration of pleasure without fear or guilt.

Until now, our social interactions have been characterised by an endless game of reaction and retribution through our fear and sense of lack. In feeding into fear, we have absolved ourselves of responsibil-ity and justified our actions at every turn. For some, the guilt of pleasure—and the fear of sin—has led them to darken its manifestation in the worst way possible. Current alarming rates of child pornography and paedophilia amply exemplify this. Aside from the shocking implications this has on our society and our children, there is a sense of irony to this present "trend." If we are so afraid of "sinning," how is it that some have distorted pleasure to such monstrous proportions? Fortunately or unfortunately, the answer to this is clear. In suppressing our natural desires and vowing celibacy from pleasure and ecstasy, there is a repression of the innate aspects of our natures that were once free. Over the centuries we have turned all that is natural into something unnatural, and today find ourselves face to face with the very "devil" from which we were meant to be protecting ourselves. This distortion of our natural desires simply indicates that in spite of the measures undertaken in history to deny their expression, our innate longings have remained with us.

Riane Eisler argues, "The bottom line about all our ethics and standards of behaviour is that we have based all our behaviour on pain rather than pleasure."[8] We have been taught to associate pleasure with such terms as hedonism and narcissism, or the belief that one person's pleasure signifies another's pain. Eisler suggests that, in order to change our ethics, we need to move away from viewing our relationships in dualistic terms of right or wrong, moral or immoral, and to define them in terms of being "caring and ethical, or unfair, uncaring and unethical."[9]

In other words, what we are seeking to regain is a sense of compassion and a less arrogant, hegemonic approach with which to infuse both our environment and one another. If we continue to regard ourselves as invincible and superior to our surroundings, how can we learn to behave in ethical, caring, and equal terms with each other?

As we have seen from observing the characteristics of the hunter, what we have been lacking is a sense of respect and responsibility for nature, each other, and ourselves. When we operate from a place of self-respect, we bring a sense of dignity to our lives from which we no longer feel the need to dominate and suppress. Indeed, the expression of our strength is innate and free flowing. Furthermore, our sense of what is ethical and caring emerges naturally as we act with compassion and respect for one another's positions and needs. As Riane Eisler points out, "Fully experiencing pleasure entails being present, sentient and aware."[10]

When we realise that our actions are constructive and not destructive to others, we naturally eradicate the guilt of pleasure from the human psyche. While this may appear idealistic, it is worth noting that people who uphold the Old Ways as a way of life abide by these very principles and subsequently hold no guilt in their attainment of pleasure or their interactions with the environment. As we succeed in liberating pleasure from fear and guilt, we can renew our sense of celebration with the environment and nature's cycles through ritual and ceremony.

Celebrating Our Bodies Through Ritual and Ceremony

As we have seen, some of our sexual practices have become twisted in a power game while we have lived by the ethos dictated by the warrior. In being led to believe that our bodies and their natural cycles are unclean, we have lived with a perpetual anxiety of guilt in relation to our giving and receiving of pleasure. Moreover, the domination and subjugation of women has continued to vilify the female body through pornography and other forms of exploitation, giving many men a false sense of the erotic. While we persist in mutually objectifying each other's bodies, we remain consistently disconnected from the sense of pleasure that we are seeking to experience—the reason being that, in order to attain the true nature of pleasure, union and communion are required. Hence, so long as we continue to deny our relationship to the earth and do not take the steps to make the necessary connection, we cannot experience what we seek.

For those who follow the Old Ways, there is no separation. The body is the vessel of both ceremony and pleasure; they are one and the same. When we talk of pleasure, we assume that we are strictly talking of sexual pleasure, and our society mirrors that back to us on a regular basis. Pleasure is pleasure in itself; how we choose to manifest it and enact it varies. Essentially it is about union, sentience, allure, and allowing ourselves to fully merge with the life force around us, as well as inside us. Separation is an illusion—it is not an option in this experience. Remaining separate, be it from each other or the environment, out of fear, pain, or subjugation, simply averts our experience of true pleasure.

In mutually honouring sexual practices, people come together in sexual union as equals and as freely determining individuals. Through reciprocal respect, energies are able to flow naturally. In the absence of any semblance of control and domination, our bodies can be truly explored and celebrated for our differences and for our ability to respond to, and attain, ecstasy. When we open our minds, bodies, and emotions, we seek a deeper connection to each other as to a spiritual force, and we lose ourselves in rapture rather than commanding each other into submission. As we attain true pleasure we open to the sacred dance of life, the spiral dance, in which everything is interconnected, moving in a pattern of cycles in tune with the rest of creation. It is this dance that renders our connection to the forces of nature, as to each other's bodies, ecstatic.

Therefore, while we can seek pleasure in its carnal form, we can also attain ecstacy by opening ourselves to our surroundings through ritual and ceremony. Ecstacy is about union and sentience, and not only the physical. Shamanic ritual practices open the senses to ecstatic states of awareness, within which a connection to the creative source is made. As there is no separation between the self and the environment, the body also encompasses the four natural elements, and from this knowledge communion is attained. The earth is our body, water our blood, air our breath, and fire our spirit. As we enact ritual, each of the four elements is revered outside as inside our bodies.

Connecting to our inner and outer worlds, we also begin to celebrate the rites of passage our bodies undergo through our life's cycles. From birth through puberty, adulthood, old age, up to and including death, we celebrate and honour the forces of nature that reflect these life passages back to us.

Despite what society has led us to believe, there is much cause for celebration in the first blood of a young woman. "A [woman's] body, its odours, secretions, and menstrual blood are sacred, are worthy of reverence and celebration"[11] This is her time of coming into her power as she begins the transition from childhood into womanhood. At this stage of her life, she begins her personal connection to the cycles of the moon that regulate her monthly cycles. In many traditional societies, as well as Western Pagan practices, a girl's first bleeding is a time in which the female elders of her tribe welcome her into adulthood and women's ways. In the case of the Bambuti Pygmies, the young girl and her friends are taken to a special woman's hut, where older female friends and relatives teach them women's arts and crafts and songs.

Emma Restall Orr describes a women's ceremony in which, in her role as celebrant, she assists the initiation of a pubescent girl into womanhood.[12] For the young woman, this was a time of establishing her connection to the moon, the earth, and water. While guided by the celebrant, the young woman opened to her own power of self-determination as she chose flowers and words to mark her transition. Interestingly, neither the young woman nor her mother were practicing Pagans, but reflected the present need in society to reclaim ritual and celebration in life.

Through such techniques we once again honour the sacredness of a woman's blood from its beginning to its end. In some Native American traditions, a moon lodge for women is not only a place to share women's lore, but also a place in which a menstruating woman can honour her blood and return it to the earth. Ceremonies can also be held to honour the end of a woman's moontime. In so doing we remove the curse from the "curse." In this way, rather than being cast out of the social circle, the girl/woman is celebrated and her relationship to the moon venerated.

As women are reconnecting with their bodies through ceremony, so too are men. Ritualised tattooing to mark a boy's transition from puberty to manhood is still carried out by many societies around the world. Similarly, the practice of circumcision, however controversial, is equally enacted as a rite of passage for boys from birth to adolescence. Men's circles and lodges are also finding new ways to celebrate and recapture the true meaning of manhood. Many indigenous traditions of sending young men into the wilderness to quest for a vision are still enacted today. While this may occur in mixed-sexes or men-only circles, the separation between the boy and his mother is made. Here the pubescent boy enters manhood by leaving the women's circle behind. As he joins the men of his tribe, he learns their practices and roles, and connects to his own heritage.

Rite-of-passage ceremonies teach us to connect to the changes our bodies undergo and to honour the gifts they bring at every stage of our lives. Moreover, they acknowledge the beauty of our bodies as well as our own journeys through the cycles of birth, life, and death. Celebrating these transitions from one state to another allows us to explore and cultivate the emerging qualities of our psyches and the spiritual riches they bring.

The enjoyment of pleasure in itself allows us to commune with each other and to mutually and individually celebrate our bodies rather than objectify them as ornaments of desire. As men and women celebrate their bodies, they are able to once again reconnect to the divine union between god and goddess in which all is sacred and nothing is profane.

The illusion of separation from the environment as from our own inner qualities and traits has kept us locked into a conflict in which we have ultimately only fought against ourselves and lost. Moreover, as the quest became a battle, people's sense of respect and compassion rapidly diminished through the tactic of enforced victimization.

The presence of guilt in much of the collective psyche also poses an interesting question as to its origins. While we can trace its institutionalisation back to biblical times and the inception of patriarchal monotheistic religions, it poses the questions of why and how this guilt became an issue in the first place. Did the story that patriarchal monotheism presents us of a banishment from some mythological "paradise" perhaps stem from the fact that some had, in fact, "sinned" as they pillaged and destroyed the earth in a quest to control it? Could it be that this guilt became a cancer on the collective conscience, and the need was felt to remind ourselves that we had behaved in less than compassionate ways towards each other and our world?

It is evident from our relationship to pleasure that guilt stops its attainment in our lives. Be it sexual or otherwise, society has ritualised the association with pleasure in terms of "numbing out," as many continue to separate themselves from its complete experience. Indeed, for a majority of people, enjoyment and pleasure are associated with drug use and alcohol, which further disconnects them from the "sentience" to which Eisler refers.

One of the reasons why sex and pleasure are considered "Pagan" practices (even pastimes or obsessions!) is that ritual opens the senses to feeling, be it sexually or ceremonially. Sentience is increased not due to insatiable desires, but insofar as "numbing out" simply impedes the sense of communion that ritual seeks to attain.

Therefore it is not the case that those who live by the Old Ways are "horny little devils," but that they recognise pleasure and its appreciation is a natural state of being.

Despite the dominant paradigm that has sought to suppress desire with fear and guilt (and by denying the open reverence to the goddesses and gods), the Old Ways have nevertheless remained alive—however occult—through the ages. In reconnecting to the hunter, we remind ourselves of the open and free relationship towards pleasure as well as the environment that was once enjoyed. In order for us to rectify our relationship with pleasure and move towards a sacred dance of the sexes, we need to remember our connection to the whole earth and render an impassioned sentience as our new way of being.

Notes

1. Bolen, *Gods In Every Man: A New Psychology of Men's Lives and Loves*, 192–193.

2. Eisler, *Sacred Pleasure: Sex, Myth & The Politics of the Body, New Paths to Power and Love.*

3. Bolen, *Goddesses in Every Woman: A New Psychology for Women.*

4. Walker, *The Woman's Encyclopaedia of Myths and Secrets*, 614.

5. Eisler, *Sacred Pleasure: Sex, Myth & the Politics of the Body.*

6. Starhawk, *The Spiral Dance*, 99.

7. Nelson, *Make Prayers to the Raven: A Koyukon view of the Northern Forest*, 23–25.

8. Eisler, *Sacred Pleasure: Sex, Myth & Politics of the Body*, 328.

9. Ibid., 307.

10. Ibid., 328.

11. Starhawk, *The Spiral Dance*, 101.
12. Emma Restall Orr, *Spirits of the Sacred Grove: The World of a Druid Priestess*.

Bibliography and Suggested Reading

Bolen, Jean Shinoda. *Gods In Every Man: A New Psychology of Men's Lives and Loves.* New York: Harper Perennial, 1990.

————. *Goddesses in Every Woman: A New Psychology for Women.* New York: Harper Perennial, 1984.

Bonewitz, Ronald. *The Mayan Prophecy.* London: Piatkus, 1999.

Conway, D. J. *The Lord of Light and Shadow: The Many Faces of The God.* St Paul, Minnesota: Llewellyn Publications, 1997.

Eisler, Riane. *Sacred Pleasure: Sex, Myth & The Politics of the Body, New Paths to Power and Love.* Shaftsbury, Dorset: Element Books Limited, 1996.

————. *The Chalice and the Blade.* London: Thorsons, 1998.

Faludi, Susan. *Backlash: The Undeclared War Against Women.* London: Vintage, 1992.

————. *Stiffed: Betrayal of Modern Man.* London: Vintage, 1999.

Markale, Jean. *The Great Goddess: The Reverence of the Divine Feminine from the Palaeolithic to the Present.* Rochester, Vermont: Inner Traditions International, 1999.

Nelson, Richard K. *Make Prayers to the Raven: A Koyukon View of the Northern Forest.* Chicago: University of Chicago Press, 1983.

Reis, Patricia. *Through the Goddess: A Woman's Way of Healing.* New York: The Continuum Publishing Company, 1991.

Restall Orr, Emma. *Spirits of the Sacred Grove: The World of a Druid Priestess.* London: Thorsons, 1998.

Starhawk. *The Spiral Dance: A Rebirth of the Ancient Religion of the Great Goddess.* San Francisco: Harper & Row Publishers, 1979.

Walker, Barbara G. *The Woman's Encyclopaedia of Myths and Secrets.* San Francisco: HarperSanFrancisco, 1983.

What Would Happen if Everybody Started Telling the Truth?

The Sacred Art of Communication— A Key to the Well-Being of the Future

LY DE ANGELES

For I would walk alone,
Under the quiet stars, and at that time
Have felt whate'er there is of power in sound . . .
And I would stand,
In the night blackened with a coming storm,
Beneath some rock, listening to notes that are
The ghostly language of the ancient earth,
Or make their dim abode in distant winds.
Thence did I drink the visionary power.

The Prelude (excerpt)
William Wordsworth

You all know where this is going, don't you? Where this is heading? Leading? We're being prepared!

Yes, it's all very nice, isn't it? Feel good? Feel ready, do we?

Not ready! Spouting platitudes and behaving holy—being good!

And all the while, people are being primed for a future that's devoid . . .

If you, personally, don't go to movies that reveal a future dark and dangerous, controlled and grey—with black-masked cops wielding lasers and stun guns—that doesn't mean that millions and millions of others avoid the box office and the vid store. These people are highly entertained. Some worry. A few know how close we are to that "virtual" future.

One could almost become paralysed, paranoid, convinced, because "virtual" means "almost," and I am old enough to remember that eventualities occur because of somebody's capacity to speculate. You see, I was born into a world with no plastic, no TV, no computers. Can you imagine?

So, walk a little further into the anomaly of "time" and ask yourself if you've done enough.

Imagine, if you can, the seventh generation. Does it matter that your name is not remembered? No. But I'm aware that one person (one person!) can affect an incalculable number of people with the right keys.

The very thing that affects our species the most, outside of the basic necessities of food, sex, shelter, sleep, and health, is excitation.

And what excites? Interaction. Doesn't matter with what. And what is the key here? Communication. Whether through words, gesture, expression, sensation, or manipulation, communication is our species' most exciting (and devastating) tool.

PART 1

BINAH #2

There is no anger within me but the primal spirit works through me
to touch you with the atrocities that build one upon the other to a
towering mass of dogma that blinds all from the song—the raven song,
the walrus song, the seagull and the snail song—
all are joined in majesty upon this earth within my arms,
like a newborn infant, to one who loves it so . . .
So find the beauty, for that is my way through, to love it all more precious
than the flower in the night, alone within the whisper of the wind—
But know also the truth. And subtly seek to change the lies. . ."

The Feast of Flesh and Spirit (excerpt)
Ly de Angeles

There's too much talking.

Talking, much of the time, has taken on a seriously flawed "agenda regime" of either personal or social propaganda in an era of what could be termed sensory assault. I would be naive to believe that people had not used lying, or distortions of the truth, for gain or profit (in whatever form) for a very long time, as one merely needs sufficient knowledge of both ancient and modern history to get the big picture. But . . .

At no other known time has there been an atmosphere so degraded, so filled with energetic chatter, so burdened with radiowaves, microwaves, electrical interference, etc., as now.

I'm clairaudient. This means that I rely on the energy of both sound and speech to be able to hear "deeply." This also means that I depend on silence to enable me to hear.

The Big Picture

Time and space and matter are all made up of energy in some great dance and song. Light joins the festival, telling us, as a species of life, just how fine is starlight.

Everything that *is* emits: everything in the continuum of "living" and "dying" (which are all progressions from something to something else) is embroiled with everything else in an endless season of energetic symbiosis, constantly altering, in patterns that the naked eye cannot see but that the body knows (and has always known) most intimately. Energetically, our bodies hold within their patterns the knowledge of forever ("The Big Bang" being merely a theory of possible "beginnings"—hey! What comes from nothing?).

> *Animate*: from the Latin root *animatus*, pp. of *animare*: to fill with breath, make alive < *anima*: breath, soul.

Let's throw away, utterly, the idea that anything is inanimate, because everything "breathes." Physical forms may not breathe the way that we do, but then, who would have the audacity, in a universe so complex, as to assume we were special anyway? Suns and stars and tables and worms, mould and plastic and cold, cold iron—all emit. All express energy in whatever their state of building up or breaking down in eternity's time. One photon a trillion light years away from Alpha Centauri dances a pattern that another photon, another trillion light years away, knows about because all expressions of energy nestle in a sea of infinite space that is very good at not losing anything!

Let's Localise

Earth (Anima Mundi) provides Her children with everything. If it isn't here, we don't know about it. Science is getting to the point that it knows an awful lot about energy—from particle physics and quantum mechanics to chaos theory—and more and more, the new sciences realise that energy and our understanding of consciousness are not separate. That nothing, really, is separate, merely interrelated; therefore our relationship to earth is, of course, mutual.

So what are we doing stuffing up the relationship?

Yeah, yeah, I know—add another voice to the blah, blah. Fine. Yep. But I'm going about it after another fashion because there is *too much noise,* and the full understanding of our mutual relationship to earth is as seriously damaged as a friendship where one person does all the talking and the other ends up abysmally bored because they are being treated like a wall; where lovers play "power-over" games on each other (to the eventual demise of the relationship); where politicians, pretending to listen to the people with whom they live, go ahead and make war anyway; where scientists devoutly invent another noxious toxin, telling us all the while how beneficial it'll be for mankind . . .

And hardly anyone is listening to other voices because should they, the ramifications to greed and avarice (all glamored up to sound like, "You can't live without this!") would be staggering.[1]

Let's Personalise
Check Your Current Reality: Questions to Ask Yourself
(Note: Your answers are best kept private unless you have already re-solved the experiment.)

One

1. Who do you live with, and what is your relationship to these people?
2. Is your relationship to those with whom you live different to the relationship you have with your friends? If so, how and why?
3. Do you hold a job? If so, who are you around your work-mates and bosses?
4. If you are studying, what is your relationship to (a) the tutors and (b) the subject matter of your study? Is the subject matter of your study aligned with a vocation?[2]

Two

1. What is the quality of communication like with those in question one? Is the quality based on a pecking order of apparent household authority? What are your responses when faced with dispute (i.e., debate, argument, walking out and slamming the door, waiting to see who says sorry first, begrudgement, guilt, anxiety, violence, unaffected, bored)? Is your household comfortable with silences, or do others think there's a problem if one of you is not speaking for their own reasons? Do any of you seek to interfere (in difference to discussing) with another's choices?

2. What is the "colour" of your conversations with your friends? Do you ever branch into dangerous topics that could offend another's viewpoint? Do you regularly discover "new" things to talk about? Are you comfortable with these people when there's nothing to say?

3. Does your job give you satisfaction? Why? Do you question the motives of the business with which you are currently employed?

4. Do you ever really listen to your seemingly random thoughts? If so, can you discern the different "layers" of thought?

5. Do you think about what you say when you say it, or do you find yourself repeating material in a repertoire?

6. Do you ever communicate, internally, with someone or something that you know is not you?

7. What, to you, constitutes authority? How do you relate to authority—your own or others'?

8. Do you have "original" thoughts and/or "original" conversations, or are they based on prelearned parameters?

9. Do you question everything that you are told or taught?

10. Do you question yourself on issues, ideals, ideologies, beliefs, ethics, moralities, and information upon which you base your judgements or opinions? Do you change when

the above are undermined, or do you fight like a demon to be seen as consistent?

11. When listening to another person speak, do you actually listen (without bias)?

Answering these questions can change you. Especially if you allow yourself to answer freely and to enter into debate regarding the questions, your answers, and what you really feel in the depths of yourself. Do you even care? Does it matter? Does anyone you know care? Are you living in a vacuum?

What happens next is the experiment.

The Experiment

The experiment has nothing to do with talking and everything to do with listening—listening very deeply.

Listening deeply requires that you use more than your ears. Listening requires that you use your hearing in conjunction with your eyes, your sense of atmosphere, your gut.

The experiment requests:

Section 1

- that you initiate no conversations
- that you respond only to what is said to you
- that you do not automatically think of what you will say next
- that you recognise your preconditioned biases and emotional responses
- that you respond to any and all conversations without preconceived parameters of relationship

Section 2

- that you observe the body language of the person with whom you are engaged in conversation

- that you remain aware of the spaces between your bodies, as this is a strong indicator of the emotional state of the other person towards you
- that you remain aware of your bodily responses to the conversation and learn to trust them—they are a truer receptivity barometer than your intellect when any emotional content enters into the conversation
- that you never prejudge a person by the glamour that they present, but rather remain constantly alert to the "ordinariness" of all people, no matter how educated or expressive in appearance

I never found it necessary to keep a record of my participation and observations in these experiments; rather, I discovered the ability to be free within all interactions and to respond honestly (whether it gets me into hot water or not). The people closest to me are aware of what I am doing, and in most cases they are engaged in the same experiment.

Some examples to watch for (self and others)

The Arguer: Keeping the object of debate at the constant foreground of conversation does not lead to argument unless the participants become emotionally attached to being seen as "right." It is no longer, then, a debate, but a debacle that will leave both or all parties debilitated and distressed.

The Manipulator: Emotional manipulation utilises many criteria: guilt, flattery, conspiracy, destructive criticism, arrogance, vulnerability, constant agreement, denial, comparison—you can tell which is which by the inflation/deflation ratio.

The Quoter: This person will use the "big guns" of authority by quoting the works of others as a reference upon which to base their own "authority."

The White-Lighter: Well, mostly they don't engage; they just tell you what's good for you and talk at you about stuff that makes them feel good about themselves.

The Perennial Parent: Constantly thinking one knows what's best for others, based on one's own experience, socially, spiritually, morally, and emotionally is to impose uniformity onto individuality without recourse to differences. Many politicians and religious leaders do this. So do people with something to gain; so do people who need a mirror to their own psyches.

The Victim: There are two kinds of victim in the world—those with choices and those without. Those people who have choices can choose to change their current realities, but the Victim will not; rather, he or she will use that consciousness to attract sympathy (false love).

Real victims (of any species or life form) have no choices. They are legion, and altering the ways we communicate and listen are one of their chances of escape.

They do not have a voice.

They are not heard.

What you will be doing as a result of actively engaging in this experiment is to break down, or through, a conditional "blindness." You will be altering your emission—your harmonic—and that will have an effect upon the collective field. Enough alteration equals overall change to the human harmonic affecting life.

Yep, what would happen if everyone started telling the truth?

Science and the Sacred

Clairaudience

Being a witch may not seem to have all that much to do with the subject matter of this discussion (and if you're thinking with me, it *is* a two-way conversation!), but it *so* does! Each person is born with a talent, and once that talent is realised and expressed one's life takes on meaning.[3] No one person's talent is more important than another's— they are merely different, and those differences are what make people exciting.

Sometimes a talent can seem like a gift, and other times it feels like a curse. It feels like a curse when one is unable or incapable of following through on one's realisations. For example, I can predict the future for others, but I cannot prevent what seems like misfortune from happening in that person's life; I can hear the desolation emitting from the gorilla incarcerated in a zoo, but I cannot release him; I can pick up the despair of the refugees in enforced detention centres (i.e., prisons), but I cannot prevent their lives from being disrupted. There are many examples, and most of you will be aware, as we speak, of the many times you have heard (or thought you've heard) these same things.

Witchcraft is my line of least resistance. It's what I do, just as being a witch is what I am. It simply means that when I realised that this was what I was, I followed the steps necessary for this way of life to unfold, despite what others had to say on the subject, because I heard the voices of the expressions of my goddess, and I heard the voices of the expressions of god. I heard them in my body and my psyche, and I heard them in the voices of nature. Learning to listen without bias . . . well, that took many years, and I'm still at it, but right now I've got a rainforest outside my back door because an awful lot of pot-bound, ornamental "indoor" plants yelled loudly enough for me to acquire them and plant them where they wanted to be planted. I listen to animals, and we talk the same language of feeling and sensation, necessity and humour.

It's people who are in a serious state of communication-crisis! So often, what is said is not what is meant, or is said for the sake of talking, or is what I call the "caught-in-the-groove" conversation, or what is said has hidden agendas lurking in the back alleys of "want." Conversations with people who have been emotionally damaged and who have never released their attachment to the experience that caused the dysfunction can be deeply akin to psychic vampirism. (Mostly they're unaware of this, and they are not to blame because they've never been given the tools of release.)

What all of these life forms have in common—what everyone has in common—is that they emit. These emissions are what are currently distorting life's patterns, and this will affect the future; this *is* affecting the future. This effect is similar to the theory of the Big Bang—light (energy) being the forerunner of matter. What we emanate affects what is to come (and this, of course, is the basis of spellcrafting).

What sound is:

In 1787, the jurist, musician, and physicist Ernst Chladni published *Entdeckungen über die Theorie des Klanges* or *Discoveries Concerning the Theory of Music.* In this and other pioneering works, Chladni laid the foundations for that discipline within physics now known as acoustics, the science of sound. Among Chladni's successes was the discovery of a way to make sound visible. With the help of a violin bow which he drew perpendicularly across the edge of flat plates covered with sand, he produced those patterns and shapes which today are called "Chladni Figures." What was the significance of this discovery? Chladni demonstrated once and for all that sound actually *does* affect physical matter, and that it has the quality of creating geometric patterns.

Cymatics (<Gk. *Kyma* or *ta kymatika*: matters pertaining to waves)

Cymatics, the study of wave phenomena, is a science pio-
neered by Swiss medical doctor and natural scientist Hans
Jenny (1904–72). He conducted experiments animating inert
powders, pastes, and liquids into lifelike, flowing forms, which
mirrored patterns found throughout nature, art, and architec-
ture. What's more, all of these patterns were created using simple sine wave vibrations within the audible range. So what you
see is a physical representation of vibration, or how sound
manifests into form through the medium of various materials.

Dr. Jenny's methodology was meticulous, well documented, and
totally repeatable. His fascinating body of work offers profound
insights into both the physical sciences and esoteric philosophies.
It illustrates the very principles which inspired the ancient Greek
philosophers Heraclites, Pythagoras, and Plato, on down to Gior-
dano Bruno and Johannes Kepler, the fathers of modern astron-
omy. "In the beginning was the word . . ." takes on a whole new
meaning while looking at these experiments!

Excerpts from an article by Chris and Jenny James
Sounds Wonderful Pty Ltd, Australia

Trinity: The Magic of "3" and the Principle of Creation

In the closing chapter of volume one of the book *Cymatics* by Hans
Jenny is a summation of the phenomena of three-part unity (that
which symbolises life).

The fundamental and generative power is in the vibration which,
with its periodicity, sustains phenomena with its two poles. At one
pole we have form, the figurative pattern. At the other is motion, the
dynamic process. These three fields—vibration and periodicity as the
ground field, and form and motion as the two poles—constitute an
indivisible whole. Does this trinity have something within science
that corresponds? *Yes*, according to John Beaulieu, American polarity
and music therapist. In his book *Music and Sound in the Healing Arts,*

he draws a comparison between his own three-part structure, which in many respects resembles Jenny's, and the conclusions researchers working with subatomic particles have reached.

> There is a similarity between cymatic pictures and quantum particles. In both cases that which appears to be a solid form is also a wave. They are both created and simultaneously organized by the principle of pulse. This is the great mystery with sound: there is no solidity! A form that appears solid is actually created by an underlying vibration.[4]

In an attempt to explain the unity in this dualism between wave and form, physics developed the quantum field theory, in which the quantum field is understood as the one true reality, and the particle or form, and the wave or motion, are only two polar manifestations of the one "thing": vibration.

The nature of magic is based on what is termed the Law of Threes—a thing spoken thrice, the magical plait, events that manifest in cycles of three, the symbol of *Awen* in Druidic lore, the Fates.

Sound in Relativity to Emission

The easiest and most familiar way to study vibration is through sound. Just as the many and varied alphabets of the world encompass all possible words in verbal language, the octave structure encompasses all possible vibrations of sound, and reveals the simple way that they fit together. Chaos theory might call the octave an *attractor*, meaning that all vibrations of sound, however chaotic or random they might be from one to the next, must be *attracted* into the octave structure.

An identical level of this octave of vibration occurs in the visible light spectrum,[5] where we recognise seven colours before encountering other, more subtle, levels (or octave of vibrations) such as infrared, ultraviolet, X-rays, gamma waves. Science tells us that packets or units of energy known as *photons* form the basis for light, and we now know that the *frequency* of the photons that create visible light are simply a *finer octave of vibration* than the sound frequencies of the musical octave. In other words, you could take the numerical ratios between each note in the musical diatonic scale and double them many times over, and eventually you would find the same, identical ratios between the vibrational speeds of the light spectrum. The only difference is the magnitude—sound is vibrating much more slowly, whereas light is vibrating much more quickly.

The Sound of Magic: Time
Clairaudience, clairvoyance, clairsentience: the same thing being "realised" differently.

> Philosophy is written in this grand book—I mean universe— which stands continuously open to our gaze, but which cannot be understood unless one first learns to comprehend the language in which it is written. It is written in the language of mathematics, and its characters are triangles, circles and other geometric figures, without which it is humanly impossible to understand a single word of it; without these, one is wandering about in a dark labyrinth.
>
> Galileo (1623)[6]

If, sitting here, I was to prophesy about the next fifty years only, I could do so with a probability ratio, oh, randomly, of about 99.9 percent certainty, that we're in for big trouble. It doesn't take a genius to figure out that right now, in the early years of the twenty-first century, we're at a point of environmental and social critical mass. I could throw up my arms and get really upset about all the issues facing life (*all* life), but (a) that would only add to the problem (based on the aforementioned conversation) and (b) it wouldn't make sense!

I have read tarot for other people for about thirty years. They come from everywhere, all walks of life, holding a myriad of differing viewpoints on life, the universe, and everything, and year after year, that which is foretold comes to pass. How? What is it that allows a seemingly random shuffle of seventy-eight cards to predict events that seemingly have not yet happened?

The events have already happened!

Matter and energy.

I'm going into waters that some people might consider dodgy, but they'd be mistaken. We're talking about event, after event, after event, after event—all of them unrecognisable to the person sitting opposite me at the time. We're talking some very weird stuff here!

I remember a couple of scientists talking on ABC Radio National about twenty years ago, who were visiting Australia on a discussion tour. They had done studies of differing forms of divination for a year and had come to the conclusion that "Tarot defies the laws of probability," more so than any other tool. Up until then, I'd always wondered but had never had the keys to look for answers to the mystery of this tool. I did some basic study of quantum physics, read Gleick's book on chaos theory, and pondered, in awe, such things as the Mendelbrot Set and fractal geometry.

If we take into account the theory of the Big Bang, then light (in whatever fashion, remembering that it's a *huge* thing and the naked eye sees only a very small section), which is both particle and wave, occurred instantaneously throughout the universe. Matter, on the other hand, seems to be taking its time catching up, which is why our universe is said to be in a continuous state of expansion . . . it's slow!

As I mentioned earlier, nothing comes from nothing, so we were obviously there at the time of the Big Bang, albeit in a different state of vibration: both light and matter (after another fashion) on an arrow-flight through conceptual evolution, however virtual. Now, whether we consider our current morph as human or otherwise is really irrelevant; whatever we even *contemplate* our ancestors as having been is really irrelevant (perhaps even religious!); what is most profound is our having been there, because if we hadn't been there we wouldn't be here now. The mere fact that our haemoglobin contains iron, that our insides slosh around in vast quantities of a fusion of hydrogen and oxygen (and that hydrogen is what fuels stars!) is *amazing*. The mere fact that our bodies follow a seemingly adequate set of parameters and clear reproduction indicates that they *remember* having been around forever . . . and that surely after several billion years (not even considering what might have caused the Big Bang in the first place—it could have been a god blowing up something we haven't invented yet) we've experienced most everything in one manner or another.

When a person shuffles my worn-out deck of tarot cards, they are actually sorting them into order. Because everything has been experienced, that person doesn't need to look at the images, like a very proficient pianist does not have to look at where their fingers are going (and in some cases to look would be to stop the music) because the music is *in* them. All I do is interpret what the person tells me, because quite often when you're involved in your life you are too close to be "objective."

This is where the strange part comes in. And I've wondered about this all my life (which is why I never get my "fortune" told anymore): is it a case of the chicken or the egg?

Collapsing the Wave: Thought to Speech (With a Pinch of Spellcrafting)

I walk the unwalked places
and I sense the roiling mists of things awakened
that live in dreams of those of us, forsaken;
dreams that others, hungry, have not taken
and I plant them, one by one . . .
in the memories of others,
still in slumber, of my kind
for the Way of Power dare not be mistaken.

The Feast of Flesh and Spirit (excerpt)
Ly de Angeles

Have you ever had the "superstition" thrust at you that to name the thing is to empower the thing? That to speak it will either (a) prevent a thing from happening, or else (usually in the case of an ominous occasion) (b) if you speak a thing you will cause it to happen (hence the "touch wood" phenomenon)? Well, I have!

Not only is it the basis for spellcrafting, it is also founded on an interesting theory put forward by Dr. Darryl Reanney in his book *The Music of the Mind*: thought is like light and travels at the same speed, and speaking collapses the wave, giving it a semblance of matter. Once spoken, never unspoken. Once spoken, the thought becomes interwoven with the fabric of our atmosphere as a frequency (please see Part One as a reference to babble) and can interfere with material reality.

So . . . once I speak aloud what I see in tarot (that preexisted in some ethereal dimension outside of time) it enters *into* time, still as an energy (like light) that the individual will walk into in the so-called future (which isn't, of course) and will be recognised *as it happens*, therefore retrospectively, as the present moment is already the past . . . hence it has already happened once spoken.

It's the same with causing events to occur by way of the use of verbal magic. One can enter a spell into an average conversation and probably no one else will ever know. It all depends on what is said and how it is said, but the reality is that I *know* I'm creating a loop: now→then→now. It all depends on how we understand the whole "time thing." When we *really* throw away the illusion of linear time, all things are valid; it's merely a matter of when.

To achieve a conscious transition from the fate of linear time, one simply needs to look at life, the seasons, the natural configuration of existence: it either spirals, cycles, or unfolds. When and why did the line become such a god?

Thought into Matter

Time rushes along empty gorges that once knew a river. The tired blindness of righteousness and sweet-smiling politicians dealing in clichés to satisfy the well-heeled to those who have no shoes, is a constant irritation to those who have the Sight.

You think we cannot see? You think we cannot sense them waiting? . . . the waiting ones? So long waiting for what is *said* to be the truth to *be* the truth? But the curse of Rome comes here, also . . .

And they have built bastions, and placed fences around common land, and said they own the very earth we walk upon, the rivers and the water that we drink, the air that we breathe! And that if we want to use them we must pay.

You see them in glass towers. Steel and plastic palaces and, oh la!, of course, the stock exchange.

Old men. Always old men, no matter what their age, no matter what their sex. Ugly old men. Always pleasant behind "blind eyes." But—behind the "blindness" they see, oh clearly! "Keep them away from us," I hear them think, with such distaste. "Keep them in their places!" They have *Peters-in-suits* to take care of these things. (The weapons are more subtle and more deadly . . . and yet? yet? is it not still sword and decimation?)

The edge of falsehood cuts like paper (hardly seen) into the minds of the gullible who want so desperately to be "saved," to be "acceptable." It is persuasive . . .

I really don't understand the gain. I really, really don't understand what has been achieved. Unless . . .

. . . Is it captivity? That would make more sense than all else. Captivity.

The deliberate, devious, crushing annihilation of the right to choose to be at odds with the captors. (Heretics, yes, that's the slander!)

I see it . . .

We have your soul, now. We have marked you. We have registered you somewhere. You are accountable. To us. We have your soul, in writing, and all debts will be paid.

You have agreed to this, or else your parents before you (and those before them). Why? Why your parents before you (and those before them)? How else can they live with the lie that they are satisfied unless they tell you that they are and become, therefore, justified in the continuance of the repetition of captivity. We have your soul. We have taken it from you by holding your existence to ransom against the possibility of being cast out! Don't forget, for a minute, what you could lose . . .

At least, that's what we are told, albeit by implication. Believers of what? Of the "religions of commonality," the acceptable paradigms, that seek to convince us that they are already where we desire (or are told we desire) to be? They are "better than?" And we are held to ransom by the promise of love . . . or wrath, or Coventry. We are told to watch for The-Lurker-In-The-Dark who represents our capacity for evil, or difference . . .

What do you see? Everywhere?

What do you see happening?

The Grail Queen (excerpt)
Ly de Angeles, unpublished work

Propaganda is one of the more potent influencers of contemporary Western culture. The media and the advertising industry are the current dispensers of doctrines of acceptability and yet, is it not still, "My way, not thy way?"

Throughout the centuries people have been told what they should or should not do and are threatened with the inventions of damnation (in one form or another), or starvation, for bucking the common rule.

These inventions are projections of consciousness!

I know this could sound trite, but it is people who make tables, and tables began in the mind of their inventors. Therefore, to think a thing is to trigger an act of creation when the thought is manifest into a material reality.

We hear the Economy spoken of like a god who suffers along with his people (or *because* of his people), and who has an appetite that seems insatiable, and that our tithing must be considerable and consistent to enable the beneficence of this god to bless us with Security and the continuance of Things.

Does Economy, then, exist as a manifest form? Does it have a true material essence? No. It is an entity, a ghost, a demon that is a figment of its creators. And who are they? Have we asked ourselves who thought up this entity? Imbued it with all the qualities of Man?

We are all capable of this ploy. Do we wish to use it? In my tradition we use the term *glamoring* to describe the process. *Glamoring is the conscious creation of a persona* ("person," "personality," "persona" from the *L: persona*: actor's mask, character).

The "future" is the product of all that precedes it—it is a songline. It is therefore really important that we participate in the future through our current actions and awareness. This requires conscious choices in every situation, no matter what our lot in life. It requires conscious responses to sensory input, specifically in relation to the Word, realising that the great god Logos is as easily manipulated as a puppet.

PART 2

Malevolent . . .
The stealing hand of "How do I survive?"
That chokes him like the grief of Lilith's daughter;
That takes his breath away and makes him fear;
"Is there anybody," begs he softly, "who can hear?
Someone who won't make me 'goat-to-slaughter?'
Because I'm drowning but I cannot see the water."

The Feast of Flesh and Spirit (excerpt)
Ly de Angeles

The Demon of Despair

Magic is always about connectedness. Where a sense—either person-ally or collectively—of the illusion of disconnection occurs, so also does an inexplicable disease that can manifest or express itself in a ta-pestry of dysfunction. This disease is despair.

Practical Steps to Freedom

It is a necessary step, in the eradication of the disease of despair, to first recognise that it is present, either in yourself, your family, your peers, or your community. To do this, you monitor your attitude and out-look on everything for a set number of weeks/months. You will, of course, be affected by newspapers and television which, more often than not, depict the world in a disadvantaged state, but there is no point blinkering oneself throughout this training. It is also important to keep one's eyes wide, wide open, and to learn as much as possible about the soul-illness afflicting our mutual species, which seems to present itself in several ways:

> **Apathy.** Constant assault from myriad media sources can trigger a form of apathy whereby people can watch absolutely horrific scenes of barbarity and brutality that eventually bounce off the psyche . . . but do they? How can they? What actually happens is more insidious: acceptance that these behaviours are validated by their continuation. The training you undertake in ridding

yourself of despair is all about seeing clearly what is happening but realising that you are not a participant in the process.

Accumulation (or, when is enough, enough?). Again, assault. The propaganda of advertising is not about *you* benefiting from a product; rather (duh!) it is about a chain of profit that has its own best interest at heart. That chain of profit includes people who produce *nothing* but who benefit enormously from those who do. Finding a level of contentment with your possessions and consciously realising that you need no more is a powerful thing. It allows *you* the security of simplicity, and it means you no longer feed the beast (the demiurge: Profit). To purchase your goods directly from the grower or the manufacturer means that you are honouring their work, feeding their families, and denying improper investment used for such things as war, environmental rape, the lining of the pockets of the greedy, and any of an incalculably vast arsenal of destructive research and development (including the still-prevalent use of vivisection).

Debt. Have you heard of the term *usury*? I realize that it is considered as the "illegal" charging of excessive interest on loans, but who is it that decides what is excessive? Is *"a profit of $2.192 billion . . ."* in one year excessive? Is *"The . . . bank this week announced a record $2.3 billion profit . . ."*? Do you realise that this is profit? This amount of money is *spare money*! It will be used for investment. Do you know where this money will be invested? Do you know how this profit was accrued?

Every time you take out a loan, or purchase using credit, you are indebting, even enslaving, yourself to others. In the current climate of company CEOs claiming bonuses in the millions of dollars, you might want to ask yourself: *How do I fare?* When will be your next holiday? What is your quality of life like?

I realise that I'm not necessarily talking about issues of which you are unaware but, so far, have I managed to get you thinking?

(Please note that some of the following topics will overlap each other.)

Relationships. Communicate without fear. Communicate without the need to manipulate. Respect silence when there is nothing to say.

Whether we are talking about an intimate relationship, the relationship between family, between friends, between associates—the way to understand relationships, and not "lose" yourself somewhere in these relationships, is to realise three things:

1. There is *always* going to be a "pecking order" within any relationship. This is not a power or a power-over phenomenon, but a biological one (I've been working on this theory, and testing it out, for many years). It cannot be controlled, and neither can the conflict that can, and invariably will, arise because of it. Therefore, understanding it is your first line of least resistance.
2. No relationship is permanent, and no relationship will remain fixed to any idea any of us may consider.
3. False relationships are those based on power over others through a cultural dysfunction known as "better-than, lesser-than."

The Pecking Order

Every species of animal has one. The problems for us as an animal species are that we don't remember that we *are* one, and we have been unrealistically brain-fried by propaganda instituted by both religions and the idealisation of love (in difference to the real kind). Many couples in intimate relationships find themselves in the dominant/submissive role. Very often this leads to conflict. When neither partner is willing to accept this dominance/submission ratio, this also leads to conflict. When a couple have put their "scents" onto each other (in effect: marking their territory) and others enter into the "picture," there will be conflict unless the couple band together, like a wolf pair, to attain a specific outcome (scenario irrelevant). In the case of a couple

without children, there is likely to be little conflict unless outsiders attempt to lay a scent. In the case of a couple *with* children? Well, here's
the reason for a couple of millennia of discord! In all other animal
species, the breeding female is *always* the dominant member of the
pack, herd, or barnyard, and the males will always vie for her favours,
therefore establishing their own "pecking order." This is not our history. The male of our species has been placed in an unnatural state of
dominance (and look at the mess we're in!). Currently, the Western
world is undergoing a crisis of sexuality (specifically in heterosexual
society) because, again taking animal behaviour into account, the majority of species do not take their sex lying on their backs! The flipping
of an animal onto its back is a threat!

Suggested solutions to dysfunctional relationships:

- Share your living space with several people, setting clear
  boundaries of mutual responsibility and gain.

- If assisting good friends or family to move into a new
  dwelling, be certain to make your "mark" on the dwelling
  by either cleaning, helping to place objects and furniture, or
  cooking a meal for them using their appliances—this will ascertain that you feel and are welcome whenever you return.

- Respect each others' needs for independence and spontaneity;
  do not lean or rely on each other; rather, be together for the
  sake of simply that.

- Recognize the pecking order that is *natural* between you and
  your near associates, but do not allow it to manipulate or
  override the uniqueness of each individual involved.

- Communicate freely (and that does not imply talking a lot),
  but do not invade another's need for solitude or silence when
  that need is obvious.

Impermanence

This is a very important ideal to keep in mind. I am not implying that all relationships cease to be; rather, they will definitely change over time as either/any of you explore and learn new things. You will find yourself at a disadvantage in any relationship should you place too much emphasis on that relationship to the detriment of your own journey. Many relationships *do* have a lifespan, and attempting to hold onto them when they cease to be relevant to either/any party involved is to dishonour the process of that lifespan (it can be kind of like not burying or performing an appropriate death rite with a corpse: sooner or later the thing will become repugnant). Quite often the severance process at the completion of a relationship is painful. So be it. Mourning is a natural way of dealing with letting go. Respect for both the self and the process of change is how one transforms through change.

False Relationships

Our culture is full of these. To avoid them, simply don't do them.

We encounter them at all levels of society—governments, business, family, institutional religion, within many education systems, socially. These superficial hierarchies are established for the purposes of control or greed (perhaps both). In an ideal world, there *is* a need for leadership, but that leadership ought to be based on the transparency, wisdom, and proven adroitness of the individual. In an ideal society, those leaders are not better than anyone else but are clear on the responsibilities—based on honour and integrity—that others lay upon them. Leaders are good leaders when they don't *need* to lead, and they recognise that they are merely good at what they do and are reliable within the expertise of that leadership.

Parents quite often demand that their children conform to an "authority" not gained through example but through force (sometimes physical, usually psychological), as do many institutionalised educators, as do politicians and bosses. Observation, on your part, of the behaviour and body language of others will allow you to understand any situation and to either extricate yourself from it or mould your behaviour (not necessarily your true self) to fit the circumstances.

A Few More Despair-Demonic Considerations
Death

Despair often walks with the person who has been taught to fear death. Through consciously realising the organic nature of death (and that everything does it, therefore it is natural), and deciding to live your life gloriously, death can be recognised for what it is—a breaking down of organic matter into that which it is forever becoming: something else!

There is a huge focus in our culture on retaining one's individuality (as it is understood) after body-death, and there are, therefore, a plethora of ideologies and theories concerning an *Afterlife*. I ask you to contemplate: When is there no life? What constitutes no life? When is there *not* life? Is it necessary to *believe* in an *Afterlife* as distinct from life? Do we know all there is to know? There is nothing "after" life because life is perpetual, eternal.

And besides, it's not like body-death is something anyone really ought to worry about, because it's going to happen sooner or later. In the meantime ... what about the *quality* of living?

A Lack of Knowledge Concerning Our Own Bodies

When our health or well-being is taken out of our hands; when we do not know sufficiently about our own bodies to ascertain their functions; when we accept, blindly, the authority of others over our own, we allow the Demon of Despair to have itself a party!

Change the situation. I was once told by a doctor that throughout the entirety of his medicinal training he spent only somewhere around twenty hours learning about nutrition. Circumstantially, I studied this subject (I was intensely into weight training for several years), and I was able to advise my eldest son, who had been diagnosed with "killer cholesterol" and given a prescription for medication, on a fitness programme and a nutritional regime that both he and his girlfriend could enjoy. It took him three weeks to reduce his cholesterol to "normal." He has since continued his exploration of such things as triglycerides, good/bad fats, protein/carbohydrate effects upon the body and has also rid himself of a ten-year high-blood-pressure problem (bearing in mind he is a young man).

That death thing we were talking about a moment ago is an integral facet of good health. Without sufficient decaying matter (compost), the earth's ability to sustain and grow food is diminished, as are the food's nutritional elements when they are consumed. Growing one's own food is an unsurpassed act of creativity, and as Frank Herbert said in his unpublished notes, *"A requirement of creativity is that it contributes to change. Creativity keeps the creator alive."*

> *Mulengro:* (The spelling of mulengro is a shortening of the form *mulengero*. This shortened form is used quite commonly in some varieties of Romani < *mulhengero mulo* (fog ghost) < *Mulengero Di* (All Souls Day) < *mulo* (dead) [these terminologies are from the Burganland Romani dialect]

The Mulengro, as an entity, moves through our culture like a curse. I have discussed it in detail in my book *Witchcraft: Theory and Practice.* It is like a disease passed from one person to another through the use of seven dysfunctional manipulations: *envy, greed, guilt, deceit, denial, expectation,* and *assumption.* Each time an individual seeks to entice, control, coerce, or otherwise twist "reality," they will perpetuate one or more of these functions. The only way to stop the Demon of Despair from dominating our well-being is to cease allowing Mulengro into our lives. I've done it; several of my students have done it; most of my friends have achieved release from the clutches of this

entity. The outcome of being infected by Mulengro is *always* resent-
ment, rejection, blame, and, needless to say, despair.

The carrier of this disease will always attempt to "pass it on." I could
write an entire book on the "games" that people play on both themselves and others in this fashion, but I'm sure with contemplation and
practice you can recognise Mulengro when it is present in your dealings with others.

Authority?

What a strange word. What connotations! The word has come to
represent a pinnacle—the epitome of "a powerful person." I rather de-
test the word, and I would, perhaps, ask you to develop a healthy ob-
jectivity regarding this concept. The word *authority* is very different, in
truth, to a *master* (such as a master carpenter, a master of the sword, a
master chef) because a person who has mastered a skill is a practitioner
whereas, in many instances, an authority is someone with an opinion
who confers with other people with opinions and who, therefore,
could be considered to be educated in opinions. *Of course* I'm general-
ising, but it's worth your consideration, as quite often those who consider themselves authorities do not condone having that authority
questioned, and *that* is, and has been, despotism or tyranny. Whether
the presumed authority is a parent, the president of a company or
country, an educator, a five-star general, or a pope, it is the responsibility of a truthful person or society to consider the individual, or the institution, open to fallibility.

I remember sitting in the loo at a friend's house in Victoria pondering the poster he had on the back of the door (and, therefore,
prolonging my stay in that tiny room). The image on the poster was
of a skeleton in a bathtub in the bathroom of a hotel that is discovered in the far distant future by a team of archaeologists. They document the sarcophagus (the bathtub), the roll of paper used to send
messages to the gods via an aqueduct (toilet paper and flush toilet),

mirror used for divination, various sacred objects (like razor, tooth-brush, etc.) kept on the altar, the obvious sacredness of water (re-alised, of course, from the profusion of taps), the quirky plastic crown worn by the king or priest of this temple (the shower cap) . . . on and on went the description. I realised that no one could truly under-stand the "past" from the standpoint of the "present" and that all such sciences employ educated guesswork.

When I see a documentary on "ancient man" depicting bent-over, ugly, hairy primates I tend to cringe, as nothing in life is un-gainly in its natural habitat. So why depict humanity alone as having been so? And "primitive" is merely deemed as derogatory in com-parison to us now!

To take upon oneself the responsibility of informed questioning ensures that "authority" does not take upon itself the title of "better-than"—it allows for possibilities, it allows for alternatives, it allows for error, and it ensures that the authority remains accountable.

Religion

I hear and read the ways the liars rewrite history. I'm sickened. How can we speak?

When the people of each tribe and clan cried out, "Murder! Murder!" their voices were silenced with sword or decimation. Now it's done with bullets and beads. Now it's done with soft soap and the "promise" of a bargain. Now it's done with the propaganda of "security"—and still it's done with sword or decimation.

And the good men die. Again and again. When the Messen-ger speaks he is shot down. Every time.

You think that the might of Rome declined and fell? It just passed from father to son and changed its name to suit the season.

No one is in control; they're too busy taking over; one against one; the bigger the one, the better. Unification, merger: ruthless! And always the game is, "Divide them to conquer them!"

Listen to the passage of the journey: from Sumer through Egypt, from Babylon to Canaan, from Judea to the lands of Gaul, to the Sacred Isle of mists and lakes and standing stones—to cities sprawling like coffins, to the forests of their pasts.

From the ghetto to the slum, to the hopeful little village, not yet surrendered (for they sleep in mediocrity).

From war zone to war zone, diaspora after diaspora—look you!

From bad to worse. Don't shut your eyes!

The Inquisition is not over: it teaches but it does not educate; it sanctifies the slave trade; it takes the tribes of every land and shackles them to dogma or to death. It moves!

From apartheid to Auschwitz, from the black Mariah on a Saturday night to the Ebola virus, from epidemic population to zero sperm count.

And always the missionaries ply their propaganda. And still the innocents are slaughtered.

And always, riots in the streets cry, "Murder! Murder!"

And still the Romans send children out to kill.

And still the women weep behind the veil, cloistered and appropriated in the name of some god or another.

Religion? Justification!

Believers of what? Of an out-there, one-god? Of the priests of religious ceremonies that attempt to convince us that they are already where we desire (or are told we desire) to be? Better than. Held to ransom by the promise of this god's love . . . or wrath? Told to watch for The-Lurker-In-The-Dark who represents our capacity for evil?

What do you see? Everywhere?

What do you see happening?

And now, ask you, to whom do you bow? No, not to "whom," to "what": When is it enough?

The horror of the effigy of a dead man on a cross? How come you to this? You have exonerated Rome. You have agreed to their ways and means of torture—you have given it holiness!

How can anyone love life while they bow to the art of cruelty (and condone its apparition)?

War has raged before this, and war has raged since this, and war has raged because of this.

What idol is this, that man has created? What does it say? I know what it says, and it is what the persecutors of love and the dividers of a people demand that it say:

No matter what you believe in, no matter who you think you are— you cannot win. Rome is "god." It can topple kings and don't you dare speak out against it! And this is a mandate for debasement.

. . . And in my dreams I have lifted "him," whoever he may be, from off that tree of hopelessness, and I have held him in my arms, and kissed his stone-dead eyes. I have cried for him and said, in silence—for there was no life there to hear me—"Oh love me, love me." Because man, not god, is calling out from Absu, "Don't do this anymore!"

Oh, where is there a rising up? Don't you understand that this was never meant to be?

Put religion, in your time, in a lead-lined, metal-banded box, and bury it beneath toxic waste a mile below the surface of the earth. And fill the hole with concrete. And mark the grave with crosses all around, on every side!

And place a fence of steel about it all. And nail a sign of triumph on the fence that reads: *None may come this way, for herein lies the demon who enslaves the mind of trust! This, here, is the pit the prophets talked about. This is the gate of the "hell" of desolation.*

Then go, and tell the Earth, and what forests still remain, that it is done.

Know freedom from tyranny by recognising its "sweet, sweet face" and its "ever-present smile"—it guards the treasury that rightly belongs to your children (not your fathers!).

It tells you, "you must . . ." "you have no choice . . ." And it holds a flag of guilt before your eyes and says, "Christ died for you, therefore . . ."

Just recognise the lie.

The Grail Queen (excerpt)
Ly de Angeles

What Was Said?

"It has served us well, this myth of Christ." What pope said that, or weren't you listening?

The Jesus Myth

Pope Leo X, who reigned 1513–21, once said: "It has served us well, this myth of Christ." By this he meant that over the centuries, the Vatican had managed to acquire enormous wealth and power in the name of a figure called Jesus Christ. In this century, the man most responsible for making the Vatican the financial powerhouse it is today was its investment manager, a financial genius by name Bernardino Nogara. Speaking of him, Cardinal Spellman of New York once said, "Next to Jesus Christ, the best thing that ever happened to the Catholic Church is Bernardino Nogara." Anticipating that Europe was heading for war, Nogara invested heavily in armaments factories, buying several of them outright. This allowed the Vatican to reap huge profits when Mussolini invaded Abyssinia in 1935 and in World War II later.

Christ and Chistianity in the Year 2000
N. S. Rajaram

Religious Fundamentalism and Dogma: Bigotry

It is in children in war-torn countries, brainwashed into hating one another without knowing why. It is the arrogant racist who believes in an imperialist, white supremacy that presumes anything can be bought. It is in the neo-Nazi and the Ku Klux Klan. Fundamentalism is in the office worker next to you who feels her faith is superior to yours and that you will go to hell and she, heaven. Fundamentalism is the reason people mail anthrax to abortion clinics because they don't believe a woman should have a right to choose. Fundamentalism is the man who bullies, beats, or represses his wife because he believes women are inferior—the source of all wickedness—and passes on seeds of tyranny to his children. Fundamentalism is the people who mock same-sex love; people who shun unwed mothers, the poor, and those infected with the AIDS virus, calling such things "the wrath of god." It is people who smile politely to those of another race in public, but condemn them in private purely because of the colour of their skin or their religion. Fundamentalism is in everyone who labels people as feminists, socialists, communists, and other boxes and throws them down the river.

Religious fundamentalism; religious laws, rules, arrogance, moral condemnations . . . It's a very good way of controlling people, don't you think?

Divide and conquer?

> Originally a Latin saying, "*divide et impera*" ("divide and rule"), the phrase has been in common use since "M. Hurault's Discourse upon the Present State of France." (1588)
>
> *Random House Dictionary of Popular Proverbs and Sayings*

A future where wonder is revered and the wildness and the beauty of life is honoured, where such terms as *"Man conquers . . ." "In the battle to control . . ."* and *"In the war against . . ."* are no longer used to discuss natural phenomena like mountains, space, death—actually, let's not use this terminology for anything!

Religions? What *is* valid about them? Whom do they serve? *Why* do a vast percentage of humans insist on bowing to seemingly omnipotent and, to be honest, terrifying deities that have no connection with the rest of nature unless "he" uses it to wreak havoc on "his" enemies?!

Whatever happened to "Shit happens"? Why seek cause or blame that are human dysfunctions and impediments? What about the big picture? Does it not all come down to a fear of death and the idea that it is unnatural?

I have no problem with the *theory* of "religion" (L: *religare*, to bind back, indicating, it seems, a tradition; a legacy) except in the hands of humans! This writer is a witch and a priestess of a magical way of living, but not a religion.

Religions demand worship. They demand divisions and employ dualisms like good and evil, us and them, sacred or profane. Us and them. Why? Religion and the words *worship, faith, belief* all go together. Inherent within these words is possibility of doubt.

PART 3

ALIVE IN ME

And in a dream we sat and talked of another lifetime,
Deep and mystical and long ago;
A time when song and dance and laughter meant more than just
freedom;
A time when solitude was beautiful, gathering was spiritual,
And love was only ecstasy.
We sat and thought on forever years, when time was not a fear;
To sit and sing from dusk till dawn did fit the tune so naturally,
We loved for reasons far beyond one lifetime's iron grasp,
We moved with beauties ever-sung till body death surpassed.
And in this dream we sat in silence, speaking not a word,
Remembering times when speech went dry we'd sing a while instead,
Never a need to fill the spaces with a soulless tongue's escape.
And in this dream we said goodbye, till next time we do meet;
The binds of time do not remain in the darkened realms of sleep.

Earthbound Angels
Ren de Angeles

When I was first asked to participate in this anthology I thought *Arghh! Ten thousand words? No way have I that much to say!* But then, I thought that about everything I've written so far.

This section is actually the epilogue. I was reading a novel before I went to bed last night and in between sentences, I drifted. I realised that I hadn't mentioned a very important thing to you in its fullness:

The Power of One

Please don't think that because you are one person you cannot have a potent and intense effect on the future.

My grandmother started me thinking about things mystical and magical when I was just eleven years old. She'd never taught her stuff to anyone before me, and she never taught anyone else after me (she died!). I've ended up teaching thousands of people throughout my lifetime, and even more thousands whom I've never met have read the books I've written. I didn't start out thinking that was what was going to happen, and ultimately it doesn't matter to me because I'm merely doing what I'm doing.

There is nothing without consequences, and everything that you do will have them. If none of us change the way we communicate between ourselves and our world, then we're in an avalanche of trouble.

I remember thinking, one time, on the eve of a rally on human rights, *So what? It doesn't matter if I don't attend, what's one person less?* Of course it was just a fleeting thought, complete with chuckle. I knew I'd go, because if I didn't and nobody else did . . . One becomes two, two become ten, ten become ten thousand . . . and apartheid falls. Ten thousand become one million, and one million becomes humanity's next step to change.

AND FINALLY . . .

Silence

Silence is, without doubt, the most important form of communication.

In silence we can think. With silence we can dare to explore the thoughts deeply buried within ourselves that may hold answers like the truth in a situation of falsehood. Through silence we can also hear other things so vitally important, like wind and rain and birdsong. Within silence is heard the voices of the gods and the warnings of our ancestors and the siren songs of the muses.

I am forgotten until you remember me.
I am the living root; the forever Tree—
I await beneath the senses for the soul who truly listens with an ear to
hear my mystery . . . and in the song of such a one I am remembered;
and remembering will set the sacred free . . .
to walk through dreams that can rebuild the ancient trackways,
to awaken memories of fires on the hills,
to call the Faidh and the Ceoltoiri to attend me
As I plant the living legends in the places of the deep,
(where the forgotten ones still sleep)
of the forest of profusion of the ever-living Tree.
I am the Lady of the Gate—I am not found in any book already
written, already printed, already bound
but in the spaces yet to be heard;
in the mystery of the yet-to-be-written word.
Ancient Now. Alive divine.
Prepare a place for me—a face for me.
Deny me not—I am the legend of the Vine
And I am yours, beloved—you who hear me . . .
And in an act that holds to nothing—we entwine.

The Feast of Flesh and Spirit (excerpt)
Ly de Angeles

Notes

1. *Glamoring* is the art of creating a personality not "naturally" your own for the sake of an effect.

2. Vocation: a calling [<L *vocatio, -onis* <*vocatus,* pp. of *vocare:* to call]. I mention this so that it is understood that we are talking about sound/harmonics again and not simply employment or career.

3. *Talent* is one's natural ability to shine in an area of expertise *particularly* rather than generally. It is something one is born with that can be enhanced with experience.

4. Beaulieu, *Music and Sound in the Healing Arts,* 40.

5. Though electromagnetic waves exist in a vast range of wavelengths, our eyes are sensitive to only a very narrow band. Since this narrow band of wavelengths is the means by which humans see, we refer to it as the *visible light spectrum.* Normally when we use the term "light," we are referring to a type of electromagnetic wave which stimulates the retina of our eyes. In this sense, we are referring to visible light, a small spectrum of the enormous range of frequencies of electromagnetic radiation.

6. Machamer, *The Cambridge Companion to Galileo,* 64–65.

Bibliography and Suggested Reading

Beaulieu, John. *Music and Sound in the Healing Arts.* New York: Station Hill Press, 1995.

Braden, G. *Awakening to Zero Point* (revised edition). New York: Radio Bookstore Press, 1997.

De Angeles, Ly. *Witchcraft: Theory and Practice.* St. Paul, Minnesota: Llewellyn, 2000.

———. *The Feast of Flesh and Spirit.* Australia: WildWood Gate, 2001.

Gleick, J. *Chaos: Making a New Science.* London: Heinemann, 1988.

Jenny, Hans. *Cymatics.* Newmarket, New Hampshire: Macromedia, 2001.

Machamer, P., ed. *The Cambridge Companion to Galileo*. UK: Cambridge University Press, 1998.

Quinn, Daniel. *Ishmael*. New York: Bantam Books, 1995.

Rajaram, N. J. "Christ and Chritianity in the Year 2000." *The Sword of Truth*. <www.swordoftruth.com>.

Reanney, Darrel. *Music of the Mind*. Australia: Hill of Content, 1994.

Saul, John Ralston. *Unconscious Civilization*. New York: The Free Press, 1999.

I Am the Mountain Walking

Wombats in the Greenwood

DR. DOUGLAS EZZY

Mountains do not walk. Not in the sense that most people think of humans walking. But that is precisely the point. If you assume that only humans are truly alive, that only humans are active, that only humans think, feel, and have emotions and hopes, then the rest of the world looks lifeless. But what if not only dolphins, whales, and chimpanzees, but also trees, orchids, creeks, rocks, rivers, and even mountains were alive? What if they were "people" with purposes, activities, and "spirit," just the same as humans?

Or to put it differently, what if I am not only human, but also part of the mountain, and the mountain is part of me? From that perspective, mountains do indeed walk. When I walk, the mountain also walks, because the mountain is part of me. I am the mountain walking.

I live in Hobart, Tasmania, Australia. Hobart is a long, thin city wedged between a very big mountain (The Mountain) and a very big river mouth. Every house in Hobart is only a short drive from either The Mountain or The River. I grew up in a suburb on the foothills of The Mountain, and The Mountain was the main view out of my childhood bedroom window.

I am part of The Mountain, and he is part of me. This is true on a number of levels. The water that I drink every day, that becomes my very lifeblood, is sourced from streams that flow down The Mountain. The air that I breathe typically comes in cold winds blowing off The Mountain. Much of the food I ate as a child was grown in our backyard garden on the slopes of The Mountain. Physically and biologically, The Mountain is part of me.

The Mountain is also a central part of my worldview. When I want to know what the weather will be like in Hobart, I look at The Mountain. If it is raining on The Mountain, it will probably rain soon in the city. If blue sky can be seen over The Mountain, it will probably stay sunny. If I become disoriented in the city, then I simply look for The Mountain, and I know where I am. Whenever I travel away from Hobart I always look forward to seeing The Mountain again as I drive back into the city. I feel that I am "home" once I can see him.

The Mountain is my friend. I still remember the day of my eighteenth birthday. Many people celebrate that day by inviting friends to a big party. I didn't. I went walking on The Mountain. I could think of no other person I wanted to be with on that special day. When a close work colleague committed suicide, I went to The Mountain to voice my hurt and anger. He listened. When I fell in love, I talked to The Mountain about my joy and pleasure. He understood. When I am depressed, he encourages me. When I am foolish or think that I am more important than I really am, The Mountain rebukes and reminds me of my place. He is a true friend.

The Mountain is my god. What does that mean? For me, gods and goddesses are not beings in another world, but part of this world. The Mountain provides me with a set of experiences and a way of thinking about my life that gives it meaning. The Mountain is bigger than me, but I am also part of The Mountain. The Mountain is a spiritual being that plays a central role in my spiritual life.

These three points are all closely related. First, I am part of The Mountain. My physical, social, and spiritual life develops through an intimate relationship with him. Second, The Mountain is a person. He has his own purposes and activities that I try to understand and respect. Third, in the same way a husband may consult his wife before making an important choice, I take into account the concerns and needs of The Mountain in choosing how to live my life.

The spirituality that I am describing here is often called "animism." Animism is the belief that not only animals, but plants and rocks, rivers and trees, have spirits—they are "animate," or alive. It is often assumed that animism is a "primitive" belief system, and you will still find references to this in some encyclopedias. It was thought that modern science and philosophy had shown animism to be wrong. However, increasing numbers of well-educated Westerners (like myself) are identifying as animists. Also, as modern Western science and business are causing huge ecological destruction, growing numbers of people are wondering whether the animist beliefs of indigenous cultures may be wiser and more insightful than was previously thought.

"Anthropocentrism" describes a way of living in the world in which humans are central. From an anthropocentric perspective, plants, rivers, and mountains are important only insofar as they serve the interests of humans. A forest does not have a right to exist of itself. Rather, if a forest is to be preserved it must have some value to humans—for example, as a place where new medicines may be found. In the Western world anthropocentrism dominates nearly all discussion about forests, rivers, oceans, and mountains.

In many ways, anthropocentrism is the opposite of animism. Animists take into account the lives of other-than-human beings such as wombats, hedgehogs, and wild orchids in their decisions about what to do. In contrast, people who are anthropocentrists are not very interested in these other-than-human beings. Christians are typically anthropocentric—the main thing that matters to Christians is that a person is saved and is going to heaven. What happens to orangutangs or the rare swift parrot or The Mountain, in this world, is not really that important. Business leaders and politicians are also typically anthropocentric. Their main motivation is to make money *for people*. They seek to improve the wealth and quality of life *of people*. Mountains can be turned into metals, trees into woodchips and paper, and profits.

I remember the first time I took a close friend walking in the wild places of Tasmania. He was studying geology at the time, and he took particular delight in annoying me by describing the various metals that might be mined from the rocks we were walking over. I tried to show him the beauty and depth of the life of the mountains and forests. It is an issue of perspective. What do you see when you look at a mountain or a forest? What do you think about? The geologist thinks about the minerals that may be in the earth. That is what she is trained to do. The manager of a woodchip company thinks about the possible profits from cutting down the forest. That is what he does to make money. But, an animist sees the complexity and beauty of the life in a forest. I think of the spiritual experiences I have in these places.

Some animists may be hunters. They kill animals for food. However, the approach is different. It is common to ask permission of an animal before it is killed, and to thank it for its life. Similarly, as an animist, I would not argue that all mining or all forestry is wrong. Rather, I would argue that the rights, values, and lives of forests and mountains need to be considered as part of the decision-making process.

Graham Harvey has described the "Greenwood" as a place where Pagans "experience and celebrate the Earth's life."[1] "Other-than-human persons" inhabit the Greenwood: "plants, insects, animals, birds, fish, and of course, the teeming bacteria in the soil." The Greenwoods are those places that remain where other-than-humans still have a life of their own. Greenwoods include places like old forests, perhaps a significant tree in a city park, and, for me, The Mountain.

Graham Harvey suggests that Greenwood Paganism is more like "sitting among trees" rather than a "spiritual path."[2] What he means is that Paganism does not look for a path to lead humans out of this world. For Greenwood Pagans, this world is already home, it is already good and holy, and there is no need to travel anywhere on a path. Rather, Greenwood Paganism is about being and celebrating life here and now.

These three things are all linked: anthropocentrism, the desire to find a spiritual path to escape this world, and the destruction of Greenwoods. Humans often look at trees, or mountains, or rivers, simply as resources, as things that can help humans obtain what they want. The need for more paper, more gold, more water for irrigation are all justifications for the transformation of Greenwoods with lives of their own into resources to serve human interests. If God, or "home," or "enlightenment" are in the next world, what does it matter if humans destroy the Greenwood? I don't think that trees, mountains, rivers, and wombats should be made to always serve the interests of humans. The wombat's experience is a good example of the problem confronted by anthropocentrism.

Unlike Australian possums, and squirrels in the Northern Hemisphere, who have adapted well to urban life, wombats do not like urban environments. One of my regular walking tracks on the outskirts of Hobart takes me past several wombat burrows that are now unoccupied. The encroaching houses have driven the wombats away, or they have been killed on the roads.

Wombats are Australian marsupials about the size of a medium dog with a solid build and short legs, a big head, and very powerful digging claws. They live in burrows that can be many metres long, coming out to feed on grasses during the night. They are not dangerous, unless you pick one up, which is hard to do as they can run very fast. Wombats have very distinctive cube-shaped droppings that makes it easy to tell if they are living in an area. Wombats live in a wide range of habitats, from the warm coastal scrublands to the snow-covered peaks of the alpine areas.

I have met numerous wombats. Wombats fascinate me. However, they don't seem that interested in me, or in humans in general. They have their own lives to get on with, eating, sleeping, burrowing, mating, and raising their young.[3] When I meet a wombat in the forests of Tasmania they mostly ignore me, or run away. I sometimes see evidence of wombats on The Mountain, though it is too rocky and too close to suburban Hobart for them to be comfortable. I usually meet them in other Greenwoods, more distant from humans.

I was walking in one of these more distant Greenwoods recently, a forest in southern Tasmania. It was easy to see that wombats lived in the area; their distinctive droppings were not hard to find on the sides of the track. The area was under threat from a logging company. Logging in Tasmania is practised in a particularly destructive way. Not only do they take all the old-growth timber, mostly to be woodchipped, they also cut everything else down and leave it on the ground, and then burn the remains in a high-intensity fire by using a substance similar to napalm. The reason for this is to kill off all the variety of native species so the area can be replanted with a eucalypt monoculture. Worse still, the foresters then lace the area with blue carrots poisoned with 1080. This is to kill off the native animals so that they don't eat the shoots of the plantation trees. So while the wombats may survive the fire by hiding in their burrows, they won't survive the poisoning. Their death is slow and painful.

Beyond questions about the economics of logging (it seems to benefit a few wealthy individuals rather than the community as a whole), and the ethics of poisoning native animals (death by 1080 poison is not humane), there is a broader issue about what really matters. For Greenwood Pagans, the lives of wombats and trees have value in and of themselves. When an economist looks at a forest, he typically thinks only in terms of the money that can be made. When a Christian hears of ecological destruction, it often does not concern them. Although there are some ecologically minded Christians,[4] surveys have shown that conservative Christians are much less likely to be concerned about the environment than people who are not Christians.

For me, as a Greenwood Pagan, what really matters is to live in the world respecting my community—that includes other humans, animals, forests, rivers, and mountains. I do not long for heaven, nor do I anticipate that becoming fabulously wealthy will solve all my problems. Rather, I long to spend time in the Greenwood, to sit and listen, laugh and dance with my friends, human and other-than-human. I do not expect to control the other-than-human world. Although we at times work together on projects, I do not want other humans to be my slaves. Similarly, I do not want wombats, King Billy Pines, and The Mountain to serve only my interests, although I may use some harvested timber or metals mined from mountains in some of the things I do. I think that my life, human lives, will be richer, more pleasurable, deeper, and more satisfying if they are lived in

community with other-than-human peoples, rather than by oppressing them, silencing them, or making them extinct.

Economists try to dominate and control the world. Many busi-
nesspeople seem to think that new technology will solve any ecological problems that arise. This is a very anthropocentric view of the
world. It assumes that the only people with good ideas or with important things to do are Western businessmen. For Greenwood Pagans, this is a strange idea. Our aim is not to dominate, but to live in
a respectful relationship with other-than-human peoples.

Westerners often assume that indigenous cultures, such as the forest dwellers in northern India,[5] should abandon their animistic beliefs and adopt Western beliefs and practices. Of course, it is assumed
this will make them wealthier. However, in almost every case when a
forest is cut down for woodchips, or a region is opened up for
tourism, or a traditional fishing ground is fished commercially, the
end result is that the indigenous peoples become poorer. They lose
their traditional sustainable sources of livelihood in exchange, if they
are lucky, for a one-off payment that never lasts very long. Sharma
argues that this form of "development" is not worth the costs.

In the same way, I argue that Westerners have forgotten that the
endangered Hairy-Nosed Wombat, or the Eastern Barred Bandicoot,
or the King Billy Pine, or the Great White Shark, have values in and
of themselves. When these other-than-human beings are made to
serve the interests of humans, many of them find themselves on the
edge of extinction. We humans have acted in the world in a very anthropocentric and selfish way.

When we cut down an old-growth forest to make woodchips we
are making a decision that the wealth and pleasure of particular groups
of humans are more important than the lives and pleasures of the
other-than-human inhabitants of that forest. I would rather give up
television, newspapers, and glossy magazines than give up my respect
for wombats and my friendship with The Mountain. I am not arguing

that we should stop all forestry, or all mining, or all fishing. Rather, I am pointing out that most humans completely ignore the lives of other-than-human beings in their decisions about what forests to clear, mountains to mine, or fish to catch.

The modern mass media, and in particular television, encourage people to be selfish and to just think about their own pleasure. Big business and marketing companies do not want people to consume less, or to be satisfied with the clothes, car, computer, or hairstyle that they already have. They want people to buy more, so that they can make more money. Politicians are always offering tax cuts as an incentive to seduce people to vote for them. In our obsession with our own human pleasures we have typically ignored not only the quality of life, but often the complete extinction of our other-than-human friends with whom we share this world.

Joanna Macy describes a Buddhist concept of "dependent co-arising."[6] Humans do not exist alone, or independently, but arise with, alongside, the other beings in the world. Humans are dependent on other beings. A person does not need to read very much zoology, botany, and ecology to understand that this is not simply a religious idea, but a very sound scientific approach to the place of humans in the world. Humans are part of the web of life. This understanding of our place in the world leads to a very different approach to the relationships of humans to other-than-human beings.

Is it fair to cut down the Amazon forest so that Americans can have cheap hamburgers? Is it right to destroy the old-growth forests of Tasmania so that we can have cheap woodchips for cheap paper? Is it right to allow the livelihoods of wombats to be destroyed to create monoculture plantations of eucalypt trees? For me, these are as much religious and ethical questions as they are economic and scientific ones. The Amazon forest, the old-growth forests of Tasmania, and wombats have a right to exist in and of themselves. They have lives of their own, and they should be allowed to live them.

Perhaps they will share that life with us. Perhaps they will give up their lives for us at times. But it seems strange, even evil, to think that all that matters in this world is the wealth and pleasure of humans. Surely we humans should be prepared to reciprocate and give up a few of our own pleasures so that the other beings with whom we share this world can have a reasonable quality of life.

What does this mean for how we, as humans, live our lives? From an animist perspective there is nowhere we need to "go" in order to be happier, not to heaven, not to a shopping mall, not to the time when we are finally wealthy. The pleasure and joy of life is to live it in the here and now. We do, however, have ideals.[7] We work toward concrete goals that involve less destruction, less greed, less extinctions, less poisoning, less selfishness.

The choices here are not just individual choices about watching less television, or eating more vegetarian food, or using recycled paper. Rather, the most important choices are made by politicians and big business. We could encourage trains rather than cars as the chief mode of transport. We could ban the harvesting of old-growth forests and poisoning with 1080. We could restrict the harvesting of certain fish species. We could subsidise farmers who grow their crops organically. Some of these actions are already in place. Such choices may make some delicacies more expensive, may require some people to change their occupation, or may hurt the vested interests of some big businesses. But these costs, which are often relatively small, are worth it because the benefit is an improved quality of life for not only humans, but all beings that live on this earth.

I do not expect everyone to become a Greenwood Pagan. In fact, I hope they do not. Each religious tradition has its own beauty and vitality. But I do hope that in the decisions about how we live our lives in this world that the voices of the other-than-human beings will be listened to more than they are at present. This is one reason that Greenwood Paganism is important. Union leaders speak for the interests of the workers. Feminists speak for the interests of women. The leaders of big business work to ensure their profits. Certainly, environmentalists speak for the environment. But, Greenwood Paganism takes this to another level, alerting us to the basic rights of wombats, mountains, and trees. These beings not only have rights, but in a very profound sense they are part of us. As such, in harming them we are harming ourselves.

Descartes was wrong when he argued "*Cogito ergo sum*" (I think, therefore I am). We do not come into being as isolated individuals through our own thoughts. This is wrong biologically, sociologically, and spiritually. Biologically we depend on the physical world around us, on a network of plants, animals, rivers, mountains, and clouds to sustain both our lives and the lives of our mothers and fathers. Sociologically we learn to think, to speak, and to be a human through relationships with family, friends, and work associates. Children cruelly locked in cupboards from a very young age do not learn to speak, think, or act as humans. Spiritually, we develop through our relationships, our encounters with other spiritual beings. As Buber argues, "In the beginning is the relationship."[8]

What do I do? I speak kindly to my friends, such as The Mountain and wombats. When they welcome me I visit them regularly. What should you do? A good start, I suggest, is to find a Greenwood and walk or sit in it regularly. Then, listen. Listen to what the other-than-human people there have to say. For me, Paganism is about living a good life in this world. Defending the rights of other beings in this world is part of what I do. But perhaps more importantly, I share my life with those I love.

I am the mountain walking.

Notes

1. Graham Harvey, "Gods and Hedgehogs in the Greenwood: Contemporary Pagan Cosmologies," in *Mapping Invisible Worlds,* ed. Gavin Flood (Edinburgh: Edinburgh University Press, 1993), 90.

2. Ibid., 91.

3. James Woodford, *The Secret Life of Wombats* (Melbourne: Text Publishing, 2001).

4. Dieter T. Hessel and Rosemary Radford Ruether, eds., *Christianity and Ecology* (Cambridge: Harvard University Press, 2000).

5. B. Sharma, "On Sustainability," in *This Sacred Earth: Religion, Nature, Environment*, ed. R. Gottlieb (New York: Routledge, 1996).

6. Joanna Macy, *World As Lover, World As Self* (Berkeley: Parallax Press, 1991).

7. Starhawk, *Webs of Power* (New York: New Society Publishing, 2002).

8. M. Buber, *I and Thou*, trans. R. Smith (New York: Collier Books, 1958), 12.

Wild Spirit,
Active Love

DR. SYLVIE SHAW

We've been hiking in the mountains for four glorious days. Today is our last day. It is also my fiftieth birthday. The hike is a gift from my friends Ed and Sue, who know the land intimately. Both have been actively involved in local environmental campaigns for the past thirty years and are passionate about this place. As we walk up the steep slope towards the top of Mt. Bogong, the highest peak in Victoria, two eagles fly above us, leading the way.

From here the Alps stretch out as far as you can see; but dotted amongst the seemingly endless blue-green hills are patches of bare earth where swathes of the hillside have been cut away and left desolate by logging operations. We eat lunch by the rock marker and watch the eagles as they circle languidly overhead. Now there are four of them. After lunch we hold hands and say a small prayer of thanksgiving to this stunning place and the end of our journey. The prayer ends with the words "We thank you for our lives."

One of the hardest things to do after such a significant time in the bush is to go back home. As we stepped off the edge of the plateau and began to descend the trail known as the Staircase, the eagles seemed to shadow us. Now there were six. "Was this a birthday greeting from nature?" I wondered. The eagles soared upwards on the wind, then disappeared out of sight.

While driving away from the mountain, I realized that the eagles were not simply there for us. They were searching for food. There had been a severe drought in the area for several months and food was scarce. This realization jolted me out of my human-centred romanticism and brought me down to earth. How easy it was to assume nature was there for my own use—how easy to overlook the sacred interconnections of the web of life.[1]

Living in the city, away from the wilds, we are cut off from the fragile life support systems which sustain the earth. Spending time in wild nature, or finding pockets of the wild in the midst of the city, we become more attuned to the subtle changes in the seasons, more responsive to the flow of the natural world, and more responsible for the earth. In becoming aware of the delicate nuances involved in sustaining the land, in frequent encounters in wild nature even in our own backyards, in sacred rituals that revere the earth, in joining in actions to restore degraded landscapes or protest against environmental desecration, we discover the relationship between sustaining the earth and sustaining ourselves.

Immersions in Wild Nature

The wild is a powerful place, and a place of empowerment, an adventure for mind, body, heart, and soul. Wild places are breathtaking, magical, beautiful, spiritual places which delight the senses and ignite the spark of imagination, playfulness, and creativity which epitomize the essence of wildness and Pagan spirituality. Connecting with wild places engenders a sense of mystery about the natural world. People report feeling a sense of connectedness or oneness with their surroundings.[2] They have a belief in a power greater than themselves, a feeling of humility in the shadow of nature's power, and an appreciation of the beauty in nature. These experiences spark feelings of inner peace, hope, joy, and empowerment; they promote physical and emotional well-being and bring about significant changes in attitude and behaviour.[3] People become enthusiastic about their nature experiences and pledge to make nature a part of their future lives. A word of warning: such wild and sacred places may begin to suffer from overuse. If we see the wilderness simply as a place of healing and personal transformation it may become just another commodity, unless people engage in wilderness preservation as well as self-preservation.

Over the past few years I have interviewed many nature religion practitioners and environmental activists involved in a whole range of earth-caring activities. They are adventurers, artists, ecologists, farmers, gardeners, campaigners, and ritual makers who care about what is happening to the environment. Whether they are involved in front-line action, land restoration projects, outdoor pursuits such as bush-walking, surfing, gardening, or earth-centred rituals, they share a deep love of nature and a desire to change things. So, they try to find more ethical and sustainable ways to live, as well as work to repair the damage being done to the earth. Caring for nature is an integral part of their lives; as they work to safeguard and restore the land, they are enhancing and restoring their relationship with it.

Nature carers, as I call them, act out of a sense of love, moral outrage, social justice, anger, and despair for the planet's future. They are highly educated, strongly motivated, self-reliant, altruistic, and deeply concerned individuals who find inspiration in the intricacies of the natural world. They love its awesome beauty and have a deep respect for its awesome power. They say that spending time in wild places recharges their batteries, renews their commitment, and sustains their capacity for action. Some prefer to get involved in what they see are "constructive" rather than confrontational activities and choose tree planting and earth-honouring rituals over frontline protests. Some climb into trees in order to save them; others organize dance parties, write poetry, grow gardens, and encourage their children's curiosity about, and adventures in, the natural environment.

Most describe the natural world as a living entity of which humans are only one part. They use expressions like interconnectedness, love, respect, right relationship, balance, power, and passion, terms that are also at home in the spiritual arena. Their environmental concern was sparked through a variety of experiences, notably by frequent and sensitive contact with wild nature, or all too often, by witnessing nature being destroyed by human intervention and experiencing a deep sense of loss. Their spiritual awakening came about or was deepened through several different processes—through workshops, introductions from friends, reading books on nature and nature spirituality, and especially through immersions in wild nature. In the case of Pagan participants, awareness of their sacred nature connection was something they had always felt and known.[4] Whatever direction they came from, all have a profound belief in the sacredness of nature.

The Sacred in Nature

Spirituality, for me, is a process of creating relationship with what we hold to be sacred. By sacred I do not mean something set apart from this world, but something inclusive of, or interactive with, the everyday—something held dear, to be respected, revered, treasured, and protected. In this definition, the sacred winds through the ordinary and the everyday as an animating, vital life force or spirit. It inspires us to act and care. It encourages us to build relationship with special places and other species, and as we do, we learn more about ourselves and our connection to the cosmos.

Eric, one of the nature carers I interviewed, lives on the edge of Victoria's marvelous alpine region and works in the local nursery with his partner. He's a longtime environmental campaigner who's passionate about the mountains and knows them intimately—a great benefit when you're on top of a mountain together, it's blowing a gale, you're freezing cold, and you need to find a campsite quickly. In the midst of this stunning terrain, Eric introduced me to his sacred and special place.

> I found a special place in the bush where I can go and do ritual. It's a kind of intimate space, not a grand space. It doesn't have the kind of feeling that a cathedral has; it's a little area where the trees are quite stunted because it sits on a rocky outcrop. I feel so at home there. There are spirits in that place, and there's a very benevolent feeling. I've put up an altar there. I found a big flat rock and created the altar, then started collecting things for it. I made offerings of incense, and I prayed. And I cried. I've done all sorts of things there—I've sat there naked with the wind blowing round my body, which connects me intensely with that place; I've sat there in rain and howling storms and in beautiful warm sunshine. And I've sat there and watched the sunset and the quietness descending on the land. It is a small sacred place in the midst of a big sacred place. It called me. And it's still calling.
>
> *Eric, bushwalker and nurseryman*

Eric has created a close relationship with this small wild place. It sustains him. He also belongs to a spiritual group which meets weekly for meditation and gets together to celebrate the seasonal rituals, the solstices, and equinoxes. He has been involved in local antilogging campaigns for many years, is a volunteer fire fighter and landcare worker, and takes part in a range of community projects such as telephone counselling and driving elderly people to hospital. He sees this as an integral part of his spiritual practice.

Other nature carers I met are involved in similar activities. They might enact their spirituality differently, but all share an allegiance to what could be termed "spiritual activism." Some are initiated Pagans in the Gardnerian or Alexandrian tradition; others describe their religion as "Pagan" while at the same time they may be atheist, agnostic, or involved in a variety of organized religions. What connects them is their deep spiritual feeling for the land. This is not the paradox, it seems. Organized or institutionalised religion is thought to be tied up with hierarchy and dogma, and there is a strongly-held belief that the separation of humanity from nature is largely due to Judeo/Christian religious teaching. Some regard formal religion, especially mainstream Christianity, as "not going deep enough." They long for a more profound connection and thus make a distinction between "man-made" and "earth-made" religion. Rick, a forest activist with the Wilderness Society and committed atheist, finds his spirituality in the Central Victorian landscape where he grew up. It is embedded in his commitment to saving this place and wild places further afield.

> I am an atheist. But I would also say that being out in that country is a spiritual experience. It's hard to describe except that it's a great source of strength and inspiration to be out there in that landscape; it gives me a sense of well-being and identity. I can't imagine ever leaving Victoria, because I have such a strong connection with that landscape.
>
> *Rick, forest activist*

Being in wild nature is life transforming for the nature carers. It opens up possibilities for new ways of seeing and acting where nature plays the role of teacher, healer, and guide. Although most interviewees say their experiences are more profound in wild nature, they also seek nourishment by working in their gardens and exploring remnants of bushland in their local environment. Each has found their own method of spiritual engagement, which prompted the environmental educator Marigold to comment, "The spiritual quest is individualistic. What matters is not which path you choose, but the action you take as a result of that."

Sacred Connections

The ocean is the favourite naturescape for the majority of nature carers. It is a place "to clear away the cobwebs," to delight in the wind and revel in the power of the waves. Sabin, a scientist and Wiccan in his late thirties, says his spiritual path is "about preserving the environment as well as about enhancing [his own] psychological development." He lives in a tiny cottage near Melbourne's Yarra River with a flourishing garden of native plants and animals and two huge old oak trees. These trees play a central part in his Wiccan rituals. During seasonal celebrations and earth-honouring ceremonies, Sabin "merges with the forest in a physical way, using the earth and leaves" as part of his garb. He rubs or "scents" himself with plants and soil, getting covered with dirt, then crawls back home at two in the morning for a bath. Although Sabin is a scientist, he sees "no disparity between practising both Wicca and science" because of his "understanding that everything is interconnected." This understanding extends to his other passion, surfing, where, accompanied by his spirit animal the dolphin, he dances with the power of the waves and the cycles of life and death.

With surfing there's always a possibility that you are going to die. It's quite an experience to go under for the third time thinking that if another wave comes, that's the end of it. Surfing puts everything into perspective. It puts me in a place where I realize I'm mortal. And there's that sense of smallness you get when you feel the ocean's power. At other times, if I'm surfing well or I'm in the flow, I feel like I've become one with the ocean, that we're communicating and working together in a kind of partnership. It's always an invitation that's been extended from the ocean to allow me to play in this way.

Sabin, scientist and Wiccan

Surfing can be risky, but the risks are submerged in the passion of the sport with surfers like Sabin feeling "at one" with the ocean, being absorbed in "the flow" and "playing" with nature's power. Going surfing is an integral part of his spiritual practice, and he likens the activity to a ritual, where the surfboard is his athame cutting through the waves and creating a space between worlds, between sky and earth, between death and delight.

The ocean is Mother, womb, originator, Tiamat, The Deep. She is soul source, at once comforter and destroyer, sustainer and lifetaker. She supports and buoys; she pulls under and takes away. She washes away the mundane soot and leaves a fresh skin of briny translucence to the true self beneath. She shows me how to be a witch.

Sabin

There is deep reverence and respect in his account, and other soul surfers that I spoke with would agree. They regard surfing as a spiritual experience, describing it as "blissful," "unbelievable," an "incredible love." "It's cleansing you, washing all your cares and worries away." Shelley is a surfer and canoe instructor in her early thirties. Originally she trained as a chiropractor, but became disillusioned at what she perceived was "a lack of holism" in her profession, so she decided to work for a while as a gardener. Spending time outdoors was the catalyst she needed. She went back to school and became an outdoors educator. Now she works in adventure therapy with adults with mental illness, commenting, "Helping people spiritually is so much nicer than listening to their back pain." Shelley started surfing a few years ago following the death of her father, and she believes the power of the waves was the balm that helped heal her.

> I found surfing probably about a month after my father died of cancer. I was in a real mess; it was a really tough time. I'd always wanted to go surfing, and when Dad died I got the opportunity to learn. And I got into it in such a big way. It was such a deep healing for me. I still find that now. Simply being in saltwater and surfing is a healing experience. Being in the power of the wave is amazing. Sometimes I just need to go surfing. I just need to go out there. It's a real cleanser.
>
> *Shelley, outdoors educator and chiropractor*

What is apparent from these stories is that being in nature can be spiritually uplifting, physically engrossing, energizing, and healing. It awakens all the senses, which for the forest activist and biologist Beth, includes fear. Not long after getting involved in the campaign to save the southwest forests in Western Australia, Beth decided to leave her laboratory job to live in the forest, high up in one of the large old-growth trees. Her first night on a wobbly platform many metres above the ground was a frightening experience. Although Beth had grown up on a farm and was used to the vagaries of the weather, a huge storm on that first night tested her resolve. She saw it as a special kind of initiation.

> That first night we had the biggest storm in twenty years. Everyone begged me to come down, but I wasn't sure if this storm was anything out of the ordinary, so I decided to stay. Most of the protestors evacuated the campsite that night, and they were so lucky. Huge trees came down really close to

people's tents and caravans, but no one was hurt and nothing was destroyed. We felt like we had been protecting the trees for so long and now they were protecting us. There was a really strong feeling of reciprocity.

Beth, biologist and forest activist

Two important issues are at play here—respect for the power of nature and the notion of reciprocity. The desire to give back to nature and the belief that nature is somehow assisting the protest are common perceptions among nature carers. For Tim, a forest activist turned wetlands ecologist, this reciprocal or two-way relationship is manifested in quite an unusual way. I met Tim on the banks of the Yarra River, where he was working to restore the riverbank and flood plain. As the ducks quacked behind us he told me about the strong connection he has with tiny yellow wetlands plants known as "Billy Buttons." He explains it is a kind of "dreaming connection" where he dreams about the plants, then wakes up knowing they are in need of help. Not knowing exactly where they are located, he begins walking in the direction he feels they are growing, and invariably when he finds them, he also finds the area is threatened with immanent destruction.

I just wake up thinking about the Billy Buttons, and then I go out and find them. It's like a normal dream in reverse. I might go out into the bush and see a particular species, and that night I'll dream about it. The dreams about Billy Buttons just happen in reverse, where I dream about it first, then I go out and actually find it. I wouldn't say the Billy Buttons are telling me directly about what is happening, but they are communicating in some way at a very deep and unconscious level. Once I went out and found the Billy Buttons were part of an amazing intricate swamp, and then I found out there were plans to build a shopping complex on it. So I started a community group and we ran a campaign for about two years, and eventually we had the swamp protected. It was just such a stupid thing that they were going to build on that swamp.

Tim, wetlands ecologist

Tim is the only person I spoke with who has this kind of "dreaming connection" with the spirits of place and plant deities, although others certainly communicate with the devas and spirits of the land. Among nature carers, psychic as well as direct sensuous engagement with nature is part of their activist toolkit. Symbolic ritual action, meditation, and prayer about sacred places or impending damage are seen to be effective through the belief that everything is interconnected, so a change in someone's understanding about environmental degradation is also seen to effect a change in the wheel of life.[5]

Other nature carers work for change through environmental education, running deep ecology workshops, organizing community festivals, writing songs, working on land revegetation projects, carrying out environmental audits at work, and taking part in demonstrations, or by lobbying in other ways, such as writing letters and casting spells. For instance, Tamsin, a Wiccan, forest activist, and active fisher, casts a "magic circle" before she writes letters to politicians, so the energy from the ritual is "charged up" into the letters. For protest marches Tamsin makes "banners symbolizing fish, to remind people about the fish and the oceans which sometimes get forgotten." She has also made "paper flowers and charged them up in circle and handed them to people on the street watching antinuclear protests," and she's worn an old gas mask to so many protest that it has now "built up a kind of ritual regalia significance." Tamsin's actions reveal an ethic of care and responsibility where there is no distinction between her spiritual practice and environmental activism.

Her other passion is rock fishing. There's the added excitement of climbing down the sea cliffs in the blustery wind, with the sound of the waves crashing on the rocks below. Tamsin is deeply respectful of the fish she catches, never taking more than she needs, and she comments that the only fish (and meat) she eats are the fish (and other feral animals like pigs) she catches herself.

> It's the thrill of hunting and catching fish in all kinds of environments that is exhilarating. There is a deep, deep connection to the ocean when you visualize your line in the ocean and your bait at the end. As soon as I visualize the fish swimming up and eating the bait, my senses become one with the ocean. The boundary between land and sea merges, the world swims in the water and I am connected to all life.
>
> *Tamsin, Wiccan, activist, and fisher*

Integral to the interviewees' spiritual repertoire is the process of developing a relationship with the natural world, getting to know the neighbours—fish, rock, bird, and human—observing the patterns and subtleties in the local terrain through the changing seasons and shifting starlight, and relating with their senses wide open. Once nature has woven its magic spell and they become more aware of what's going on in the wider environment, they recognize the link between individual responsiveness and environmental responsibility and return again and again to be filled, nurtured, and nourished.

Being Immersed in the Elements

Being immersed in the elements, whether fishing, surfing, hiking, or meditating in sacred places, is an essential part of nature carers' lives. They do it for fun. For adventure. For inspiration. For healing. For love. Most describe their deeply felt experiences in wild nature as a transcendent spirituality, a belief in the mystery of the cosmos that is beyond understanding. Others practise a more Pagan-inspired or immanent spirituality, but they too mention moments of self-transcendence in nature, reporting them as "epiphanies," as "mystical," "numinous," "magical" or "blissful" episodes. These experiences of the sacred do not take us out of this world into some other world of disembodied spirit, but affirm our fleshy, visceral union with nature. They are characterized by flashes of illumination; a feeling of unity; a sense of joy, bliss, and peace; a transcendence of time and space; and a sense of the numinous where the perception of "otherness" disappears and a change in attitude and behaviour emerges. Cara is an herbalist, scientific researcher, teacher of Goddess spirituality, and avid gardener. She was camping in South Australia's magnificent Flinders Ranges, and on a hot spring day was transported by the elements of that place.

> I've often had numinous experiences in nature where I have been overwhelmed by nature and transported to another realm. I think there is something in being open and also in putting yourself in physical situations where that is possible. So you've done something really strenuous to get there; you've put aside other obligations; you've made a physical effort, and you've also welcomed it as if this is a really special time. We were quite high on the rim and sat watching the hawks cruising on the hot currents, swooping and diving. We were looking right down on them. It was an extraordinary experience. There was something that was completely magical for me. I was very much part of that landscape and was delighted to be part of it. It is about connection with the cosmos, about being contented, and about having a physical experience that keeps me grounded in the cosmos.
>
> *Cara, herbalist and scientific researcher*

Cara's connection is at once physically grounding and spiritually uplifting. She sits on the edge of the rocky escarpment in the heat, in a heightened state of awareness, and experiences something "magical." The expressions she uses such as "being overwhelmed," "transported to another realm," "being part of the landscape," "connection with the cosmos," and "extraordinary" are reminders of the possibilities for personal transformation and spiritual insight that come with connecting with wild places. Mystical experiences like Cara's are also termed "peak experiences."[6] But this expression seems somehow disconnected from the lyrical, magical, and transformative qualities that nature carers use to explain the precious feeling of being connected with the rhythms of the earth.

As the herbalist Cara explains, moments of such divine illumination can often occur after demanding physical effort, and this is exactly what happened to the activist and writer Vivianne. Now in her mid-fifties, Vivianne joined her family on a hiking trip in one of Tasmania's glorious national parks, where an encounter with a tree led her to reflect deeply on her own attitude and behaviour. It was a tough hike in more ways than one.

> I'd gone on a five-day hike with my kids, and I thought I'd die on the first day. Here I am, over fifty years old, with a bad back, and you have to carry all your food up this very steep mountain. When we finally arrived, I was exhausted. But by the next day I had recovered enough to go walking through an old pencil pine forest, a wonderful old-growth forest. I found a really old tree that looked so amazing, with branches hanging down to the ground, that I decided to sit under it. But as I sat down, the tree rebuked me. It was so humbling. The tree said, "How dare you just blunder in and sit down without asking permission! Don't you realise there is a whole community of beings you've just sat on?" It was the most extraordinary rebuke for someone who's supposed to be pretty ecologically aware. It was really powerful. Immediately I jumped up and apologised to the tree and approached it again, this time properly. Then, very chastened, I went on with my walk. When I came back a few hours later, there was a hawk feather right where I'd sat. It was such a stunning lesson. Now I always ask permission. It was a sacred place, but in my delirium I just assumed I could go in there and be blessed.
>
> *Vivianne, activist and writer*

There is a valuable lesson here about humility, patience, and awareness. Despite years of environmental, spiritual, and social justice activism, Vivianne realized she needed to be more respectful of the spirits of place, to treat the land "properly," to be mindful and ask permission. But in asking permission, we should not assume it will always be given. The Victorian Pagan/earthcarer Yarrow suggests that we may need to get more acquainted with a place or a particular tree before being accepted.[7] It was another lesson Vivianne was about to learn.

On another occasion, when walking by the ocean and contemplating a difficult personal issue, she was confronted by serious environmental damage. At the same moment she felt drawn to an old and gnarled Banksia tree. She buried her head in its branches, begging its forgiveness. It was, she remembers, "a profoundly religious and moving experience." She felt her apology had been accepted when, a short while later, she came across a tree alive with birds. "The whole tree was singing. There were hundreds of birds, and the tree was pulsating with song," she recalls. At first, Vivianne found a force in nature which humbled and chastened her. As she learnt to act "properly," she was blessed with the celebration of "treeness."

The Journey's End

We are part of nature, yet we need "the otherness" of nature to remind us of our humanness. Nature, especially in wild places, has the power to teach and delight us, but it also has the power to destroy. The cycles of life and death through nature's beauty and awesome power are acknowledged by the nature carers. Eric, who's sacred place is in Victoria's mountains, sees "destruction as a natural force which has to take place to have a rebirth."

> I've been in bushfires and floods, and I've seen the awesome power of nature. I've seen the awesome destruction, and yes, the awesome rebirth. You are totally helpless. You can't do anything,

but it has to take place. I'm not saying I like destruction, but there has to be a balance. It's like the tall trees which are so aloof looking down on you saying, "What are you doing here? Have you asked permission to come here?" That is the land speaking to me.

Eric, environmental campaigner and lover of mountains

The evocative stories shared by the nature carers have shown the depth of their commitment and connection. They have found that being in nature, particularly in wild places, restores their energy, strengthens their resolve, and sustains their capacity for activism. It helps them cope with the pain of environmental loss. It connects them to their sense of what is sacred in the world. It empowers their beliefs with a sense of purpose—they are impelled to act. They join with others in a range of earth-honouring activities from protest action to land restoration, from community gardening to celebrating community, from ritual worship to festive dance. Through all these practices they are creating a partnership, a sacred relationship, between themselves (as human nature) and the rest of nature.

The people I've interviewed care for nature wherever they are. They protest to save heritage buildings as well as to stop uranium mining. They create community gardens, restore local habitats, and perform ritual actions to protect sacred places in the city as well as the wilderness. I remember one moving ceremony which took place under the spreading branches of the 120-year-old oak tree on the edge of the Yarra River at Melbourne's innovative city-based Children's Farm. This area was threatened with immanent development. We circled slowly round the expansive trunk of the tree, holding hands. Then we lit small candles and walked slowly outwards to the perimeter of the tree. It was a clear, cold night. We could see our breaths in the moonlight. We stood in quiet contemplation of this place, honouring the spirits of the land and the community involved in protecting it, until the candles burnt out.

There are many pathways to spiritually-engaged activism. American Earth First!er Dave Foreman says that in order to protect the environment, four qualities are necessary—passion, vision, courage, and action.[8] These are also the qualities that I found among the nature carers. They act not out of heroism; they act because this is what they need to do to be true to themselves. But there is something else that characterises the nature carers. I call it "active love."

> When we make a ritual for the earth, that's active love.
> When we walk with others in a demonstration;
> Or live up the tree to protect the forest, that's active love.
> When we plant a tree in thanksgiving;
> When we make love to the rocks, or delight in the waves caressing our body;
> When we dance naked in the rain and the water pours over us;
> When we get covered in mud and relish in the muckiness,
> That's active love.

Active love is deliciously active. It throws mud in the faces of those who contend we shouldn't romanticize the natural world. But at the same time, it is not sentimental, idealized love; it is far more subversive than that. It inspires resistance—a resistance evident in the stories of commitment to an ecologically-sustainable and peaceful, socially-just world with all that it entails. Nature carers are working at many levels at once—to protect the forests, to save endangered animals, to ensure clean air and water for the city, as well as to enhance the quality of all of our lives. By choosing the path of wild spirit and active love, they are sustaining themselves and the earth for generations to come.

Notes

1. Throughout this chapter I use the term nature to mean nature "out there" in remote areas as well as nature "in here"—in the city and suburbs, and closer to home, within our instinctive sensual bodies.
2. Stringer and McAvoy, "The Need for Something Different: Spirituality and Wilderness Adventure."
3. Fox, "Enhancing Spiritual Experience in Adventure Programs"; Roberts, "Place and Spirit in Land Management."
4. Adler, *Drawing Down the Moon*; Matthews, "Neo-Paganism and Witchcraft."
5. Harvey, *Listening People, Speaking Earth: Contemporary Paganism.*
6. Maslow, *Religions, Values, and Peak Experiences.*
7. Yarrow, "Sacred Landscapes."
8. Foreman, D. *Confessions of an Eco-Warrior* , 8.

Bibliography

Adler, M. *Drawing Down the Moon*. Boston: Beacon Press, 1986.

Foreman, D. *Confessions of an Eco-Warrior*. New York: Harmony Books, 1991.

Fox, R. "Enhancing Spiritual Experience in Adventure Programs." In *Adventure Programming*, edited by J. C. Miles & S. Priest. State College, PA: Venture Publishing, Inc., 1999.

Harvey, G. *Listening People, Speaking Earth: Contemporary Paganism*. Kent Town, South Africa: Wakefield Press, 1997.

Maslow, A. *Religions, Values, and Peak Experiences.* Columbus, OH: Ohio State University Press, 1964.

Matthews, C. "Neo-Paganism and Witchcraft." In *America's Alternative Religions*, edited by T. Miller. Albany, NY: State University of New York Press, 1995.

Roberts, E. J. "Place and Spirit in Land Management." In *Nature and the Human Spirit: Toward an Expanded Land Management Ethic*, edited by B. L. Driver et al. State College, PA: Venture Publishing, Inc., 1996.

Stringer, L. A and L. H. McAvoy, "The Need for Something Different: Spirituality and Wilderness Adventure," *The Journal of Experiential Education* 15, no. 1 (1992): 13–20.

Yarrow. "Sacred Landscapes." In *Practising the Witch's Craft: Real Magic Under a Southern Sky*, edited by D. Ezzy. Crows Nest, NSW: Allen & Unwin, 2003.

Dancing in the Daylight

A Role for Shamanism in Social and Environmental Change

GORDON MACLELLAN

We live in a world of wonders and marvels—a world that deserves to be celebrated, not necessarily because it is useful or valuable, but simply because it is a place of glory in its own right. Many of us, however, do not seem to recognise that. Oh, we recognise some of it. We treasure wilderness, preserve the last of things, not acting until it is almost too late: whales, tigers, rhinos, peat bogs. But the wonder is everywhere. City streets, town squares, wide open monocultures all, too, hold life, all cultivate wonder. And we spray toxins on the dandelions, mutter about pigeons on the street and the moss in the lawn, and do not applaud the persistence of cockroaches and the resilience of rats. At the same time, we talk of estrangement, separationn, and loss. People feel "out of touch" with the world, it seems, but that world itself marks no separation. Has it ever dropped us out of touch? (Two useful tests: Still breathing? Then you are still part of it all. Dead and decaying? Still in touch.) That world, that vibrant, rich, and changing world has continued going about its business of adapting and absorbing and sliding into every niche in every new situation we have offered. And us? We have gone on hammering it, living off and not living with, pushing ourselves away from the life-pulsing beat of the earth, away from recognising what we are doing, the impact we are having, away from accepting responsibility for how we live our lives.

The situation is changing, however. It feels to me that we are living on the edge of something. A world balanced on a precarious brink. The edge of what? Destruction? Another mass species extinction to rival the loss of the dinosaurs or the earlier and even more dramatic end of the Palaeozoic world? Or something more unexpected? The brink of a caterpillar metamorphosis, perhaps? Or maybe that edge is just a small ridge, not a precipice, and our world may stumble and then stagger on, much as before. I do not know. An edge is an edge. I am, possibly, a shaman, and we work with, live with, that sense of balancing on the edge of the cliff. The next step is into the unknown. We may guess possible answers. We may predict outcomes of eagle flight or pebble plummet, but really we do not know. The situation is changing. People care. They do care and are beginning to realise it, and are finding their own ways of approaching the edge of the cliff. And no one knows if they can fly until they step off the edge.

People care. They turn around, are turning, looking anew and with senses rekindled, exploring with renewed wonder the world around them. The inspiration for this seems to come from all sorts of directions: growing "green" consciousness, community development initiatives, spectacular wildlife documentaries, sudden bursts of personal creativity. They all seem to contribute, and when asked, people may or may not articulate some source of inspiration. Sometimes, however, it just seems that this is the right time to open our eyes and look at our neighbourhood and at each other. This essay is not about charting the background to new environmental consciousnesses, but about drawing upon my own experiences as someone working within that air of change and renewal, and reflecting upon the relation between that movement and the Pagan and magical communities.

I am not an academic or some researcher who tries to look at the whole of this process. My experience lies at the leafy ends of one branch of that spreading tree. I work with groups of people to find ways of celebrating the places where they live, work, and play. I am brought into such groups as an environmentalist, an artist, and a creator of celebrations to guide an adventure, providing skills, confidence, and experience in expeditions that are community and individual centred, artist guided but community led. The relationships are subtle. The apparent patterns of "who is in charge" are very fluid, but the essence of the work remains rooted in the community; and like a shaman, the artist or celebrator is there to serve the community and the place where those people live. Again, shamanically, our job is to facilitate the exploration and, hopefully, renewal of a creative relationship by those people, between themselves and the land they live with. "Community" might be anything from a local history club, to a school, a group of schools, a whole housing estate, youth groups. The heart of the work lies in helping whoever wants to be involved to find ways to explore their own relationships with place; and in the process, they will often find new ways of relating to each other and to themselves as thinking, perceptive, creative individuals. The whole process that I will discuss here is both new and not new. We may create celebrations to replace or accompany older ones, or devise ones that have no historic context at all but feel necessary and relevant to our modern communities. I am fascinated by how much "established" celebrations evolved and went on evolving as ideas and relationships changed. It is very easy to think of "heritage" as a fixed unit: "This is how it is done, and has always been done." There is a great security in referring to the sanctity of established practice when often the practice is not nearly as established as we would like. So we should not be afraid or ashamed of new shapes in old celebrations or scared of creating new ones. Perhaps environmental celebrants like myself are needed simply because we have skipped a few generations of the relevant perceptions and skills, and in time we may become cheerfully redundant as communities take over their own celebrations again.

New celebrations? They take many forms. There might be lantern processions that plunge us into the depths of cathartic despair before scaling the dizzy heights of the temple of love and passion. We might tell through dance and poetry the story of a stone that someone picked up in a car park. Several hundred people may become a river dancing down to the still waters of a reservoir and blessing the new reservoir with dreams and stories it has not yet had time to grow for itself. We might unfold fern-uncurling imaginations, the tales that explain the savoured treasures and spooky corners of our neighbourhood. We might simply turn ourselves into the animals and plants of our home and listen to them as they speak, or become those who we would welcome in to walk our streets and rest in our gardens again.

This work, these adventures, provide hope that participants will review where and how they live. They do not set out to ask people to list "ten things I can do to save the planet." They aim to inspire and move people, giving them a chance to experience the world they walk in, add verb the air they breathe, and explore their own feelings for that world. For myself, that carries a hope that people will come out of the experience wondering at their world, and wanting to act and to help, but I accept that this may not be the result. My job is to build the boat that sails us on our adventures: where we go and how we are changed on the way is up to the sailors themselves.

"Celebration" to many people seems safe, frivolous even, when there are so many more "serious issues" that need addressing. Personally, I feel celebration needs to come first. I feel there is a great need for that sense of wonder, and of caring, and of valuing, and maybe an attendant desire for change. We can go ahead and plant trees or recycle everything in sight, but when these initiatives come from other organisations and are, effectively, imposed (even for the best of reasons), there is often no underlying community commitment to the process. It was not something that people chose as part of their vision for their homes. Tree planting is a wonderful thing to do, but if we want people to accept trees as their own, to respect and care for them, it should come from the desire of that community to have more trees around them. Of course, there are exceptions. Some of those wonderfully envisioned trees might still be ripped out and torn down, while those trees some company walked in and planted all over the local rough football pitch might survive and be loved. There are no absolutes in this work. There are people.

So much happens in the process of building a celebration. Participants explore the places around them (and often there will be surprise, dismay, and delight in those occasions alone). They gather skills that might be useful anywhere, or work to become puppeteers, musicians, singers, and storytellers. Perhaps that will be for just this one occasion, but with creativity comes confidence, and with participation comes an awareness of the right to be heard, of the right to a personal interpretation of the world. It may not be rooted in scientific understanding or technical knowledge, but people find their view of their world is as valid as anyone else's. The process is a delicate one and is very dependent upon having facilitators dedicated to the growth of people rather than the glory of the artist's own art. To offer people the freedom to speak and be heard and to be a part of planning, growth, and final celebration can offer a profound realisation for a society steeped in "given" information and opinions. Now people are given the chance to look around for themselves and find their own awareness of the value they place in the world on their doorstep. That sense of value is often there: "my" groups may not live in beautiful landscapes or spaces precious to anyone else, but celebrations start on doorsteps, and we find that there is wonder everywhere. People do care for their homes and neighbourhoods. Letting people remind themselves of that sets many things in motion. Celebrations are frivolous, but their effects may be profound. Within a cavalcade of laughter and noise, there may be the silence of reflection. Time to be still. There may just be lots of laughter—or fears being whispered to the ancient stones of a wall, or floated away in a flotilla of paper boats down the river. Under it all lie seeds of change, small caterpillars of transformation. Celebratory work can be waved away, but it carries an impetus for personal and community growth and change that runs deep, quiet, and powerful.

Effective celebrations encourage people to change. Spiritually and politically, celebrations can set all sorts of things in motion. I do not think people need to be told how to change or to be given some new vision for the future. People are quite capable of finding and owning their own vision of what might be, and a celebration can be one way of setting these thoughts in motion. The results are often unpredictable, perilous even; not being told or instructed as to what the outcome should be, people might take unexpected paths. A whole celebration can go dragon-stamping off in a new direction as people begin to think for themselves and perhaps find that what matters to them about "here, there, and now" is not this but is definitely that, and, "Why can we not celebrate something else altogether?" The artist's role is to facilitate, to guide the practicalities, and to respect and support those unexpected turns of creativity. The whole process should generate confidence and direction. People start deciding for themselves what they want for their community. "Community consultation," for some of those groups who endorse it, can be a dangerous thing: local government, bigger organisations, and landowners claim to support it, but once the celebratory, consultative dragons come out of the cage, they do not necessarily belong to the people with the money. They belong to the people with the fiercest imaginations and the greatest sense of "this is our place," and who are prepared to ask, "What do I care for here?" And, "How would I like my home to grow?"

The growth of individual and community into confidence and readiness to act may be slow, but here we are investing in a future and hoping our way of being lasts long enough for these seeds to grow to maturity, as children grow up celebrating their world, not just grabbing everything they can from it. Nebulous. Difficult to pin down. How do we know it matters? Can we quantify that? Probably not.

There are no quick answers here and no apologies for the mess that we continue to perpetrate. To celebrate is not to deny the destruction our society is wreaking, but it is to try to work around that and change those directions by appreciating what is there, living and wondrous, around us, rather than trying to "guilt-trip" communities into modifying behaviours.

I work in a world that revolves around renewing and maintaining wonder and excitement in the world. I work with a wide range of groups, but am often left wondering, "Where are the Pagans?" "Are the magicians out on the streets?" They are probably "my" community as much as anyone else is. I call myself animist and Pagan, and possibly shaman. This Pagan community describes itself as earth-loving, and I look out and ask, "Where are we?" Where are these people who say they belong to a nature based religion? Oh yes, sometimes we are there. There are magnificent exceptions who give me hope, but overall, the question remains, "When will the Pagans step outside and join in?"

Joining in. That seems to be the challenging bit: being a part of a bigger community. Not our own small secretive world, but joining in with "ordinary folk." Nonmagical types. Even Christians. It is not necessarily about campaigning for our rights as Pagans and making sure that people know who we are and why we deserve the right to live, believe, and worship as we will. That is a battle that we do still need to fight, and I know and acknowledge that sometimes we stay hidden for very good reasons. But come on. To join a lantern festival you do not need to wear the tall pointy hat and flowing robes. You do not have to be loud and extrovert to see yourself as musician, artist, leader, or anything other than "myself." You just need to be there. You just need to join in, to share experiences with other people, and remember that "community" can include anyone.

So maybe people are there anyway, and I just do not notice. Easily possible. But if they are, why does it not show up anywhere else? Why do we not hear people celebrating all that excitement in our small Pagan circles? Are we so advanced in our ritual that we cannot learn and grow and change and draw upon the experiences to be gained from watching whole groups of people with no "ritual training" or "ceremonial experience" finding new ways of celebrating the earth we profess to love and honour with our teachings and workings?

I suspect the reasons lie in awkward and irritating areas like "respect" and "integrity," and maybe "power" and "humility" as well. I think I measure the quality of a belief system by how it encourages the individual to look beyond themselves and toward the quality of life of those around them and those who may yet come to live here, and by how much such principles also apply to more than just human communities. I am "Pagan": the heart of my experience of the world and of my way of being in the world lies in seeing, valuing, and celebrating the richness of this planet's biodiversity and the dynamic systems that support the fragile webs of life that hold it all together. It is a source of much joy and excitement to meet human communities looking beyond themselves and appreciating the world they live in. The imagery they use to express their relationships is seldom "Pagan," but we revel in connected experiences, sharing delight in different languages. Their beliefs are not animistic, and to presume to describe them as such would, for me as a celebrator and shaman, feel a betrayal of their trust. How you define yourself is up to you, but the consequences of that definition are what the rest of us can, hopefully, enjoy.

What does it mean if you see yourself as "powerful," feel yourself to be strong in your belief and in your magic? In your magical practice, do you work for yourself, for your own growth and delight, or do you grow to live more closely, more fully with the wonder of a living earth? I hope that I work for the earth, for the freedom for the earth and those living here to grow, working to give myself away, to always move closer to being part of the patterns of the life unfolding around me. Perhaps to become "powerful" is to serve more deeply, more fully. Perhaps humility reeks a little for us of Christian monasteries and imposed value systems telling us to be meek and mild and not to shake that system, but humility may also lie in joy and delight in anything, everything, including yourself, rather than a strained determination to be meek, mild, and not shake the system.

How can we not act?

Out there in the wide world there are people finding their own ways of doing things, of touching and feeling, that seem to me to be close to some of the core principles of Paganism. Love. Respect. Honour. Integrity. No, the people involved are not Pagan, and some would be very offended to be described as such. We have no monopoly on earth-love, but I would hope that an active sense of connection is central to our world, whatever form of Paganism we profess.

So while the people we live with are out there, or are ready to go, adventuring, should we not remember that people are part of the pattern, too—that they are part of that enchanting web of woven life? And should we not jump up and go adventuring, too?

Perhaps we do that already? Perhaps in our hidden house temples and with carefully planned, taught, and received ritual cycles we are serving the earth in our way. Does doing this excuse us from other action? Why should it? The ceremonial patterns may be rich, rewarding, and strong, but there is more to it all than that. If we are "Pagan," and if we are people who listen to the heartbeat of the earth, how can we not join in when other people start to stamp an earthbeat of their own on the ground? Not to convert, corrupt, or lead, but simply to be part of the process, part of a waking and a growing. We have experiences to share and ways of working that can be valuable. Detach all that ritual pattern from the ritual words, and realise that we have a lot of skills in planning ceremony. Many people go through life being led: being told in church, school, work, wherever, "This is how you do things," so when the time comes to try shaping something new, they have never had to look at the structure within a way of doing things. I hope we have—that we can talk about beginnings, middles, and ends, about people, lanterns, masks, banners to marking spaces, about sharing experiences, valuing silence, encouraging group participation.

This does not mean we have to abandon all our existing practices, but I would expect us to challenge ourselves and ask why we do things. It takes a hard edge of personal questioning to separate (if they can be separated) "What do we do for ourselves and our personal relationship with the earth?" from "What do we do for the earth who nourishes us?" and "What do we do out of habit and because it is safe and gives us a sense of power and mystery in ourselves rather than in the wind that blows cold through the thorn trees?"

We are Pagan, and there may be questions to ask here about where our beliefs lead us. Where do those Pagan paths go? For me, they lead me to move deeper into a sense of the stillness, the shifting tranquility that lies within movement and change, learning to listen, to feel the movement of the patterns of life around me, learning simply to "be." My magical practice is not to mend or heal or change, but to navigate, to sense the paths and patterns of others and not to alter those, but to help people find their own ways of sensing the paths they walk, finding their own ways of moving with some degree of grace and beauty within the world. Given all that, how can I not act? To celebrate the world is at the heart of who I am and what I do, and that celebration needs to be as embracing and as encompassing as I can manage it.

We are Pagan. To new celebrations we can bring our own wider experience as well. As a shaman, I try to listen to the earth and to the nonhuman worlds, and to find ways of letting their voices be heard in my work. We can encourage an appreciation of the world from other perspectives. Celebrations may be held by humans, but they can embrace all of the world, and we can create opportunities for people to offer warmth and appreciation to the world and to genuinely thank, in their own way, the world for being there.

I am a shaman. I tend to work outside the boxes from a very fluid, shifting, growing place that shapes itself to suit the needs of the moment. So it is easy to point accusing wands at the likes of me and say we are anarchic and do not appreciate or understand the subtlety of formal ritual or the importance of it in some greater scheme of things. Shame. Maybe I have no appreciation. But also I am used to working with groups of people and to seeing the skittering evasions people use. "I can't draw," "I can't sing," "I can't dance, make things, stand up in public and speak," or "I don't know anything about trees, about anything." Other people get past all of those things and touch their world and are touched by it. Other people take those personal risks, face those quests, and are changed by their action. I have to wonder how much more scared our people are, or how much more self-satisfied, having got that whole "in touch with the earth" bit sorted already.

And no, this is not an invitation to High Priestesses and Priests everywhere to put on their crowns of power and flounce out to lead the masses. It is a challenge to all of us to be ordinary, to join in where things are already taking shape, or maybe to start celebrating the ordinary places and ordinary things as ordinary people. To participate. Not as an excuse to wave a Pagan flag, but because other people are finding new ways of valuing their home spaces, our home spaces; and if we care, if we really care and commune with and belong to the earth and to nature, how can we not be a part of new ways of celebrating all of that?

Our celebrations, our rituals—and that includes me as well—are so often part of the darkness, of the magic that moves in nightshadows under the moon. We dance in the darkness with glory and excitement. Maybe the biggest challenge now is to be brave enough to be ordinary and to dance in the daylight.

Pagan Politics,
Pagan Stories

An Interview

STARHAWK

This interview was conducted in mid–December 2003, in Lismore, New South Wales, toward the end of Starhawk's Australian tour.

Thom van Dooren:Your approach to the global justice movement incorporates many aspects of contemporary Paganism, such as ritual and an awareness of energy dynamics and their effects on groups and society at large. Do you see these to be important aspects of the movement?

Starhawk: In the global justice movement, or in any kind of movement that involves direct confrontation with oppressive powers, it

really helps to understand energy dynamics (*laughs*). Just on a pure
survival level, grounding—being able to stay calm in moments of crisis—is what I fall back on again and again. It's what I teach in every
direct-action training, and people will always come back to me and
say, "Thank you for teaching me that, it really helped when the riot
cops were beating on me, I was able to stay calm," or, "When the tear
gas came I was able to figure out what to do." So yeah, that's a really
important tool on a number of different levels. With Pagans, of
course, it helps to keep our energies together and focused. That shifts
the energies of what's happening.

We've also seen that a lot of the younger activists, who may have
started off really antispirituality because they identify it with oppressive, patriarchal kinds of religions, also have spiritual needs and have
a need to confront those intense things that happen in life. Certainly
they come out of these actions often needing a lot of healing and are
often hungry for that kind of thing. When it's offered in a way that's
not authoritarian or rigid and doesn't involve adopting a whole external belief system, people are often very open.

I've been asked to do healing rituals for forest defenders who have
suffered horrific violence. I was in occupied territories in Palestine a
lot last year and spent a lot of the time doing support for some of the
teams—like the teams that were with Rachael Corrie when she was
killed by an Israeli bulldozer trying to stop a home demolition, and
the teams that were with Tom Hurndall and Brian Avery when they
were shot. Sometimes that involved formal ritual, and sometimes it
just involved fending off other people who think they know what's
best for somebody in a state of grief and trauma, and are actually trying to take control of the situation. Sometimes it's saying, "Go away;
stop imposing your thing." Sometimes it involves saying something
as simple as, "You know what, maybe you actually know best what
you need right now, not what everybody else thinks you need."

What advice would you give to Pagans who are already involved in protest and direct action but would like to incorporate more of their Paganism into these actions?

I think that actions speak louder than words in terms of bringing stuff into these groups. If you are an activist, and people know you and respect you in that way, then they will be more open to sharing your spirituality. We have always tried to share things in ways that are not imposed on a group. We won't say, "Okay, now everyone's going to do this ritual," but more, "Okay, we're going to go over there and do this ritual, and we invite anyone who wants to come and join us." That has worked very successfully.

And think about being flexible in our ritual form. We don't have to be wedded to waving our swords around and invoking this and that in ways that people don't understand, or using specific deities when everyone might not be a Pagan or a witch. Instead we can go back to the things that are common to all of us, like the elements. I often talk about invoking a nonspecific goddess and thinking about what's sacred to each of us, what we each care about, what we will take a stand about. It is also important that rituals be open to people who may or may not have a certain belief system.

We did a really great Black Bloc/Pagan Cluster ritual in Miami. The idea came from some of the Black Bloc, some of the hardcore anarchists, who really wanted to do some kind of a ritual. We had a lot of discussion about what would work. We decided not to start off with everyone standing in a circle holding hands and intoning things, because the anarchists would have just felt uncomfortable or laughed. Instead we decided to start with creating an energy base through drumming, then put stuff in the centre and let people do what they felt like. The Pagans had had some discussions about holding a coherent energy base in a chaotic situation—which, of course, is what you need to do in an action anyway. And it was beautiful. It was really wonderful, a magical ritual that just flowed completely spontaneously. We wove a web and we danced and we lit fires and we hit plastic barrels and released rage and transformed it into beautiful, wonderful, compassionate singing and chanting energy. It came out of years of trust building and solidarity with different groups, which was not about our attempting to get other people to do ritual. It grew out of the numerous other occasions of front-line street solidarity. "The cops are targeting these kids; let's link each one up with someone from the Pagan Cluster and walk them through this police line; let's put our bodies between the cops and the kids in the Black Bloc and stop them getting beaten up." That built the base for being able to do ritual together, and for different kinds of work together in the future.

I think that maybe part of the reason that ritual hasn't become such an important part of these sorts of actions in Australia, and some other parts of the world in which protests are not greeted with such a direct violence, is because the situation is perceived not to be so desperate. We are obviously part of a world in which the situation is desperate, but it often doesn't seem that way here because there are no rubber bullets or tear gas.

Well, we've also done plenty of rituals in situations that weren't so desperate. It wasn't always like this in the US. Back in the 1980s, when we were doing blockades and things very similar to the things that you have done here, we would offer a ritual for the camp for protection or for empowerment. Again, we would never do it as, "Let's everybody do this ritual," but more, "Hey, over in that field *(laughs)* we are doing a full moon ritual and anyone who wants to come is invited. The intention is to raise energy and protection for this action." Then people would come. Often what would happen is at first some people would come and other people would say, "Ah, I'm not into that stuff." Then people would come back and say, "Wow, that was great, that was wonderful." Those other people would say, "Gee, why didn't I go to that?" and then they might come to the next one.

How would you conceptualise the relationship between Paganism and politics?

For me personally, my activism comes out of my Paganism. It comes from my sense that we are part of a living being that is the earth, and that we are all deeply interconnected. So I can't sit around and watch idiots destroy the earth or see people in suffering without trying to do something about it. Also because, as a Pagan, I don't believe that there is some heaven somewhere later on where everything will be all right. I believe that the terrain of the sacred is right here on earth. Here is where we need to act. This is where we need to create heaven and beauty, in balance and delight.

At the same time, my political activism is helped by my Paganism. It's what helps me sustain my energies. My activism has also informed the way that I practise Paganism. Reclaiming, which is the network of people I work with, is very much modelled on the structures we learned from doing nonviolent direct action. We work by consensus, we work in small groups. We have spokescouncils and representatives. We work on creating an antiauthoritarian Pagan culture that mirrors antiauthoritarian political culture. We work on some of the same internal issues around our own divisions, prejudices, and limitations that we do in larger political work. That, I think, has given our ritual practice a real sense of aliveness, spontaneity, and creativity that otherwise tend to get lost when things become dogmatic or hierarchical.

In approaching these issues you have often spoken about the need to challenge consumer culture and reprioritise values by beginning to envision, tell, and live alternative stories. This is a big question, but could you tell us some more about how this might be approached?

For Pagans especially, we have a religion where we say we worship the earth and that nature is sacred, but a lot of Pagans don't actually know anything about nature (*laughs*). I'll see Pagans driving their SUVs (sport utility vehicles), and going home and playing their computer games, and spending all their money on fancy Pagan jewellery and stuff, and not composting their garbage. You have to stop and say, "Wait a minute, this isn't an abstraction. It isn't just an enlarged fantasy game. It's about really thinking about the way we live. It's about living in a way that's as integrated as possible with those natural systems that we say are sacred to us." When you do that, one of the things you find is that your sense of what creates abundance in your life changes. It's no longer about what you buy or what you wear—although I think that people will always like to dress up (*laughs*). Maybe it's also no longer about going out and eating at a fancy restaurant. Maybe instead it's about being able to go out to your yard and pick a fresh salad and put it on your table within ten minutes, and eat something that you can never get at a fancy restaurant. Maybe it's no longer about having the newest, biggest size car. It's now more about having a little more time to spend with your kids, your family, your friends, or your circle.

I think there is a potential within Paganism to really shift people's values. There are a lot of Pagans who voluntarily spend their spare time doing things like thinking up new rituals and getting people together for events. They are sharing and celebrating and getting people together to create a sense of community, when they could be spending all that time watching TV (*laughs*). So there's a strong potential, and sometimes it gets realised more than others. I think one of the things that we need to think more about as Pagans is how we actually root our spirituality in the real earth, and not just in our abstract ideas about "earth." Not only about how we invoke water, but also about conserving, saving, cleaning, and returning water to the environment, as well as working on issues of water policy in our home communities.

And the new stories just flow from this experience?

Yes.

In your work you have also advocated a strong program of localisation with regard to lifestyles and trade, supporting the development of stronger "bonds with place." Why is it that you see a stronger localisation as an essential aspect of an equitable and sustainable world?

We have to begin to see that something like food is not just a bunch of isolated commodities that can be transported all over the world and bought and sold for profit. Food is a living system that is part of sustaining life, and that system has to be rooted in place. Growing food is not just about producing a banana. It is about producing a whole web of interrelationships between plants, animals, soil, worms, microorganisms, human beings, communities, the people who do the work of growing the food, and those who do the work of distributing it and preparing it. All of those things are like a web; they're interrelated. When you start pulling apart little strands of that web, it no longer holds up. So, it's not that I would say, "Nothing should be traded." I think trade can be a really important means of enriching our lives. But certain things really belong at home, and need to be rooted in home.

Many of our problems are global in both their causes and impacts (for example, global warming). Is it not essential that we "globalise" and shift our focus to a global system of governance and trade in order to approach them?

There are definitely global agreements that we need, for example, the Cochabamba Declaration that came out of Bolivia after the local people retook their water supply. This document calls for a global agreement to secure our right to water—water as a human right—as well as protect the world's water supply and oppose its privatisation. There are certain things like the global declaration of human rights that I think are really important steps in that kind of direction. But before we set up a new global governing agency, I favour putting more control back into the hands of local communities around important and vital aspects of life, like production and control of their resources.

Certainly what we see happening in the United States is that the further up the scale you get, the more money and influence come into play—particularly money—and until we deal with that issue (*laughs*), a global system is only going to make it worse. If we could figure out how to actually have democracy in the United States, then I would be more favourable towards thinking about it at a global level. But we don't have democracy in the States; we have plutocracy. We have rule by money. On a local level you can sometimes get around that, and we have some good things happening on a local scale. But as you move up the scale it gets harder and harder because the amounts of money, influence, and power brokering, and the ruthlessness with which they are employed, are just so overwhelming and enormous.

So is this type of localisation in part also a way of moving power away from the federal level and into local communities?

It's a mixed bag. It's not that I totally advocate at this point moving all of the power away from the federal government. There are places in which the federal government is the only thing that protects people locally against the power of ruthless corporations. Certainly there have been times in our history, like the civil rights era, where you had some very bad local governments and the federal government could step in to ensure more justice and equality. But what we see right now is that power is being shifted from individuals and communities, preventing them from actually having a say in things like how their needs are met and how their resources are used. That has to be redressed. Again, we don't have a democracy. We don't have a system where people actually have a voice in the decisions that affect them. We have decisions being made by elites on multiple different levels, from the WTO to a corporation that decides to move out of town and relocate in Asia, where they can pay workers twenty-five cents an hour. We need to rethink the whole way that our economy is structured, to move away from a system where our only intention is to produce short-term profits for major transnational corporations. We need to look back to a system where the goal is to meet the needs that people have and produce the things that we need—to produce in ways that provide a livelihood of dignity and security for the people who do the work.

Towards an Activist
Spirituality

STARHAWK

No sane person with a life really wants to be a political activist. When activism is exciting, it tends to involve the risk of bodily harm or incarceration, and when it's safe, it is often tedious, dry, and boring. Activism tends to put one into contact with extremely unpleasant people, whether they are media interviewers, riot cops, or at times, your fellow activists. Not only that, it generates enormous feelings of frustration and rage, makes your throat sore from shouting, and hurts your feet.

Nonetheless, at this moment in history, we are called to act as if we truly believe that the earth is a living, conscious being that we're part of, that human beings are interconnected and precious, and that liberty and justice for all is a desirable thing.

When we founded Reclaiming two decades ago, our intention was to bring together the spiritual and the political. Or more accurately, some of us for whom the spiritual and the political were inseparable wanted to create a practice and community that reflected this integration.

Now, with the Bush forces engaged in aggressive wars, with horrific environmental and social problems left unaddressed, the need for activism is stronger than ever. The stakes have never been higher, and the sense of urgency is palpable.

Reclaiming folks have been out there—taking part in marches and demonstrations and protests from Seattle to Washington DC, bringing magic and ritual and spiral dances into what sometimes seems like the zone of battle. And doing the proactive work beyond the protest—helping to organize our communities, provide healing, food, nurturing for children, music, art, and ritual—all the things that embody the world we want to live in.

The integration of magic and activism sometimes means bringing magic into an action—doing a spiral dance in the midst of the tear gas of Quebec City, or in Grand Central station surrounded by riot cops. It might mean starting our strategic planning with a trance or a tarot reading, or invoking water as we work against the privatization of water resources.

But that integration also means that our rituals are informed by our activism, and by the real-life issues that we address. It means a different conception of spirituality—that spirituality and ritual are not something removed from the world, but are deeply embedded in it.

Reclaiming is founded on earth-based spirituality, which rejects the split between spirit and matter, and claims nature and the physical, material world as equally sacred with the spirit.

We don't ideologically believe in the separation of spirit and matter, but in practice, we still tend to think that things that are too material, too real-life, are somehow not as spiritual. So a trance to Faery is perceived as "spiritual," whereas a trance to a Brazilian favela slum is not. We can argue about the reality of Faery, but the favela is undeniably real. If we truly believe that our spirituality is about deep interconnectedness, maybe it's more important for us to grapple internally with the reality of the favela than to dance with the faeries.

Of course, visualizing the faeries generally makes us feel good, whereas thinking about slums and wars and international trade agreements often makes us uncomfortable. Even angry or sad or hopeless or guilty.

Much of our magic and our community work is about creating spaces of refuge from a harsh and often hostile world, safe places where people can heal and regenerate, renew our energies and learn new skills. In that work, we try to release guilt, rage, and frustration, and generally turn them into positive emotions.

Safety and refuge and healing are important aspects of spiritual community. But they are not the whole of spirituality. Feeling good is not the measure by which we should judge our spiritual work. Ritual is more than self-soothing activity.

Spirituality is also about challenge and disturbance, about pushing our edges and giving us the support we need to take great risks. The Goddess is not just a light, happy maiden or a nurturing mother. She is death as well as birth, dark as well as light, rage as well as compassion—and if we shy away from her fiercer embrace, we undercut both her power and our own growth.

There are times when it is inappropriate to feel wholly good. Now is one of those times. As the saying goes, "If you aren't angry, you aren't paying attention."

This doesn't mean that we need to be in a constant state of rage or irritability or guilt. It means we need to use our magical tools to

face the stark and overwhelming realities that confront us, acknowledge our feelings, and transmute them into the energy we need for
change.

Last fall before the Spiral Dance, we received a letter strongly ob-
jecting to an invocation from the year before, when we had staged
a mock march to invoke water, complete with a river of cloth and
chants that began, "No FTAA, No WTO, No privatizing, Let the
river flow!" The writer objected to the ritual being turned into a
"pep rally."

I never had time to reply to her letter, but I was grateful to the
writer because it stimulated a lot of thinking for me. Everyone has
the right to their own opinion about a ritual, and to their own aes-
thetics. There's generally at least one invocation in every ritual that I
could personally do without. But what interested me about the letter was her unspoken assumption that an issue such as the privatization of water was somehow an extraneous element that didn't really
belong in ritual, and turned it into something else.

For those of us who created the invocation, the privatization of
water is a deeply spiritual issue. Because the water we hold sacred is
not some abstract image or fantasy of water, but the real stuff that
we need to drink and bathe and grow our gardens, that provides the
crucial habitat for fish and plants and thousands of other creatures,
that is the earth's literal life blood.

If two-thirds of the people on the earth don't have access to the
water they need—as is predicted within another decade or two—
and I am integrally connected to those people, that's a spiritual crisis as well as a physical and political crisis. And if I've been engaged
with that issue politically and magically (as we have been in many of
the actions around global trade agreements that further the corporate takeover of the planet's water), I need my rituals to reflect that
struggle and energize my work.

Another common, unspoken assumption is that spirituality is about calm and peace, and conflict is unspiritual. Which of course makes it hard to integrate the spiritual with the political, which is all about conflict.

In New Age circles, a common slogan is, "What you resist, persists." Truly spiritual people are never supposed to be confrontational or adversarial—that would be perpetuating an unevolved, "us-them" dualism.

I don't know from what spiritual tradition the "What you resist, persists" slogan originated, but I often want to ask those who blithely repeat it, "What's your evidence?" When it is so patently obvious that what you don't resist persists like hell and spreads all over the place. In fact, good, strong, solid resistance may be the only thing that stands between us and hell. Hitler didn't persist because of the Resistance—he succeeded in taking over Germany and murdering millions because not enough people resisted.

On some deep cosmic level, we are all one, and within us we each contain the potential for good and for destruction, for compassion and hate, for generosity and greed. But even if I acknowledge the full range of impulses within myself, that doesn't erase the differences between a person acting from compassion and love, and another choosing to act from hate and greed. Moreover, it doesn't erase my responsibility to challenge a system which furthers hate and greed. If I don't resist such a system, I am complicit in what it does. I join the perpetrators in oppressing the victims.

I am often astonished at well-meaning, spiritual people who advocate beaming light toward world leaders, who scold activists for expressing anger toward authorities or police, who define compassion as loving the enemy—but somehow lose sight of the need to love our friends, our allies, and those who suffer at the hands of the perpetrators. I really don't feel much call to beam love and light at Bush or Cheney or the directors of the International Monetary Fund. Whether or not they suffer from lack of love is beyond me. From my perspective, they suffer from an excess of power, and I feel called to take it away from them. Because I do love the child in Iraq, the woman in the favela, the eighteen-year-old recruit to the Marines who never dreamed he was signing up to bomb civilians. I can't love them, or myself and my community, effectively if I can't articulate the real differences in interests and agendas between "us" and "them"— between those who have too little social power and those who have too much.

To equalize that power means changing an enormous system. And systems don't change easily. Systems try to maintain themselves, and seek equilibrium. To change a system, you need to shake it up, disrupt the equilibrium. That often requires conflict.

To me, conflict is a deeply spiritual place. It's the high-energy place where power meets power, where change and transformation can occur.

Part of my own spirituality is the conscious practice of placing myself in places of conflict. As someone in the Pagan cluster said after the February 15, 2003, antiwar rally in New York, which was seriously harrassed by the police, "When everyone else was running away from trouble, we were running toward it." I run toward it because I generally believe I can be useful there—sometimes de-escalating potential violence, sometimes just holding a clear intention in the midst of chaos, sometimes just serving as a witness.

Our magical tools and insights, our awareness of energies and allies on many planes, can deepen and inform our activism. And our activism can deepen our magic by encouraging us to create ritual that speaks to the real challenges we face in the world; it offers the healing and renewal we need to continue working, and a community that understands that spirit and action are one.

Previously published in *Reclaiming Quarterly,* Fall 2003 © Starhawk

Place, Politics, and Spirituality

An Interview

DR. VAL PLUMWOOD

This interview was conducted in mid-November 2003, at Val's living place near Sleeping Woman Mountain in New South Wales, Australia. At the time, literally thousands of cicadas had come above ground for a huge mating session, and their calls overwhelmed the ear and filled the forest (as anyone who has experienced this event will know). The interview questions were structured around the desired end goal of introducing Val's ideas to a Pagan audience who may be largely unfamiliar with the many important developments she has made in her philosophical work. At a few points in the interview, the local bird and animal life made its presence even more apparent than usual. At these times I have left our brief discussions in the text as they often beautifully highlight the way in which the broader environment enters into our conversations.

Thom van Dooren: You have spoken about the "fracturing of place" in modern societies, and the way in which most of us now dwell in a group of places. The "home place" with which we interact on a daily basis is no longer our "economic place." What do you mean by this?

Val Plumwood: There are many important historical factors here, in particular the rise of capitalism, and the industrial revolution, which moved work out of the home and into a separate work place which was controlled by the manager. There's a very interesting paper by Steven Marglin, a classic paper called "What Do Bosses Do?" in which he looks at this move of work out of the home and into the factory and argues that there really wasn't any basic economic reason for it.[1] Rather, it was done for reasons of control, because it enabled the manager, or managerialists, to take control of the production process. When this move occurred in the eighteenth century, it was resisted very strongly. People wanted to keep control of their work and keep it in the home, or associated with the home. This move into the factory—which is a really crucial part of what we take to be modernity—is associated with rationalism, too. A lot of the rationalist position is a justification for managerialism, what the manager contributes is rational control over all of these other bodies, hired hands, the "body people."

The move from the home to the work place is a part of the fracturing of place, but, of course, it also took place earlier, in class society: for example, when class society instituted a division between those who lived in the city—the gentlemen, the citizens—and the people who worked on the land, who were often slaves or had no political rights. So the masters took no responsibility for their own "bread labour" and for the places that produced it. And then, of course, we get the market as an extension, or inclusion, of both of these trends. The dominant concept of property doesn't in itself give any recognition to place. Place becomes this sort of interchangeable profit production potential—real estate. The particularity of place is lost. But globalisation introduces a big further fracture.

Another important fracturing is a form of mind/body fracturing, which occurs between the place that you identify as your own place and the place that actually supports your life—this is where the concept of an "ecological footprint" becomes useful. This fracturing goes back a lot earlier than globalisation. If we look at the ancient Greek city, it is already there to some degree. Of course it is vastly worsened when you have a market in which you have no idea where the product comes from, where it is completely anonymous and detached from its place of production—you can't even find out if you try. I asked the fish man, when I was buying my fish, where it came from, and he just got angry with me *(laughs)*—and this is a local market, so in the global market there's not even anyone to start asking.

So the fracturing between what supports your life and your home place is really a version of the mind/body split, I think. This fracturing is one reason why an approach to environmental problems which says "what we need is a better sense of place" is problematic. Because of this fracturing I think there are severe limitations to the extent to which we can replace "ecological discourse" with "place discourse." Of course, indigenous societies don't seem to have this fracturing, and they are our best examples of societies that don't have it and seem to have very strong spiritual connections with places and with the land. But I see the market as a "place-fracturing institution" because it establishes a pattern of relationship in terms that disregard and override place and treat place as the interchangeable production potential, particularly the global market. We have to be very aware of this fracturing of place, because it imposes a lot of limitations on the extent to which

indigenous models can be applied to the situation of people living in
a market society.

This is also where postcolonial critique has a lot to contribute.
Colonisation is place-fracturing because it gives people (both colonis-
ers and colonised—in different ways) a false consciousness of place
and their relationship to it. The coloniser conquers other places to put
them at the service of his "one true place"—the place that in the
colonising imaginary is the centre of empire—and sees potentially
colonisable places as "development potential," as vacant land empty of
(worthwhile) projects or presences other than his own and inviting
occupation. He "denies prior presences" in order to lay claim to these
very strong, unconstrained concepts of ownership. The colonial mind
tends to admire the universal, and to devalue the local, especially the
local landscape and vegetation, and to subordinate it to the colonial
centre and to its rational ordering of places in terms of a currency of
"economic values." The colonised can easily be deceived by buying in
to this framework, for example, or reversing it into a "local is everything" perspective.

*To what extent then is it valuable to get rid of the market society and return,
well, "return" might be the wrong word . . .*

To a unity with place?

Yes, or in other words, what do we do about this fracturing of place?

I think that there is more than one answer here; I don't know that
there is a unique solution to this problem (*laughs*). Well, obviously returning to a unity with place is the ideal. Indigenous societies probably
varied in the extent to which they had unity with place, but in our
minds they have a unity with place; it's the ideal (*laughs*). There was all
kinds of trade going on—but I don't know that trade itself necessarily
fractures place in a very damaging way. I think that there can be all

kinds of patterns that underlie trade, not just the modern "market"—by which I mean a capitalist market based on lowest prices and biggest profits and so on. There are entirely other bases for a market, so it seems to me that it's not so much trade itself that we should be looking at here, but the "market," or a capitalist-based form of trade. The basic problem with this market is that it eliminates any kind of "place pattern," any sense of responsibility for place, or even knowledge of the places which support our lives, and instead presents an anonymous commodity, so the commodity form is part of the fracturing of place.

In short, I find the idea of "one"s place," "your place" to be problematic. The idea of "your place" is probably far less problematic for those communities whose economic, social, spiritual (if I can use this term here) and environmental lives all revolve around a piece of land that they can grasp as singular, as country. What is so wonderful about this is that the place they love and cherish is also the place that provides for them. But that's not our situation. So inevitably when one talks of "one's place," one is tending to favour a notion of "one true place," which is a singular or monogamous notion of one's place as their place of consciousness, and so in a sense, to speak this way is to collude with the suppression of the other places that nourish one's life. I don't want such a singular ideal of place, and this is why I find the term "one's place" very problematic. I want us to acknowledge responsibilities of care for multiple places, the places of the ecological footprint. An ethic of singularity of local and home place attachment has potential for a conservative politics, whereas for an ecological consciousness we need an ethics of respect for complexity and multiplicity of place, human and nonhuman, local and nonlocal, and attention to local, regional, and planetary contexts.

Although, I have to say, it is quite difficult for me to resist the "one true place" way of thinking because I have a very strong relationship with this place. It is such a strong relationship that in a sense this place is my family—it is a totally absorbing place. I put much of my day's work into this place, and it's always immensely satisfying, which is one reason why I can live alone; in a sense, it has replaced a whole lot of other relationships, my relationship with this place. That is not a normal life for our society, although I know a few other people around here that live it. It's kind of a strange relationship. It's almost like the place is your partner in a sense. That's why I don't really have any space in my life for another person, or don't seem to have any space, because it's taken up by this place.

So that's my relationship with this place, but in an important sense this is not "my place." I get some of my food from here, but a lot of it comes from elsewhere; all my other goods come from other places, so there's a lot of input from other places to my lifestyle in this place. So it would be pretty unsatisfactory for me to think about this as "my place" in that simple way. It is easy to fool yourself about this and act from the false consciousness of place that is promoted in colonial and commodity culture.

It seems that different approaches to this fracturing of place, although often not articulated in this way, are in the background of many of the different positions in the global justice movement, such as the ones that emphasise globalisation or localisation . . .

See, if I'm right, it's not so much a question of globalisation or localisation, but one of the form of exchange. I don't think it's exchange itself that's the problem. Where do you take the antiexchange thing? Do you take it right down to complete individual family self-sufficiency? I'm somewhat against that. I think it's very nuclearising. It's atomising to some extent. So the emphasis on small local communities can be another form of atomisation. It can be another form of saying, "Well, we'll just have this one unit that is self-sufficient." It's not an individual person, but it's an individual community. That worries me; it doesn't acknowledge relationships. I'm not convinced that exchange has to be demonised. I think it's a particular form of exchange that has fractured place, and exchange itself could even be a way of celebrating place—ritually, for example.

So it seems to me that the "reversal" terminology of "localisation" versus "globalisation" leads one to see it as a problem of scale, when really it is more a problem of the type of exchange, not its scale. So I think commodity forms of exchange are the problem here.

Is the alternative a type of "trade" that has more respect for what is exchanged? I'm reading Vandana Shiva's Water Wars *at the moment and she talks about at least two different ways that we can think about water. One is the sale of bottled water in capitalist society, and the other is the "water temples" in rural India in which water is given to everybody; it's a common good.*

Yes, and this is because the dominant commodity form is not only highly individualist but also highly reductionist of what it commodifies, not wanting to admit that anything is left out of the commodity. It has to be reductionistic and instrumentalist (e.g., about water)—making things out to be less than they are and conceiving them as reducible to human use—to give permission for commodification. (This is one of the connections between ethics and politics I pointed to in my last book.) Whereas the "water temple" is a very antireductionist way to think about water.

The dominant commodity form also embodies hegemonic conceptions of agency in production and ownership that background or disappear the contributions of those classed as lesser, e.g., as body or matter—for example, the "hired hands," the maintenance labour of women, the contributions of the nonhuman sphere. Production agency is attributed to the "entrepreneur" as the agent who makes things happen. This backgrounding of others facilitates exploitation in the economic sense, and claims to exclusive property.

These features of capitalist forms of exchange are aimed at max-
imising private ownership and private control over resources as opposed to acknowledging and developing public goods. So it's a neoliberal form of the market as well; it's a neoliberal commodity, and
we could get more specific about it again. The basic feature of the
commodity and its anonymity is precisely this overriding of place,
and that's now enforceable in the global trade rules which demand
various kinds of equivalence and exchangeability that are not actually present, in a way that ignores environmental costs in particular
places.

In short, we need a relational concept of the self which acknowledges that we are in exchange with others—so I'm a bit opposed to
the self-sufficiency concept. To the extent that we are thinking about a
unitary community that is self-sufficient, we are going back to atom-
ism again. We'll never be able to dispense with the problem of responsibility to downstream communities, which self-sufficiency models
refuse to recognise. We need to separate exchange from the particular
form of it that we now have. Exchange doesn't have to be energy intensive either. The particular form of it we have now is, but it doesn't
necessarily have to be.

Energy intensive in terms of transportation?

Yes. It doesn't have to be fossil fuel based; it could also be based on
items that don't require fossil fuel exchange. If one thinks about a society in which transport is not based on fossil fuels, then exchange
isn't necessarily environmentally damaging. Using things like "dyna"
ships, which is quite an exciting proposal, in which shipping is trans-
ferred to a hydrofoil type technology that's guided by computerised
weather forecasting. It's really pretty up to date, using a lot of solar
power, so we could get rid of the fossil fuels used in transportation
almost entirely on that scenario.

I heard the other day that the shipping of goods around the world produces about the equivalent amount of greenhouse gas emissions as all of the cars in the US.

Right, and of course it's absolute madness. It has to come to an end. The whole balloon is going to be punctured as soon as the energy costs rise sufficiently, as the current regime is based entirely on the assumption of endless cheap energy, which is not going to last more than the next thirty years, even if it lasts that long. So it's all going to have to change.

I'm looking forward to the demise of fossil fuels. Then maybe we'll be able to work back towards a more egalitarian world. Nothing could more clearly condemn the standards of justice and democracy in fossil fuel culture than the fact that the peoples of the third world—whose countries hold the oil resources that the privileged find precious—are likely to see these resources plundered while their own living standards plunge, their governments are corrupted, and their distinctive cultures destroyed. In places like Nigeria, those sections of the country that have oil deposits have seen disastrous drops in their living standards—the Ogoni people, for example, in Nigeria. (This is the process now being inflicted with exceptional severity on the unfortunate people of Iraq.)

Much of the energy usage we are persuaded to see as "unthinkable to be without" is wasteful, unnecessary, and maladaptive—for example, personal climate control and huge SUVs. Fossil fuel and commodity culture together enabled increasing remoteness from the effects of consumption and consequent ecological irresponsibility. The prospect of moving out of fossil fuel culture should be a source of hope rather than dread, especially if we can manage the switch to sustainable and smaller-scale resources in the right way. And if the chances of doing that improve the sooner we start, we should start now.

The fossil fuel patriarchy form of colonisation has been based very strongly on the denial of prior others, prior presences, especially in the form of the forests whose ancient labours produced the oil-bearing strata. What could more clearly illustrate the ingratitude and lack of understanding of this culture than the way it now destroys the forests, using the very energy sources the forests laid down.

Perhaps since the publication of Lynn White's article "The Historical Roots of Our Ecological Crisis" in the early 1960s it has been widely acknowledged within academia that both religion and spirituality are intimately bound up with our current ecological problems.[2] Along similar lines, you have argued that not all spirituality is helpful to our current environmental situation, and that some may in fact be harmful. Why is this?

Yes, I must admit I was one of the people who really liked Lynn White's article "The Historical Roots of Our Ecological Crisis," although it set up an industry of refutation. Perhaps it was a bit too single-minded in identifying Christianity as the sole problem. I would want to enlarge that in a whole lot of ways—to monotheism, patriarchy, and, of course, the domination of nature. But certainly the connection between monotheism and the environmental crisis seems to me to be pretty well made out.

One of the things I really liked about Lynn White's article was his identification of the otherworldly orientation of Christianity as an environmental problem. I think it certainly is. The fact that the otherworld really is the one that is valuable, and not this one—it's not an earth-friendly religion, it's absolutely not. But it goes back well before Christianity, even to Plato.[3] It's rationalism, the splitting of the mind from the body and reason from matter, and the exclusivity of the value attached to the first one. We can see these elements in Christianity, too, with its emphasis on spirit/matter dualism and the spirit being disconnected from the material world, from the world of matter, from the world of now and the world of nature, and the value of the afterlife, which is abstract and immaterial—subordination of the world of the material to the world of spirit.

There have been other religions that have had more than one world in their way of thinking, like some indigenous native American traditions. It is the relationship of subordination of the material world to the afterworld that is particularly problematic, though— the devaluation of this world. So, it is possible to have more than one world, as long as you don't use it to devalue the material world of earthly life in which we all have our being.

Some of the American Indians actually use the afterlife world to permeate and add an extra dimension to this world, to value it. It is a way of making a connection to the past, to the ancestors. To have the past world permeate the present world, it is more of a way of deepening the concept of the present material world than of devaluing and renouncing it.

One of the most important things about monotheistic religion is the way in which it drives the sacred out of nature. It empties the sacred out of the world and concentrates it in a single point of divinity, so there is a centralisation of the sacred. So that involves removing the sacred from nature, from the more than human world and the other forces in our lives which are not respected. The centralised divinity then gives the sacred back to some well-behaved parts of the world, if it chooses. It's a position that relies on polarisation and exclusion.[4]

How often do we hear people, especially Green Buddhists, condemn "materialism" as the source of our woes and propose to combat it by "spirituality." I think this colludes terminologically with mind/ body, spirit/matter dualism and the devaluation of matter. Consumerism, commodities—these may be bad, impoverishing things, but they are not the fault of matter, but of a particular culture. In consumerism, it's not just material objects that are deemed valuable (e.g., stones, leaves, bits of wood and bark), but rather certain status goods that are accumulated. It is not valuing all "matter" that is the problem, things like grains of sand and marbles (etc.), so it is a bad bit of terminology. It is not more matter they are after; it's status and social standing, commodities.

Spirituality has become the flavour of the month, as a word. The other aspect of its problem is the "extra ingredient" connotation. So we can give the term spirituality all kinds of different meanings. Some of them can be helpful; others are not. If we don't want one put over us, I think we really do need to be clear about what we mean by spirituality. If we mean by spirituality "religion," then it is quite clear that this is not a solution to our ecological problems because many religions have not been earth-friendly. Take Christianity, for example. We can think about St. Martin of Tours, whom I have proposed as the patron saint of forestry (*laughs*), whose speciality was cutting down the sacred groves of the Germanic tribes to demonstrate how powerful the Christian God was. The logic was, he wasn't prevented from doing it, so his God was stronger than the German ones—a great kind of spirituality involved in that, eh? And he's a saint, according to Christianity—so he should be spiritual if anybody is, shouldn't he?

So if we're going to be sloppy about spirituality, then we get all kinds of arguments like that coming through, that anything that can pass as some kind of religion becomes a solution to our environmental difficulties. So I think we need to be fairly clear about what we mean by spirituality. If we just mean by it a faith, or commitment to a religion, then I think it is not convincing at all to suggest that it has anything at all to give in this situation. I think it is very important to take up the question of what kind of spirituality it is, what kind of belief about the world it is.

There are also, of course, "blood and soil" spiritualities—even a land spirituality isn't necessarily innocent. This land has the blood of our ancestors who fought for it in various wars; we can think about

Bosnia and the Balkans as an example of that. Land spirituality can be used to make people chauvinistic. So we really need to be careful about what we're doing here, and we're not getting that care in the use of the concept of spirituality. We need a much more critical concept of spirituality.

One concept of spirituality that I like, though, is the concept of spirituality as gratitude, an indigenous suggestion from a North American Indian writer who defines spirituality as being "inclined to honour, respect and acknowledge the elements of our universe (both physical and nonphysical) that sustain and nourish our lives."[5] So this fits very nicely into a philosophy of "mutual life giving" between humans and the nonhuman world. I like the concept of gratitude, too. This, of course, will have to include gratitude to the nonhuman world which supports our lives. You have to bear in mind, though, that, using this definition, many conventional religions would not be spiritual. So the problem with the looseness of the term spirituality is that it is used to sell the idea that conventional religious arrangements are environmentally sound, or are contributing positively to our lives—when they may in fact be doing the opposite.

As you have pointed out in relation to some religions that are less ecologically desirable, there is a strong connection between religion and our current ecological crisis. With this in mind, why do you continue to endorse any variety of spirituality at all in our approach to environmentalism? Would we not be better off simply abandoning spirituality and adopting a more hardline, scientific approach?

Ah, (*laughs*) where did you get that question from?

It seemed like a good "devil's advocate" type question.

Ah, hello, we've got a visitor.
(A bright orange cicada lands on our table.)

Wow.

This is what they do when you pick them up—they object . . .

Wow, I've never seen one alive and up close before.

These are the drummers down here that they make all the noise with . . .

That's incredible. I didn't realise they were so bright.

Yes, and they are quite cheeky, too.

Do they all look like this?

No, there are green ones as well, and there are black ones and red ones, but this is the most common colour around here.
(The cicada flies away.)
(Back to business . . .)

   Well, I don't like the contrast between spirituality and science. This is a bad way to set it up—spirituality versus science. It seems to me that from an ecological point of view they are often not opposed, but in collaboration. Human-centred religion joins with human-centred science to give you a generally messed-up world. So it's not as if we are looking at a contrast here; very often the same kinds of things are at work in both of them, as far as things like a critique of human cen-teredness are concerned. For example, I see both dominant forms of religion and those of science as evolving together in a way that is built on human/nature dualism.

   This is a Western-based cultural formation going back thousands of years that sees the essentially human as part of a radically separate order of reason, mind, or consciousness, set apart from the lower order that comprises the body, the animal, and the prehuman. "Inferior" orders of humanity, such as women, slaves, and ethnic Others ("barbarians"), partake of this lower sphere to a greater degree, through their supposedly lesser participation in reason and greater participation in lower "animal" elements such as embodiment and emotionality. Human/nature dualism conceives the human as not only superior to but different in kind from the nonhuman, which as a lower sphere exists as a mere resource for the higher human one. This ideology has been functional for Western culture in enabling it to exploit the nonhuman world and so-called primitive cultures with less constraint, but it also creates dangerous illusions in denying embeddedness in and dependency on nature, which we see in our denial of human inclusion in the food web and in our poor response to the ecological crisis.

Ancient Greek society was androcentric, anthropocentric, and built on slavery. Its democracy privileged the 30 percent of the population allowed to vote—the elite males who saw themselves as representing spirit, mind, and reason. The remainder—women and slaves—were identified with material, bodily labour and led highly separated, confined, and devalued lives. Correspondingly, in ancient Greek philosophy, the earthly, material world of materiality and embodiment is seen as not only inferior but corrupting, and those who leave it behind on death pass to a higher and purer realm of immateriality beyond the earth. Plato's philosophy is dematerialising, treating reason—lodged in a pure realm of immaterial, timeless ideas—as opposed to or threatened by the corrupted material world of "coming to be and passing away," the biological world of nature and the body.

The hyperseparation and devaluation of the body and matter are not confined to ancient philosophy, but are widespread in Western culture and were inherited by the dominant Western religious movements of Christianity. In the spirit of the classical Greek tradition of earth denial, Christian ideals of salvation and transcendence of the material subordinated the "unimportant" earthly world of nature and material life to the next world of heaven, the immaterial celestial world beyond the earth, where nonhumans could never go. In the ascent to a better world of spirit beyond earthly, embodied life, matter would ultimately be conquered by the opposing elements of spirit and reason in a process of dematerialisation.

With modernity, reason as modern science began to rival and replace religion as the dominant belief system. Western science replaced but also built on this earlier religious foundation, transforming the idea of conquering nature as death by subordinating nature to the realm of scientific law and technology. Modern science, now with religious status, has tended to inherit and update rather than supersede these oppositional and supremacist ideals of rationality and humanity. In the scientific fantasy of mastery, the new human task becomes that of remoulding nature to conform to the dictates of reason to achieve salvation—here on earth rather than in heaven—as freedom from death and bodily limitation. This project of controlling and rationalising nature has involved both the technological–industrial conquest of nature made possible by reductionist science and the geographical conquests of empire.

The idea of human apartness emphasised in culture, religion, and science was of course shockingly challenged by Charles Darwin in his argument on the descent of species that humans evolved from nonhuman species. But these insights of continuity and kinship with other life forms (the real scandal of Darwin's thought), remain only superficially absorbed in the dominant culture, even by scientists. The traditional scientific project of technological control is justified by continuing to think of humans as a special superior species, set apart and entitled to manipulate and commodify the earth for their own benefit. Against the evidence that animals like birds are just as evolved as humans, human-centred culture assumes that humans are the apex of creation, more intelligent, more communicative, more important and much more evolved that other species.

This sense of apartness is challenged by the new science of ecology that stresses the importance of biosphere services and ecological processes, and the dependence of humans on a healthy biosphere and a thriving more-than-human world. But the influence of dematerialising philosophers like Plato and Descartes who treat consciousness, rather than embodiment, as the basis of human identity, continues in a false consciousness and mode of life which fails to situate human identity, human life, and human places in material and ecological terms.

So, would I wish to adopt a hard-line scientific approach? I think this is the reason versus emotion dualism that we have probably got here as well: dispassionate science as rationality versus spirituality as emotionality. It seems to me that this is the "extra ingredient" approach to spirituality in which there is something missing from our world and we'll try to get it in terms of spirituality. There is an awful lot missing from our world. In many ways, our dominant lifestyles are very impoverished ones, in terms of contact with nature and acknowledgement of the places and of the forces that support our lives, very often in terms of extreme individualism as well.

But with regard to a scientific approach, again I'm unhappy here with the two underlying contrasts, which are reason versus emotion and religion versus science. I think these are both false contrasts.[6] I don't think I would agree at all that science is dispassionate; three out of four scientists today are working for corporations or the military and they are not dispassionate. I would also want to supplement this with a critique of the way in which emotion is treated in the dominant culture as something that is private and individual and is untrustworthy and shouldn't be allowed to come into judgements or be expressed in any formal way. This leaves the field to various "hard" things, such as making a profit, competitiveness, things that are interpreted as being rational. So I think that these are all false contrasts, really. Hard-line science, well that is part of the problem, isn't it? Another science is possible, and another science is needed, but we haven't got it. Instead we have science hand in hand with capitalism; they work together very closely, in my opinion. So I think the idea of a dispassionate, hard-line science is misplaced. A mode of knowledge that is appropriate to our current situation has to take account of emotion as well as being reasoned, and has to take account of the various others that contribute to our lives, such as nature. So the word "hard line" makes me very worried here. What does hard line mean? I think a contrast between hard and soft can't be good news. It points to many things being excluded that are likely to be needed. But, generally speaking, I think that the contrasts between religion, spirituality, and science are badly constructed.

Some recent discussions of the global justice movement have dismissed the importance of redefining individual lifestyles—such as one's spirituality, and even what we consume and where we live—instead insisting that our focus must be on direct political action. You, however, have for the past thirty-odd years, lived in a stone house in the middle of a large section of Australian bush with a very small amount of occasional electricity from solar power, a composting toilet, a vegetable garden, and frequent wombat visitors. What do you think the value of this lifestyle is?

It seems to me that individual lifestyle change can be political action, so I wouldn't agree with that contrast. But a critical analysis that involves structural change I agree with, but it can't just be a matter of changing individual lifestyles, although it can include it, and it can be important. There are limits to what we can do on our own as individuals, and after a while you reach those limits. For example, taking the issue of improving your energy use, on your own you could decide to ride a bicycle, but maybe you're not in a physical condition to do that. There are a limited number of people who can decide to ride a bicycle, but you can't decide on your own to take the bus because that is partly a matter of how society structures the bus service, and whether it has enough buses or whether it actually has any buses at all, and so on. These things require structural community action, political action if you like, so I don't think it can be done just in terms of individual action. A whole lot of decisions have to be made in terms of the way that the community is structured.

Well, I guess what I wanted to get at with this question is: is there a value that is not a direct political value in cultivating a sort of relationship with place through spirituality, in deepening one's awareness of place? Maybe even as a motivation for other political action?

Well, I think there is a value in deepening our relationship with those elements that support our lives, which is a better understanding of who you are and what makes you what you are. (We might bear in mind here the postcolonial critique of the "inauthentic" or self-deceiving individual with a false consciousness of self or place.) Those elements that support our lives are not just found in nature, but in the human community as well, and those elements are usually very much suppressed in the dominant culture—this is part of the cult of hyper-individualism; they are often just not visible to us. That type of spiritualty involves a deep quest to uncover those things, and I think it involves a critique of the dominant culture's erasure of them, too. So that's why I would say that individual lifestyle change is political, if it goes deep enough.

In the final chapter of Environmental Culture *you endorse a "materialist spirituality of place"—which I think most Pagans would feel right at home with. Can you explain to those unfamiliar with your work what you mean by this concept, and how it differs from more "traditional" Western understandings of spirituality?*

This comes back to my critique of the spirit/matter dualism implied in a certain type of widespread critique of materialism which demonises matter when what it should be looking at is consumerism (which I argue in the book is itself actually a kind of spirituality, by which I mean if you define spirituality widely enough to mean a faith or belief in a system of some kind that will benefit you, then consumerism is a kind of spirituality). So it's not so much spirituality versus nonspirituality, as looking at various kinds of spirituality (in the context of this broader definition of spirituality at any rate). So, in a materialist spirituality I'm trying to set up a few paradoxes, or get to the bottom of the fact that this terminology is not very well thought out, and not very well historicised. A materialist spirituality is really an attempt to get at some of the dualisms here and bring some of them back together again, resisting reductionism but also resisting the splitting of spirit and matter through a richer conception of materiality.

For example, if we define spirituality as a discipline of recognising the elements that support and nourish our lives (which has got to include human and nonhuman elements, as well as some recognition of matter and its sacredness), a materialist spirituality is an attempt to undermine the dualism of spirit and matter. Part of this, of course, is the respect/use dualism, the hyperseparation of respect and use, in which the reductively conceived things of everyday use don't have any basis for respect. Here a materialist spirituality tries to restore the respect, and some would say "sacred" element, of the things of everyday use.

A materialist spirituality also recognises ourselves as embodied, as part of the earth, and undermines the conception of ourselves as "set apart." My materialist spirituality involves recognising that on death we become a part of the earth, we nurture other species in a process of mutual life giving. That is my materialist understanding of it. Also trying to recognise the way that matter has been put down as "mere matter," and the way that it nourishes our lives, too, and we can nourish it back—matter, and of course the earth itself, and the dirt, the land. Other people have pointed to the extraordinary way in which our culture treats dirt: dirt is dirty, which, when you think about it, really is extraordinary. One might contrast this with the way in which some indigenous people feel nourished by sitting on the earth and are born onto the earth, so they want to make that link with the earth, seeing it as a source of respect.

And is that tied into a particular place for you? For indigenous cultures it is, or at least has been, or is it just tied into a more general . . .

It works best, is clearest, when you have a single place which nourishes you and which you nourish in turn. I think it's clearest, but of course ultimately we're always nourished by the larger earth even though we don't recognise it. The commodity appears as something anonymous and remote. We don't need to find out about its production process, where it came from, or how it arrived here. This business of suppressing the elements that support our lives, the failure to recognise nature and its contributions is very much a part of the environmental crisis and is a sort of modern disease: the fact that we just don't seem to be able to recognise that we won't continue to live without nature, and our illusions that we can go and live in space are also tied up with the way in which nature's contributions are made invisible through commodities, and in many of the ways that we live. So a materialism would hope to bring that out and therefore restore gratitude.

This seems to be tied in with the way that our culture deals with death more generally.

Yes, it really offers us two choices: either of continuing our personal story in an immaterial realm, or, that of the dominant "atheistic" form of rationalism which rejects continuity and says that death is the end of the story—your real self just ends right there, there's no more. This is a false choice between immaterial continuity or material discontinuity. I think it's good to have a narrative of continuity, which the conventional atheist loses, and that it's quite possible to have both materiality and continuity. This false choice comes from buying a transcendence/immanence division that I think is also false. I want to say, "No, death is not the end of the story, it's not final—you do continue, not in another immaterial realm, but right here in this realm—nourishing life in a different species form." So there can be a continuing story. In a sense I think that the idea that death is the end of the story comes from having a sense of identity that is very cut off from other beings, so your story cannot continue in another form. Your story is this hyperindividualised, consciousness-based repetition of self again, so when you're consciousness-dead the story has to finish completely.

But if you see yourself in more connected ways, your story can go on after death. So the idea of human apartness from an inferior realm of nonhuman nature creates as its other side the discontinuity-at-death problem, which has to be solved by creating a mind/body split within the self, the material, perishable body and the imperishable, immaterial soul. And the other option, of course, is that identity is tied to a transcendent consciousness which continues in an immaterial realm. So if you want to reject that, you seem to be stuck with a meaningless finality, that the story ends and life is ultimately meaningless. I think that there are other options that those choices make invisible—that the story does continue, and that we continue as part of other life forms, in nourishing them. So our meaning is then tied up with a mutual nourishment story.

There is a Native American story about a mouse who goes on a long journey, and along the way he gives up both of his eyes, so that when he reaches his destination on top of the Sacred Mountain, he is blind. At this point, though, an eagle swoops down on the mouse and he falls asleep, only to awaken again with his sight, soaring above the mountains. He sees again through the eyes of the eagle, who has eaten him. There does seem to still be a strong attachment of some sort to personal identity here, but it does also show a concept of incorporation through being digested by another.[7]

Right, and what we can see in this story is the way that identity can be construed in a broader way. I think the Cartesian obsession with an individual consciousness as the element of identity leads you to this finality; either it can be an immaterial realm, or you have the end of the story when consciousness ends. But if you have a broader sense of what identity is based on, then you can still have sources of continuity and meaning in terms of nourishing the lives that have nourished you.

But I think we are prevented from seeing this option by a sense of being set apart from the rest of the universe, our "human specialness," plus the identification with an immaterialist consciousness. I started thinking about this myself because of my involvement with the crocodile.[8] Because when I was confronted with my last moments, by the crocodile, I thought, "This can't be happening because I'm special. I'm a human being; I can't be food. There is a case of mistaken identity here (*laughs*). This crocodile has mistaken me for food." That's not quite what it was. I knew that it did think I was food, but I also thought that there was some serious mistake going on.

As a culture we do that with sharks as well. They supposedly eat us because we look like turtles or seals, and maybe that's true, because apparently we don't taste too good . . .

Yeah, that's sharks, but apparently not crocodiles. They think we're pretty good food, as numerous cartoons point out. My favourite one is of two crocodiles talking to each other while these two humans walk by wearing solar topis and carrying butterfly nets, one crocodile saying to the other, "They look disgusting, but I believe that they are very good for you."

I think that you are right though, as a culture we are more comfortable if we can think about it in terms of mistaken identity.

There is a mistake here all right, but it's not in the identity (*laughs*).
The mistake is in thinking that we are set apart from others and can't
be food.

Right, and this ties into the important lesson that you have spoken about hav-
ing learned from your crocodile encounter. Can you tell us a bit more about
this?

I learned a lot, and I try very hard to pass it on to other people, but
I feel that I'm swimming against the tide as far as the culture is concerned. I think for me, what the crocodile encounter exposed was
that the world that I thought I lived in was an illusion. That sounds
like a very Buddhist thing to say, but it was my inability to see myself as food that revealed that to me. I didn't see myself in ecological
terms; my consciousness had been formed in such a way that really
stopped me from seeing myself in ecological terms. That is why I
couldn't accept myself being food. It wasn't just that I resisted it; it
was more than that. It was that I didn't believe it could be happening. The world wasn't like that. And the world I lived in wasn't like
that—I mean the world I *thought* I lived in wasn't like that. So the
whole episode revealed to me that there is a certain kind of cultural
illusion. I knew that it wasn't just my own consciousness; it was the
way that that consciousness had been formed in the culture.

I think that this illusion lies behind the environmental crisis and
our failure to respond to it. The fact that we don't see ourselves in
ecological terms, we don't have an ecological identity. It's what I call
"ecological denial." There is something very strange going on when
we hear that in thirty years global warming is going to produce the
loss of the Arctic (and not very long after that the Antarctic), and
this is a major positive feedback for climate change, and yet people
don't bat an eyelid. It doesn't even make it into the newspapers; it's
not on the front page. I think that we are blinded in certain ways. So

the crocodile encounter revealed to me that I didn't think of myself as an item of food. I thought that I was set apart.

Like all almost-terminal encounters, it has a very vivid impact on you. It's something you never forget. Those moments when your death rises up to meet you in terrifying and concrete detail are ones that can be quite life changing. Although it takes a long time sometimes to work out what they mean—I've been thinking about that encounter for nearly twenty years now. At first I was inclined to think that I had gotten into a parallel universe in which I was food, in which the world cared nothing for me and I had no more significance than a mouse. It's taken me a long time to figure out that that is not a parallel universe—it's this universe, and the illusory universe is the one that I thought I lived in, in which I was a special person whose main feature was my consciousness. In a sense it was a kind of divorce between myself as a consciousness and myself as a body, not sufficient awareness of myself as food, as a juicy nourishing body. That is not a consciousness we would like to cultivate. I've had to try and cultivate that way of looking at the world since. So my project has been reconciling these parallel universes and understanding where the illusions that I encountered in those terminal moments lie.[9]

Of course, I was also very lucky to survive, but the big puzzle that I had afterwards was why did I think about it like I did while it was happening, and why did people receive it like they did, and why did people think about it in the way they did later? There were lots of really interesting elements there. "What is a woman doing on her own in a place like Kakadu?" "Women shouldn't go into the bush on their own." "Women shouldn't do anything on their own."

In the newspapers?

Yes, there was some of that. It was more informal, though. From an aboriginal perspective, you don't go into a place like that on your own. I guess if I had known more about the place I wouldn't have gone there on my own at that amazing time, just as the monsoon rains were set to bring the huge yearly floods down from the Arnhemland escarpment to cover the vast river plain below on the Alligator River. But I don't know that being on my own was the key element. If there had been someone else there it might have worked out pretty much the same way. I still go places on my own; I haven't learned anything about not going on my own, so I didn't draw any conclusions like that.

It was interesting the way people constructed the bush as a place that wasn't for women, and that that was one of the meanings that they got from the experience. It wasn't one of the meanings that I got from it. Well, it's a very strong meaning in Australian culture. Women shouldn't do these things unless they are properly chaperoned by a male. And that was the *Crocodile Dundee* message, too. Foolish woman goes into the bush; she doesn't actually get mauled—we wouldn't want to have her beauty messed up—but she gets worked over somehow by a crocodile and is saved in the nick of time by the bushman hero.

Slightly changing the topic of conversation now, in past conversations you have been wary of the term "sacred," and the attempt to simply regard more parts of the world as sacred. Why is this?

I don't want to eliminate the word "sacred," but I think it has to be part of a multiplicity and spectrum of concepts for honouring and being grateful to the world. I think that some people try to do too much with it. The reason why this worries me is that sacredness is at the strong end of the spectrum of terms like reverence, respect, gratitude, etc., and to the extent that it has connotations of being contrasted to something that is profane, fallen, and everyday, it will be unhelpful to us in locating a life that is more grounded. It reinforces a kind of respect/use dualism—that what you honour is not what you make use of, what supports everyday life—and it seems to me that we absolutely do need to recover a sense of the everyday lives that we live and the things that support them, a sense of honouring those as well. So I think a Sunday concept of the sacred (and to an extent this is built into concepts of the sacred) has got to be supplemented by other concepts, or it becomes a figurehead concept. Like having a shrine, and having that area set aside to be treated with reverence, but everything around it being capable of being treated with disrespect, is not going to be helpful to us. We have to restore some sense of respect and honour to everyday things.

So, you would also be wary about simply regarding everything as sacred?

Well, I just don't think that this is going to be very helpful. I think we might be better off using a term like "respect" or "reverence" there. But we've got to be able to cash this out in behavioural terms to some extent. So what kind of behaviours would go with treating everything with reverence or respect? We have to think about that; otherwise it does get airy fairy. It has to be more than a matter of thinking; it has to be about having lifestyles and ways of life that honour the elements around us—the more than human world, the forces involved in our lives.

There's a bit of a paradox of the sacred, really—in that to the extent that it involves a connotation of "specialness" it doesn't help us with the everyday, which is where the problem lies. So it either has to be broadened out—in which case you've got the second problem of how it gets its meaning apart from its contrast role—or it has to be supplemented. I'm in favour of supplementing it, seeing it as part of a spectrum of concepts like honour, gratitude and so on. I don't see why you shouldn't have some parts that are especially honoured, as long as this doesn't lead you to the contrast where you have a fallen element that is devalued—the everyday.

I'm inclined to think that the reason people want to focus on the sacred alone is tied up with spirit/matter dualism, the extra element approach. We add something. I feel that this is wrong. It is more a mater of deconstructing—to use Derrida's term—what we already have, and reassembling it to avoid certain splits that stop us going forward, rather than adding an extra element, which is kind of what the spirit/matter spirituality tends to suggest, and also part of what the sacred approach tends to suggest. Thinking about more of the world as sacred would require a very big reconstruction of the way that we live our lives, our economic lives in particular. So it seems to me that it has to cash out in something structural. There is a tendency for people to want to think that a five-minute prayer will do the job, and to avoid the more thorough forms of rethinking.

Drifting over into these more structural topics, and into an area that particularly interests me, I am wondering what the kind of views that we have been discussing about the fracturing of place and the importance of cultivating relationships with place say about modern cities?

Well, there has been a lot of thinking in anarchist circles about this urban/rural divide, and I guess it is something of a dualism. The city is the "mind place" and the rural is the "body place," the place that produces for the body. Plato certainly thinks about it in those terms in *The Republic*. I think that there are several ways of trying to break that division down, which really can be quite an impoverishing division: the extreme urbanisation excluding a whole range of experiences that people find quite crucial to their development, and the rural environment doing the same. Whichever way you fit in, you only get a single part of the whole, when really you need some of each. So we can think about ruralising the city. Many people have suggested having something more like the Cuban model, where we have a lot more food production going on in the city, and a lot more nonhuman representation in the city. There is a need to recognise, welcome, and invite the nonhuman presence in the city, and recognise the way that that has been erased in the establishment of the city. On the other hand, we could have a rural life that is less an adjunct to the city, that has more independence and more of the social aspects that have been exiled or concentrated in the city, and are more available to people in the city. I think this would involve breaking down current economic models and using new ones.

I rather support Consumer Supported Agriculture (CSA) as a good move in that direction and a way of beating remoteness. Of course it has always been part of the anarchist/Marxist dream to have some kind of rotation between urban and rural life, so you could have a mixture of work arrangements that all involve mind and body work. I try to do that myself; I find that a very satisfying aspect of being able to live here. Every day I am able to combine physical work with philosophical work. I think this is good. Getting the balance right is hard, because "the world calls you"—the chooks need feeding, the greenhouse needs watering—but I think this is a really important part of a recipe for a more satisfying life and a more equal community. More equality between mind work and body work, which is part of taking responsibility for place, as well. This is why I think a unity-of-place idea is perhaps a little off the track—that some sort of specialisation, at least for the time being, seems inevitable, but some kind of mixture ultimately seems like the best way to go.

In CSA, the consumer makes an arrangement with the farmer for, say, a year's vegetables of a certain kind, and will retain a relationship with that farm. They might go up there to work, or for a weekend to take their children up and see what is happening. So you're able to take some sort of responsibility for your place. Here you can't start to see the possibility of reassembling a concept of "your place" in an honest way, because that is what eludes us, I think. The concept of "your place" that leaves out the denied elements of place, the denied elements that support our lives, is a dishonest concept of place. So is a colonial concept that establishes a false consciousness of place.

This is part of the breakdown of the anonymity of the commodity, as well as of the rural/urban divide and the mind/body division (which has ramifications in just about every area, in this case affecting the breakdown between the work place and the place that supports your life, and between the city place and the rural place; these are all permeated by the mind/body distinction).

Of course, the other aspect of living in the city is the depth of one's ability to think about death and life. If you live close to nature you come across death all the time—like the dead cicadas—you have to be thinking all the time about what this means. About death and justice. The justice of life. Unless, of course, you are insulated by the idea that human lives are separate and special and not like that. If you're not insulated by that belief, then the world around you constantly confronts you with death and with thoughts about death and justice. Job's question about the justice of life. So perhaps the country is really more spiritual than the city (*laughs*). Although city folk often see it the other way around.

Specifically, my questioning here is motivated by the idea that we have a great deal to learn from the nonhuman world, a lot of which we are missing out on by living in cities and leaving large and important parts of the nonhuman world to live "out there." In particular I am thinking of Theodore Roszak's comment that "children who grow into life without knowing wild nature will be less than fully human."[10] Ignoring this rhetoric of the "fully human," do you think it is fair to say that we are somehow diminished, both as individuals and as communities, by a lack of contact with the more-than-human?

Very much so. Well, I don't like this term "fully human." Less than, more than, fully human. I try not to talk this way myself. Partly because I don't like to see the term human used as a term of praise. To the extent that it involves a contrast with the nonhuman, I think that that takes away from the nonhuman. If we're talking about human ideals here, then I guess that is a way to put "less than the ideal human," but that's probably a little bit more honest (*laughs*). There is obviously a different concept of the ideal human here to the one that you get from the average advertising executive.

I think that we are definitely diminished by a lack of contact with the more-than-human world, and we are diminished as thinkers as well as emotionally. The range of experiences that we are excluded from is very important: contact with life and death, and the meaning of them.

I was just listening to a program last night about how insulated we are from death. If you live in a place like this, you can't be insulated from death; it's going on all the time here. You can insulate yourself, of course, by a belief in human hyperseparation; that's a cultural separation, not place based. It's not just a physical separation, but a cultural one. You might, for example, assume that the deaths you see around you have nothing to say about human death and the meaning of life. So you wouldn't learn, in that case; you wouldn't be able to reflect back and forth.

Do you think that there is a significant mind/body dualism in politics? In particular I am thinking of Hannah Arendt's reading of ancient Greek politics, and the way in which the political should ideally exclude the domestic, the maintenance and sustenance of the body. [11]

Ah yes, this is a set of ideas that she has taken directly from the Greeks, which is where some of this stuff started. The *polis* is the place of the mind, and the *helot* is the producer of the stuff for the body—they didn't have any rights, of course, they were sort of the Greek equivalent of agricultural workers. I am totally in disagreement with that. In a sense what we've got now is a version of this, where economic decisions are made at the global level and what

goes on at the national level is sound and fury. So a lot of those economic decisions that are beyond democratic control are the ones that
are about global trade and are the ones that are about supporting
your body. This is a mind/body division that is really rather damaging, because we get out of touch with what is really happening. Just
as the colonial mind and conception of place are out of touch, that
kind of global mind and conception of place are out of touch. In a
sense it is illusory.

There's a little water skink there; it's lost its tail. It's jumping and
coming this way . . . It's sacrificed its tail at some point . . . They store
food in the tail. It's a storehouse, so it's had to give its storehouse
away to something else to survive . . . The practice is called "caudal
autotomy" . . . It's hunting. I wonder what it's getting. Must be some
little insects there.

And with that, I think we'll leave it. Thank you very much for your time,
Val.

Notes

1. Steven Marglin, "What Do Bosses Do?," *Review of Radical*
   Political Economy 6 (1974).

2. Lynn White, "The Historical Roots of Our Ecological Crisis," in *Science* 155 (1967), reprinted in *This Sacred Earth: Re-*
   ligion, Nature and Environment, ed. R.Gottlieb (London:
   Routledge, 1995).

3. As Val argued in chapter four, "Plato and the Philosophy of
   Death," from *Feminism and the Mastery of Nature* (London:
   Routledge, 1993).

4. Val discusses this in more depth in chapter six of *Feminism*
   and the Mastery of Nature and in chapter ten of *Environmental*
   Culture: The Ecological Crisis of Reason (London and New
   York: Routledge, 2002).

5. This is Carol Lee Sanchez's definition and is cited by Val in *Environmental Culture*, 223–224.

6. As discussed by Val in chapter two of *Environmental Culture*.

7. This story is called *Jumping Mouse* and can be found online at <www.hyemeyohstsstorm.com>.

8. Val was attacked and very seriously injured by a crocodile in Kakadu National Park in the Northern Territory, Australia, in 1985. There have been numerous accounts (both in writing and in a documentary film) of Val's encounter. Her own written account is called "Being Prey" and can be found in *Terra Nova* 1.3, Summer 1996, 32–44. Reprinted in *The New Earth Reader*, eds. D. Rothenberg and M. Ulvaeus (Cambridge: MIT Press, 1999), 76–92.

9. Val is working on a book on this topic now called *The Eye of the Crocodile*.

10. Theodore Roszak, "Sanity, the Psyche, and the Spotted Owl," *Trumpeter*, 1997.

11. Hannah Arendt, *The Human Condition* (Chicago: University of Chicago Press, 1958).

Dwelling in Sacred Community

THOM VAN DOOREN

Ancient, once majestic forests are being cleared every day at an unfathomable rate for nothing more meaningful than to plant inefficient, monoculture crops and graze cattle for the dairy and beef industries. Species of plants and animals are made endangered or extinct as their habitats are lost, or they succumb to the hunter and human greed. Rivers are silted and polluted, fish numbers drastically decline, and incredibly intricate and beautiful coral reefs are bleached bone-white by the actions of people both here and on the other side of the globe. Animals on farms are treated in ways that are so far beyond comprehension that one must surely question the validity of any link between the word "humane" and the name of their tormenters' species. All the

255

while, on a planet that produces more than enough to feed us all, millions of people around the world go hungry every day.

These issues are not separate, and the attempt to deal with them as such is doomed to failure. The success of any movement for equality or liberation, any movement that attempts to move beyond the domination of others, is in reality dependent on the success of them all. The domination of one group or species naturally leads to the domination of others because *domination is not an action; it is a way of being in the world*. It is based on a worldview in which we are isolated, separate, and disconnected. In this way we are able to merely *use* others; we are able to distance ourselves from them and their concerns. If we wish to genuinely engage with any of these issues, we cannot, as we have for so long, attempt to simply change aspects of our society *around* this worldview.[1]

For example, the idea that in order to feed the world's human population all we need to do is produce more food would be laughable in the extreme if the consequences weren't so tragic. Already the earth produces more than enough food to adequately feed us all. Hunger is not caused by a lack of food; it is caused by inequality, economics, politics, social structures, the inability of people in positions of political and economic power to behave "humanely," and ultimately, our acquiescence to their failure to do so, that is, the failure of the people of all nations to come together and demand solutions. More food may be helpful, but it may not be; it is certainly not a solution, but at very best a Band-Aid.

With regard to any situation of domination, oppression, or inequality, technology alone is not the answer, nor is politics. Education may be helpful, but it is not a miracle cure, either. Freeing up even 1 percent of the US's defence budget may go a long way, but neither will it solve these problems. Our problems go deeper, and they are not something that can be fixed by throwing money or technology at them. In order to bring about the necessary deep and long-term changes, we will require not only these social, political, legal, and economic changes (in short a shift in social dynamics), but at a fundamental level we must also redefine our worldview, specifically the way in which we understand ourselves and our relationship with this planet. Just as domination is a way of being in the world based on a worldview of isolation, genuine equality must necessarily be situated in a worldview in which our deep kinship with others, both human and nonhuman, is acknowledged and honoured.

This intuition has required that we begin to deal with critical thought in different, less traditional ways. In philosophies such as deep ecology and ecofeminism, as well as in some of the Christian responses to our environmental crisis in the work of individuals like Thomas Berry, there is a calling into question of our fundamental perceptions of "self," and our relationship with "place." The "environment" is no longer being sectioned off as something "out there" that needs to be dealt with through political and legal channels; rather, environmentalism is increasingly being seen, in some sense, to encompass all other issues, and to be fundamental to our understanding of what it is to be human. We are attempting to reinterpret and redefine humanity in an effort to move beyond egocentrism and anthropocentrism by understanding humanity in its broader context—the environment of which it is, after all, but a small part. This understanding of humanity issues a requirement on individuals and societies to operate in different ways and to reconsider some fundamental assumptions about the way in which we live, so as to open up the real possibility of a more honest, inspiring, and sustainable future for this planet as a whole.

In this article I want to consider some aspects of this situation, specifically as they relate to our understanding of ourselves and our relationship with the broader environment. In so doing, I will attempt to draw out the fundamentals of a "Pagan environmentalism," which I appreciate is for many of us something of a tautology. I will propose a relational view of the world which I have called "sacred community," and discuss the way in which we can become aware of our existence in this type of community through making relationship with both death and life. The resulting lifestyle, which is grounded in a conscious recognition of sacred community and our place in a larger pattern, is simply termed "dwelling," and is presented as an important component to any genuinely sustainable and fulfilling worldview.

Sacred Community

All of the ideas in this article are premised on the concept of *sacred community*, which is rooted in a deeper recognition of the relational nature of the world in which we live. None of us exists as a separate entity; to be alive is necessarily to already be in relationships with others. We are conceived by others, born into the world by another, nurtured into maturity by others, and all the while we rely on others not of our species to be our food and provide our shelter, air, and water. These requirements are not at all trivial: air, food, water, and shelter are the essential biological ingredients of what it is to be human; they are fundamentals. Without the satisfaction of these needs by others, *we simply could not be.* To understand a human, or any other organism for that matter, as a "thing" that just happens to interact with its environment is to fail to look beneath the surface into what is really a far deeper and more profound interaction. To be an organism is to always already be in relationships with others. No organism is self-sufficient; we are all delicately but inextricably interwoven in the world, in a dance far older and more intricate than we can possibly imagine.

It is this understanding that lies at the foundation of an awareness of sacred community—an understanding of the way in which we, both as individuals and collectively (as societies and as a species) are in fact constituted by our relationships with others. In other words, these relationships are an essential aspect of what it is to be human.

Sacred community honours and recognises our interdependence on other life, understanding both humanity and individuality in relational terms. A community, however, is necessarily *a community of individuals.* As such, individuality is not dissolved by this view; it is simply placed within a different context, in which what it means to be an individual is not as "individual" as we may have initially thought. To lose sight of the individual in favour of more "holistic" understandings of the world is to fail to recognise and honour all of the ways in which we are different from one another, both those of our species and others. It is also to lose the concept of "relationship," which is so central both to Paganism and to an impassioned interaction with the world. Relationship with others creates the very possibility of a wide range of experiences, such as passion, love, lust, anger, and the rest of our fantastic range of human emotions; these are all modes of being with others.[2]

Sacred community must, therefore, be understood as a community of individuals, united by their commonalities and their differences, working together, complementing, honouring, and acknowledging one another. In our current discussion, the importance of an awareness of sacred community is primarily the way in which it opens up the possibility for a new depth of relationship with others. An awareness of the way in which we are involved in a process of mutual life giving, in which we all make the lives of others possible through vital exchanges, gives rise to a relationship based on a felt sense of *commonality of purpose.*[3] This awareness breaks down our estrangement from the world and from one another; it necessitates a broadening of concern for others. Sacred community must, however, exist as a *felt awareness* of community, not merely a theoretical appreciation of a biological fact. Sacred community is about more than biology; it is about *family*, and about an acknowledgement and honouring of the sacred as it exists on this planet. As such, this awareness of sacred community forms the basis of the "Pagan environmentalism" outlined here, an awareness of our "embeddedness" in the world, and of the fundamentality of our being with others. In my approach to this situation I do not simply advocate meditation and ritual (both of which can be very useful and meaningful), but rather, I outline a more active and impassioned way of life in which we honour and acknowledge our fundamental connection to others by making relationship with them in both life and death.

Death and the Art of Dwelling

As living organisms, we are part of a system in which it is necessary for us to kill and cause suffering to others in order to survive. We use others for food, shelter, and clothing; in fact, everything that we have and everything that we are, even the flesh that constitutes our bodies, has been gifted to us by the earth—in large part, *gifted to us by the death of others*. Killing, as such, is not just something that we occasionally *do*, but rather is a part of who we *are*, a part of our very nature as human beings. In our steel and concrete cities we have managed to make death into something "out there," something that happens in other places to other things. Not only do we sterilise and hide human death behind curtains and hospital walls, but even the food that we eat is grown or raised and then killed *elsewhere*, out of sight, beyond our concern. The trees are killed for timber, the metals and minerals are taken from the earth; all this takes place elsewhere. Even the incredible suffering that occurs in modern "factory farms" happens "out there." We have attempted to place death so far away that we don't even have to be conscious of it anymore; we can just pick up the timber, the veggies, or the neat cut of beef in its little package. Death, however, does not take place elsewhere; it takes place where you are—where we each are—as we cause it in countless ways every single day.

The vast majority of our society only considers death occasionally, usually when it confronts them personally, or those immediately around them. Death, however, is all around us all the time, and we are the cause of a great deal of it. Killing is, of course, unavoidable, and as such, the vegetarian or vegan mindset becomes worrying when it is considered to be a lifestyle validated by the idea that "it is wrong to kill."[4] This view misunderstands our nature as human beings, and our place within a system of which death is a necessary constituent. It attempts to exclude plants from ethical consideration, and thus make it inconsequential whether they live or die. This view dishonours the whole process of life. By removing any group from ethical consideration, and then just killing that group, people attempt to create a *comfortable relationship* with death—to make death into something they don't really cause—at least not in a *serious* way. In reality though, all of us kill. Every day that we live, we cause the suffering and death of countless others, no more desiring of death than ourselves. I maintain that the unavoidability of this situation does nothing to diminish its unacceptability, but rather makes a call on us as individuals to take responsibility for death, and to engage with it consciously, compassionately, and actively, through *making relationship with death.* The relevant ethical question then becomes not *who* can we kill, but rather, *how* should we kill? The *how* question then often implies limitations on the *who*.

In large part, to make relationship with death is to become actively involved with it—to kill that which dies for you. By being active in, or at least present at, the deaths that we cause, we come to better understand our place within a sacred community, and what it truly means to be human at a fundamental level. Becoming active in death may mean hunting or slaughtering your own animal, or growing and harvesting your own plants—but whatever form it takes, it means being there, participating, and knowing what it is to kill that which dies for you. Within our current lifestyles it is simply not possible to be present, let alone active, in every death that we cause. Every time we switch on an appliance, coal has been mined, or the earth has somehow been altered (often violently) to power it—even renewable energy systems must be built from something. Paper, wood, our furniture, and our houses are the result of the death of trees. Food means the death of all sorts of plants and animals, in all sorts of conditions and degrees of suffering. Everything that we have, everything that we know, has come from the earth in one form or another. The ideal position, therefore, cannot be to attempt to completely eradicate any impact on others—this simply is not what it means to be an embodied human on this planet. Rather, what I am suggesting is that we honestly acknowledge these interactions with others by attempting to minimise the discrepancy between the death and destruction that we cause, and that which we are aware of, by living in different, simpler, and more active ways—ways that allow more participation not only in death, but in our relationship with life.[5]

By becoming *active* in death, whether it be the death of farm animals, "wild" animals, vegetables, or trees for timber, we engage with it, and understand what it is to perform this killing. Although this will not always be possible or practical, at least by having carried out this act even once we partially understand what it involves. This participation, however, is not purely about physical participation; it is primarily about conscious and sacred *recognition*. In addition to being *active* in death, making relationship involves a thanksgiving for and a genuine awareness of the fact that the death of another who will, for example, become my food, has made the continuance of my life possible. The killing is also an opportunity to understand oneself *as food*, not only to become aware of the fact that one day we will each be food for another, but also to make the promise to those who are killed—a promise of return—that just as they die now to feed us, we will be food for others at another time.

Unfortunately, within overdeveloped societies this awareness and appreciation are largely missing. Not only are we absent in the act of killing, we are also absent in the promise and the gift of the return. In our cities, sewerage is secreted away, moving silently beneath the ground where no one need see it or be offended by it. Later it is chemically neutralised. We take the gift of life that we are given, at the expense of others' lives, and offer nothing back in return. In this way what should be a "web of life" becomes a hierarchical system, a "food chain," with the affluent of humanity firmly placed at the top. We eat and eat and then, instead of giving back in the form of nutrients for more growth, we destroy; we sterilise our "waste" so that the goodness of the world flows into the mouth of humanity like a bottomless pit. We consume the world.

We fail to appreciate that we are beings within a community, part of something larger than ourselves, something which every day gives to us the very possibility of our existence. Even when we die we lock the body away in the ground, protecting it from the soil in thick metal or wood. The earth cannot have it to feed others. The earth cannot take back the flesh that it has provided, to continue the process. Of course, ultimately the coffin will rot or be exhumed and burned or dumped, but this failure of our society to give back even in death is yet another manifestation of our estrangement from both death itself, and sacred community. We cannot be *comfortable* with death, but this does not mean that we can ignore it altogether. To ignore death, to neutralise our own "waste," is to fail to be a part of life. Our absence in the promise and the gift of return is a failure to *appreciate* that which we are given. To be absent in this way is to misunderstand life, and to misunderstand and fail to appreciate our place within the system that sustains us.

The idea here is not that thousands of tons of human excrement and an unlimited supply of rotting human bodies will somehow "refertilise" the earth, but rather that our absence in these ways betrays something deeper in our understanding of our relationship with both death and life as a whole. Perhaps our waste and our bodies are even too toxic to be useful; but then this fact highlights a deficiency in what we eat, and the types of societies in which we live. In short, the gift and the promise of the return are not simply about the physical return, but are also about the awareness and the consciousness that accompany these acts, as well as the very active presence of the *promise* to the dying.

The making of relationship with death, then, involves both an active participation in it and the promise and gift of the return. It involves an awareness (often to a limited degree), both of what it is to make another our food, and to *be* food ourselves; an understanding that humanity is not the top of a "food chain," but is rather a species like any other, dependent on others and on the entire process of which we are but a small part. Furthermore, the goal of making relationship with death is not to somehow validate or make acceptable our killing of others, but rather to do honour to others—to be genuinely appreciative and conscious of the gift of life that another has given us with their death. This awareness of the importance of the other, and the gift that they offer us in their death, allows us to more fully appreciate our place within a sacred community. This understanding, as briefly mentioned above, issues a requirement on the individual to simplify their lifestyle and begin to make more active relationships with life and the places in which they dwell. It is this process that will be the topic of the remainder of this article.

Life and the Art of Dwelling

Within the cities of the overdeveloped world, the idea that we should attempt to connect with, or become more conscious of, the places in which we live is often seen to be outdated. Modern technology has made it so that we no longer need to eat seasonally; we don't even

need to eat locally—food can be brought in from the other side of
the world. In addition to this, very few people who live in large cities
are directly dependent on the seasons or the specific locality in which
they live for their livelihoods. As such, it is often felt that there is no
need for us to be aware of the cycles of the place in which we live. We
no longer rely on this knowledge for our survival; everything can be
brought in from somewhere else.

In many ways, contemporary Paganism inherently rejects this understanding of the world. It is built into the very fabric of Paganism
that information about place and about the cycles of the seasons is
important. The four "fire festivals," among other things, speak of our
relationship with place at the most fundamental of levels, as provider
of our food, livelihood, and lifestyle. The observance of other significant events like solstices, equinoxes, and the cycles of the moon are
very intimately tied into an awareness of place, and the effect that
these times may have on us and our specific locality. So even though
we as individuals, and certainly as a society, are not so dependent on
the particular cycles of the places in which we live, as Pagans we
continue to honour these cycles. Why?

In part, I think that the suggestion that we are not so dependent on
these cycles in our modern lifestyles, something which has often been
raised with me as an objection to contemporary Pagan ritual, misses
the point. This view is based on an assumption that relationship with
place is purely about physical utility—about what biological or eco-
nomical resources the land can provide us with. This position, however, misunderstands two important points. The first is that no matter
where the fulfillment of our needs comes from, they come from
somewhere on this earth, and that fact can (and many of us feel, *should*)
be acknowledged and respected.[6] No matter how "advanced" our society has become, everything that we have is still gifted to us by the
sustenance of the earth. Secondly, and more importantly in our attempt to reinterpret our relationship with place as something beyond

mere utility, the interaction that we have with the places in which we dwell occurs on far more levels, and far more deeply, than simply satisfying basic biological requirements.

In our conscious interaction with place, we are aware of ourselves within a larger context, that of a wider environment made up of interlocking and intertwining relationships. These are biological relationships on an important level; we eat each other and rely on others for shelter, air, water, etc. On another level, however, there are important psychological and spiritual aspects to our interaction with place. What I am primarily concerned with here is the way in which these biological relationships are always already spiritual. Just as we are offered the opportunity to make relationship with death, the very fact of our nature as biological organisms gifts to us the further opportunity of making relationship with place, life, and the individual others with whom we must interact to survive. In this way, the fact that we *must* kill to survive, and thus must interact with others, reveals itself as the gift of relationship, as the necessity of being with others. It is a part of our very nature as organisms that we must be in relationships with others—relationships that depend not only on our causing each others' deaths, but also on defending others, nurturing them, loving them or simply being with them. Paganism, and spirituality more generally, reveals itself in these relationships that are so fundamental to who and what we are that they are already sacred, already spiritual, if for no other reason than simply because they create the very possibility of our living. As such, I understand Paganism not to be about worship or prayer, nor about belief in powers and forces "beyond" us, but rather to be a coming into awareness of the fact that *we are always already in relationship with the sacred.*

"Dwelling" is an expression of respect for this situation. Respect comes through embracing and honouring these relationships and living consciously and passionately in them. It is for this reason that we make relationship with place, with those who sustain and provide for us.[7] This conception is in many ways naturally a part of Paganism, as we honour the unfolding of the year, of life and of death, the seasons and the cycles that not only "surround us," but that actively "engage us." The seasonal changes don't take place "out there" as they do for some people—those who, for example, simply turn up the heating when winter comes and notice the cold only in terms of what it *takes* and what it *prevents*, as they encounter it for a minute each day on the short walk between the house and the car. Paganism, as I understand it, embraces these changes—we "situate ourselves" within them, we experience them, honour them, revel in them, live them. Every change is not necessarily "good," in terms of our own personal desires, but every change is a gift—an opportunity to dance differently, to move and live in different ways, to see different things, and to partake of something far larger than ourselves that, like death, creates the very possibility of our existing. To make relationship with place through an honouring of its cycles in both life and death is to perform the art of dwelling.

It is called an "art" because it is primarily intuitive. No two places or people are alike, so that the way in which one person dwells in one place could never be transferrable to another person in another place. There are ideas and concepts that are transferrable, but there is nothing like a "blueprint" that can simply be "applied" to all places. If we could simply apply the techniques of others, we would not be making genuine relationship with our place; we would not be listening to our place—hearing and seeing what it does. It is this active engagement with place through personal experience that ultimately provides us with an understanding of the unique experience that will allow us to live honourably within our local environment.

To "dwell," then, is to become aware of the "pattern of a place," the way that it flows and moves, and the way that we can naturally fit into this pattern.[8] This awareness must be gained from a genuine relationship with a place, from observation, honouring, celebration, and otherwise getting to know a place and what it does throughout the year. That means knowing the animals and the plants, and not just how these "wild" cycles work, but also when and how the foods and other "resources" that we are gifted ripen, or need to be collected, or planted. It is not just an abstract knowledge of what a place *does*, but is knowledge made practical by its application to the more pertinent questions: *How can I live here honourably and with respect? How do I fit into this pattern?* The experience that provides an answer to this question must necessarily be different for each person, gained in different ways through unique relationships; but one thing that remains central is a making of relationship with those things that directly nourish and sustain us.

Making Relationship with Place

The making of relationship with others offers us the possibility of a greater understanding of who we are as individuals, and as human beings. Like all living things, we are relational beings, and thus to some extent, we are defined by our relationships. Ignorance of the relationships that provide our basic needs as a species equates to ignorance of what it is to be human. Understanding of ourselves is revealed in our relationships with others. It is for this reason that doing things for ourselves, things like growing our own food, making our own homes, furniture, and clothing (or at least getting involved in these processes as much as is possible), is so important. Doing for ourselves allows us to actively enter into the relationships that are basic to our nature as humans—relationships with the raw materials of the earth: the dark, moist soil, the plants from which our foods and fabrics come, trees and the timber they provide. In entering into relationship with these things, by directly working with them, we come into a better understanding of what they really are, and the profundity of what they offer us—which is often their lives.

When we, for example, buy our furniture ready-made, we miss the opportunity to work with the tree, the timber, and the process of the crafting; we miss out on a genuine understanding of the process. More importantly, within the context of this discussion, however, we miss out on an understanding of the gift of the tree. By not interacting with the tree (or even the raw timber), we do not know it and thus cannot fully understand or respect what it offers. This is not to suggest that what is missing in buying furniture is simply the act of killing the tree; there are countless ways to enter into relationship, which, at its foundation, is simply a conscious interaction with another. Specifically what is missing, though, is this interaction: the tree is never even seen, so it cannot be understood, and neither can its sacrifice. Instead, what should be a relationship of gratitude and respect with a tree becomes a purely financial transaction in which only the humans are acknowledged. Nonhumans become resources, mere "things," to be used as we see fit, without regard or respect. Thus, in the example of furniture, the person who has made the furniture is financially acknowledged (although perhaps never seen), and the person who markets and sells the furniture is also financially acknowledged, but the tree is completely absent and unimportant.

This framework extends out into every aspect of our lives—to the food we eat, the clothing we wear, the power we use—all produced by the death and suffering of countless others who remain unseen, faceless, and nameless, and thus able to be used as mere resources. This "use" of others is, of course, something that is also done to humans, for example, to those working in "sweatshops," who cannot show themselves, who are never seen and therefore also go unacknowledged in these transactions (which are more than purely financial; they are also about respect and gratitude).

Another example of this resource-driven, disrespectful "use" mentality can be seen in attempts to breed featherless chickens. The chicken has become "pure-food," not respected in any way beyond its utility as a resource to be grown and harvested. Not only is the chicken's natural life cycle destroyed in factory farms, but now its actual being as a "chicken" is also threatened. It has been so irreversibly and inexcusably altered that it could never exist as a chicken; it could never fly, or be kept dry or warm by its feathers. It is a new type of animal produced for and suited to one environment and one purpose that has no respect or even reference to the concept of a "chicken." This is made possible by an understanding of chickens as "human resources," things whose purpose and nature are defined solely by their human use. This understanding is itself largely possible only because the actual chicken, as a living animal, is absent in almost all of our interactions with it, unrespected and unacknowledged.

To make relationship with others, like chickens in this case, is not necessarily to stop using them for food, or down, and so on, but rather to respect the chicken as something more than this as well— to understand it as another being that has desires and needs *that should be respected in as much as it is possible to do so.* This respect itself must, however, be rooted in a new depth of understanding that cannot possibly be achieved in a purely theoretical context, but must be the result of sustained and conscious interaction through relationship. At a personal level, this means beginning to make relationship with others in as many vital contexts as we can.

Technology and Relationship with Place

Just as in making relationship with death, it is simply not possible within our current society for an individual to be active in all of the relationships that are required to sustain them. The idea is that we try to become as actively involved as we can. Only in this way do we come to truly understand and respect the other, and the sacrifice and gift that they give. Our society, however, offers opposition to such attempts, opposition that is built into its very foundations. The structure of our society is such that we are expected to be part of a system that is based on specialisation, that requires us to choose a particular profession and do only that, using the money and resources that it provides to purchase all of our other needs. This model is, by its very nature, harmful to the process of conscious and responsible living.

This situation is, however, particularly problematic in contemporary society with its emphasis on technology. Specialisation of tasks and vocation has, in various forms and degrees, been an aspect of every society, and is to some extent a defining characteristic of what a society is. In the case of contemporary society, however, this specialisation has been a large part of the cause of our estrangement. As technology becomes more and more complex, even the possibility of relationship is undermined. Again taking our example of furniture, no one person in our society is any longer involved in the entire process of making a table. A group of people cuts the trees, another group processes them into timber which is transported all over the world to be purchased by companies or craftspeople who produce furniture (often on an assembly line), to be sold by yet another group of people in large stores. This process is completely dislocated from both locality and individuals (both human and tree). It is nothing like the process of a local craftsman felling a tree (or even buying timber) and then producing furniture to be sold locally. *In our current model, there isn't even the possibility to view trees as anything other than resources.*

By doing things for ourselves, however, and becoming involved from the ground up, we are allowed the opportunity to enter into genuine relationship with others and thus to understand them as something more than resources. For example, growing our own food, we are allowed the possibility to make relationship with it not only in death, but also in life—to contribute something real in our interaction. In working in a vegetable garden we are able to both better understand each of the things that we eat, and enter into relationship with them. In this way we can come to better understand how to live honourably within these essential relationships.

The value of this type of experience is manyfold. Primarily it lies in the fact that by consciously acknowledging others through the making of relationship with them, we naturally enter into an awareness of their, and our, being in a sacred community. We become psychologically "transformed"; we begin to feel our interconnectedness with others. This is a gradual development, and also often astounds me, as it grips me and almost violently pulls me into an awareness of the beauty and profundity of life. A good example of this, both because I personally find it to be a very meaningful task, and because it is a task which is central to much of Paganism, is the baking of bread. Many of my most profound experiences have taken place during, or just after, baking bread. The action of mixing, kneading, leaving to prove, and kneading again, is not only sacred in all that it has to tell us about the world and our relationship with it, but it is also deeply meditative. I remember once baking bread, home alone at a friend's house in the hills, as a massive storm was moving in overhead to signal the beginning of the wet season. As I kneaded the dough for the second time I became aware of a fly sitting on the windowsill next to me. I was drawn to the fly, and slowly leaned down until my face was only a few centimetres from it. I stood like this for several minutes, entranced by the intricacy of the fly and its tiny movements. This simplest of experiences allowed me to appreciate the beauty of this planet, and one of its smaller (and here in Australia often most annoying) creatures. After tearing my eyes away from the fly long enough to finish my kneading, I left the dough to prove again, while I went outside to feel the incredible wind and watch the clouds roll in. While taking this all in, I again became aware of a tiny movement next to my face. A spider was, with great difficulty in the strong winds, putting the finishing touches on its new web under the eaves of the house. I stood, again as close as I could, to this intricate dance, in awe of its beauty.

The significance of these experiences in this discussion is the fact that they were, in large part, facilitated by the kneading and baking I was doing, by my making relationship with the bread. It is this type of experience that is sacrificed when we substitute doing things for ourselves for either having others (either human or technological) do them for us. Importantly, it is also not just a meditative experience that is sacrificed, but all of the other aspects of a relationship with the raw ingredients of our lives and this earth. This relationship, as I have been discussing, is essential to both an understanding and an awareness of sacred community. It allows us to better appreciate the offerings made to us by others, and their essentiality to our lives. In many ways, technology is necessarily an abstraction from this process of relationship. By its very nature, technology is aimed at simplifying our lives and making things easier and quicker. In doing so, however, technology adds a level of abstraction. It separates us from the task at hand and robs us of countless opportunities such as the pleasure of the work, the opportunity to learn from the task, and perhaps more importantly in the context of this discussion, it separates us from the earth—from the wheat of the bread; the hemp of the clothing; the soil of the garden; the raw, unpolished, and rich offerings of the earth. The further we retreat into our cities and hide behind our gadgets, the less we know, the less we are able to do, and the further we diminish our relationship with the earth and consequently with one another.

There are, of course, many positive aspects of technology. What is at issue here, however, is the need for *appropriate technology*, not technology for its own sake. Inappropriate technology not only causes unnecessary levels of abstraction in our relationships with others, it also encourages wasteful and consumption-driven lifestyles. Where one appliance and a bit of know-how were once sufficient, ten appliances are now needed, and this situation can only get worse as generations go by and we forget the old skills and knowledge that past generations used.

A Vision for the Future

In order to combat this drive toward unnecessary technology, we need to focus on genuine *quality of life,* as opposed to *standard of living.* This means beginning to value and cultivate lifestyles that are inherently rich and rewarding, as opposed to simply being expensive.[9] This is not, however, as simple as it may sound within our overdeveloped societies in which status and success are usually gauged on the basis of how much a person has, and how much they are able to consume. A societal focus on quality of life, on the other hand, would require massive changes in even the most fundamental aspects of our society. For example, even the cities where the majority of the world's affluent (and thus consumptive) population lives, seemingly exist in direct opposition to the possibility of meaningful relationship with place. There are, of course, pros and cons to the city environment, and not only do many people want to live in cities, but with a human population of over six billion, it is simply not possible for us all to do otherwise. The question then, for us as a society, becomes: how is it possible for us to live in sustainable and meaningful ways within cities? This is an incredibly complex question which must ultimately be both the most challenging and the most important question that we as a society can ask of ourselves and of this planet. Therefore, I must admit to not having even 1 percent of the answer, but what is clear is that massive changes will need to take place.

For example (and these comments will necessarily be culture and locality specific), we need to question such fundamental and entrenched ideas as forty-hour working weeks, and what this fact, along with many others, has done to our personal interactions with others in the form of both family and community. We need to set aside time and space to rebuild genuine communities within cities, communities who share each others lives by working together, learning together, and helping each other. Over the period of the recorded history of our species we have seen the dissolution of the "family."[10] Where once we had tribes living and working together, then large extended families, then smaller "nuclear" families, we now have a situation in which even these are being broken down with the drive to work harder and longer at the expense of all else. To read these comments as an attack on women's liberation and a woman's right to join the workforce instead of raising a family, is not to look at the problem deeply enough. Everybody needs to work less, not just women. Everybody needs to reprioritise family and community over economics and employment, perhaps men most of all. Henry David Thoreau once asked a very simple question, which at the time that I first read it shocked me with its simplicity and insight. He asked, "How many years of your life did your house cost you?"

Of course many people love their jobs, and almost all of us need to work to support self or family, but a great deal of what we earn is wasted. It's wasted in ways that we are so used to that we don't even see anymore—the frivolities of our society. Without wanting to sound overly pessimistic, I believe that the system is designed to encourage such wasteful lifestyles. We work to earn, and are all the while being convinced by marketing and gimmickry that we need to spend this money on technology and gadgets that will save us time and make our lives more enjoyable. But then we need to work even more to pay for them, which often simply depresses us, encouraging us to spend more to find experiences that are instantly gratifying. Time is money. In the end, the amount of time that we are saving with technology is so completely overridden by the time we had to work to buy the appliance. In addition to this fact, the task that technology is now doing for us could often have been rich and rewarding, or at least as enjoyable as going to work! But this is simplistic. We work harder and harder to get promoted, to have to work less and less for more and more, but this is ultimately just another trap, and another way of locking us into an economic cycle. There have been studies done that calculate the actual speed that we travel in our cars once we take into account all of the time that had to be spent working to pay for the car and its associated expenses. The result is always that it would have been quicker to walk (or certainly to catch a bus or ride a bike), yet we don't—all around us, we witness the dissolution or stagnation of public transport and the simultaneous expansion of bigger and bigger highways to accommodate more cars. These are perhaps the twenty-first century nuances of Thoreau's question. As technology and life become more complex, how much of what we have do we really need? And what would we be prepared to give up for more *time*, more *life?*

As a society, we can begin to make these changes. We can begin to live differently. By living in community (even if we still physically live separately or in smaller families), we can work less and help each other more, spend more time doing for, or with, one another, more time teaching others to do for themselves. In large part I am sure that this is why the family and community structures have been broken down; people need to work more if they are all isolated individuals needing to call on outside (and expensive) help for all of their needs. People are, however, beginning to break down these barriers of isolation with local schemes in which individuals exchange goods and services outside of a normal cash economy. In addition, we could get involved in community garden projects, especially within cities, where we grow food together, teaching our children and helping each other (and for those of you who haven't tried growing your own veggies, it really is both simple and beautiful. The earth can surprise you with what it yields—especially in zucchinis!). Time spent in the office can then be exchanged for time teaching children in the garden—my preference should be clear. People all over the world would need to start to get involved, though, everyone would need to start simplifying lifestyles and making relationship with place, with this incredible planet, and with one another. These are options open to anyone, not just Pagans, and in fact, we *need* everyone. This is just one reason that we must start to "dance in the daylight," as Gordon MacLellan beautifully terms it in his article in this anthology. We must start to involve other people in at least some of our rituals, and get involved with building and establishing genuine community.

What About Trade in This Utopia?

Much of what is offered here, however, seems unrealistic, if not utopian. As I have previously commented, we simply cannot produce everything for ourselves and still hope to meaningfully engage with a twenty-first century society. To some extent, then, we must accept the "commodification" of our relationships with the natural world; we must be willing to buy and trade, instead of making direct relationship. Just as in the example of the featherless chicken, which has become food and nothing but food, not respected in any other way, we are witnessing the mass commodification of a variety of other "resources." Water, for example, the lifeblood of this planet, has been "privatised" in many countries, sold off to European and American companies only to be sold back again to consumers under what have often been far from desirable circumstances.[11] Ours is a world in which anything can be turned into a commodity, and anything that is not "useful" will eventually be destroyed. Many of our politicians and business people see this planet as one giant resource—nothing is sacred, and everything is up for grabs. So, even if it may not be possible to do everything for ourselves from the ground up, there can still be a vast difference in the integrity of those who we rely on to do things for us, and we can support those who operate in more sustainable and respectful ways. This support can be purely financial, but it can also be emotional, physical, and spiritual. I maintain that doing things for oneself is a vital part of understanding what it is to be human, and of beginning to develop deeper bonds of kinship with this planet. That means beginning to appreciate it as something more than a giant resource, as something that offers us our very lives. Having said this, however, when we do buy things, all companies and all products certainly were not "created equal."

Organics, biodynamics, and permaculture, for example, are all methods of growing crops which, by and large, view the world as something more than a resource, which work with a place to produce food—in this sense, then, they are preferable to my mind. Not only do I believe them to be a healthier option both for me and the environment, but they are also a healthier vision for agriculture, a statement of a healthier relationship between people and planet, in which everything is not merely a commodity. Genuinely free-range egg production is another good example; the chicken might still be an "egg machine" in some sense, but it is acknowledged to be more than this as well; it is acknowledged to have at least some of the needs and desires that make it a chicken. There are so many examples of wonderfully gifted people working in these areas—the people, for example, who used old railway sleepers to make the coffee table in my lounge room.

While looking at trade, it is important to consider the massive resources that international trade consumes. Oil for transportation, plastics for packaging, and more water than you could possibly imagine. This fact has led many to support a localisation of trade where each country (or each area within a country) provides for its own needs as much as possible, while other people instead support the globalisation of a fair trade and the reduction of the environmental costs of trade through new technologies and the wiser use of current practices. There is really no straightforward answer to this debate, as there are strengths and weaknesses in both positions. Overall, however, I feel that there is an important element that is often missing from both sides of the debate. As I have been arguing throughout this article, there is an essential need for individuals to enter into relationship with the place in which they live and those things that sustain them (which may or may not come from that place). As Starhawk points out in her interview in this anthology, what we eat is more than a mere resource; it is a part of the web of interrelations on which we are all dependent, of which we are all a part.

My Paganism, however, has taught me that a genuine relationship with a place is more easily and successfully achieved when we attempt to work as much as possible with the place in which we live, when we give to it as well as take from it. This situation was made starkly apparent to me while I was sitting on Glastonbury Tor a few years ago with a friend when I had just arrived in England for the first time. I sat down, closed my eyes, and melted into the ground, thanking the spirits of the place for the beauty of the day, for my safe arrival, and for holding me in their embrace while I was so far from home (Australia). The response that I received was not quite what I expected, and in hindsight was perhaps largely caused by the fact that Glastonbury Tor was at the time crowded with a hundred or so noisy tourists who had just trashed Stonehenge at the Summer Solstice "celebration" and were now hanging around waiting for Glastonbury Festival to kick off. The response I got from the Tor was not hostile, but it certainly was confrontational—I was challenged by the Tor to speak of what I had offered to this place, why it was that I thought I should be able to come here and eat the food, drink the water, breath the air and bring only this paper money, which meant nothing to the Tor, nothing to the land itself, with which I claimed I had come to speak. Had I planted any trees? Stopped any deforestation? Saved any water or spoken up about recycling and landfill? Had I worked with the land in any practical sense, or had I only these empty words to offer? I had only arrived three days earlier, so was a little taken aback by this "welcome," but I took it as a vital lesson about place relations. It is not just about money and economics; paying people on the other side of the world to produce something does not constitute a relationship with place, no matter how "fairly" we pay them.

There is a sacred element to trade, just as there is a sacred element to living more generally. When we support local craftspeople and businesses, we continue, to some extent, to deepen our relationship with the place in which we live, and what's more, we can also hope to exercise more control over their practices and keep a closer eye on the social and environmental costs of production. This is not a perfect answer to the issue of trade; much needs to be done to make it cleaner and fairer, and at the same time to help those developing nations who have effectively been forced into producing cash crops like sugar, soybeans, oil palm, cotton, and many others for Western markets, at the expense of producing food and other products for their own consumption. What I have tried to get at here is the importance not only of doing things for ourselves but also of looking into the companies and practices employed to produce the things that we will continue to buy, and the desirability of supporting those whose visions for the future are sustainable and whose practices are respectful. Sometimes this will mean trading internationally, but wherever possible it will mean understanding our sustenance as just one more way in which we can deepen our connection with the place in which we live: whether through doing things for ourselves, through getting our hands "dirty" in the rich, moist soil of the earth, or through supporting the farmer who does this, who respects the land which she works and the products she produces.

Ultimately what I have attempted to do here is to draw out some of the strings of a Pagan environmentalism as I understand it. I have proposed that the beginning of this environmentalism must be the making of relationship with life and death, and the cultivation of an awareness of sacred community. Technology, economics, and education are all important, but our understanding of ourselves and this planet is even more fundamental, and changes in this understanding must necessarily accompany any real long-term and deep social or personal change. The primary significance of making relationship with both life and death is the breaking down of individualistic worldviews that it facilitates. In place of these types of views we can become aware of ourselves as members of a sacred community. This awareness is accompanied by a deeper sense of kinship with others—a feeling of respect and commonality of purpose that is essential in moving beyond the domination of our environment, or in fact any group. This is the challenge that Paganism has, in many ways, presented itself with in the twenty-first century. How can we begin to understand and utilise our spirituality, our depth of relationship with the world, to move towards a more equitable and sustainable future? I hope that this article has offered some meaningful insights and additions to this discussion.

Notes

1. A great deal of this article is a discussion of the author's society. Obviously there are a wide range of diverse human societies on this planet, and while I am writing from a Western, middle-class, English-speaking background, at least most of what is said here is applicable to "developed" nations in general. To what extent it is applicable to the reader's society must remain a matter for his or her discernment.

2. Interesting discussions of relational worldviews (within a largely environmental/philosophical context) can be found, for example, in deep ecology (in which this view is usually quite holistic and is referred to as "gestalt ontology") and ecofeminist thought. My own articulation of a relational worldview is strongly influenced by the work of Val Plumwood. See *Environmental Culture, The Ecological Crisis of Reason* (New York: Routledge, 2002).

3. I owe the phrase "process of mutual life giving" to Val Plumwood's work.

4. This is not to say that there aren't a lot of other very good reasons to be a vegetarian or vegan, especially in this world of hormone- and chemical-enhanced factory farming.

5. Making relationship with life will be discussed in the second half of this article.

6. From a broader perspective we should also acknowledge the role of the sun, moon, and other celestial bodies.

7. Please also see Val Plumwood's interview in this anthology for a discussion of the political and ecological consequences of too simplistic and solitary a conception of "place."

8. Dolores LaChapelle discusses the "pattern of place" and the use of ritual in the facilitation of an awareness of one's being in this pattern. See D. LaChapelle, *Sacred Land, Sacred Sex, Rapture of the Deep: Concerning Deep Ecology and Celebrating Life* (USA: Kivaki Press, 1988).

9. This is a distinction commonly drawn in deep ecology. See for example G. Sessions and B. Devall, *Deep Ecology, Living as if Nature Mattered* (Gibb Smith, Utah, 1985), 70.

10. In the broader sense of the word, which is not limited to biology and blood links, but speaks rather of "kinship" with others, a deep sense of knowing and caring for others.

11. See V. Shiva, *Water Wars: Privatisation, Pollution and Profit* (Cambridge: South End Press, 2002); or T. Clark & M. Barlow, *Blue Gold: The Battle Against Corporate Theft of the World's Water* (New York: W. W. Norton & Company, 2003).

Witchcraft

Theory and Practice

Ly de Angeles

Here is a manual to the theory and practice of Witchcraft that is aimed at the serious student; specifically, the practicing Witch. It is written conversationally, talking to the individual, as though the student was being trained through the author's coven.

It takes the trainee step-by-step through the stages of the work and leaves nothing undone. It is a comprehensive textbook for both solitary and group practice, covering the philosophy, the disciplines involved, the meaning and practice of ritual, applicable alternative studies, and the attitudes required for successful spellcrafting (sorcery). It specifically implies that a Witch does have certain psychic powers, either inherent or that can be developed. The depth in *Witchcraft: Theory and Practice* enables it to be read more than once and it may also be used as a Grimoire.

1-56718-782-X
288 pp., 6 x 9 $12.95

When I See the Wild God

Encountering Urban Celtic Witchcraft

LY DE ANGELES

Magic and witchcraft begin with self-awareness. A crucial step toward self-awareness is recognizing the many faces of the witches' god. This book provides a clear mythology for those who need assistance in answering the call of wildness within.

High Priestess Ly de Angeles teaches beginning and advanced practitioners about the persona of the gods and the Celtic perspective of sacredness. Going beyond ordinary witchcraft manuals, she explains fundamental concepts, such as logos and mythos, the Tuatha de Danann, the Quicken Tree, immortality, animism, pantheism, and the elements. Also included are urban stories of magical realism, which take readers on a ritual journey to understanding the solstices and equinoxes.

0-7387-0576-4
288 pp., 6 x 9 $12.95

The Quickening

LY DE ANGELES

Most people see the Travelers as a ragged bunch of musicians, artists, and fortunetellers crossing the country in an old, double-decker bus, but these magical creatures are actually the Sídhe, the Fair Folk, an ageless, magical race bringing the light of the ancient mysteries to those who are lost.

On an unforgettable night of murder and mayhem, Kathryn meets the Travelers and awakens to her true Fey nature. She and her witchy friend Merrin help the Sídhe find the ones responsible for the bombs, fires, and terror wreaked on the Southside of New Rathmore. Trouble escalates when Robin, son of Puck and Hunter the forest god, is kidnapped. Is Michael Blacker's Fundamentalist Christian cult behind these despicable acts? Can Hunter and the Sídhe rescue Robin before the young god becomes another casualty of this twisted "Inquisition"?

0-7387-0664-7

288 pp., 6 x 9 $15.95

Pagan Ways

Finding Your Spirituality in Nature

GWYDION O'HARA

Do you feel the spirituality in nature? Are you full of questions about mainstream religion? Do you long to engage in rituals that have meaning for you? Perhaps you are a Pagan at heart.

Pagan Ways is your first step toward finding your personal spiritual truth. It is designed to offer enough understanding and insight to allow a fully thought out and firm decision as to whether or not Paganism is, indeed, the path for you.

Explore the history of Paganism and the founders of the modern Craft movement. Learn how the Pagan God is found in the cycles of the seasons, how to get in touch with nature spirits, what celebrations are included in the Pagan calendar, the tools used for magick and worship, how to erect an altar, how to conduct a ritual, how the eight Pagan virtues fit into your life, and what the stages are to becoming a Priest or Priestess.

1-56718-341-7
216 pp., 5³⁄₁₆ x 8 $7.95

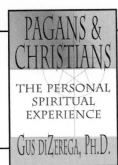

Pagans & Christians

The Personal Spiritual Experience

GUS DIZEREGA, PH.D.

Pagans and Christians have been polarized within the spiritual landscape for two millennia. Recent media reports even talk of efforts by the Christian Right to boycott the U.S. Army for allowing Wiccan soldiers to practice their religion. There is no better time for Western civilization's most prominent religion and humanity's oldest religion to enter into intelligent and respectful dialogue.

Providing something for Pagans and Christians alike, Dr. diZerega presents an important and original contribution for contemporary interfaith understanding. For Pagans, his book deepens the discussion of Paganism's theological and philosophical implications, penetrating its inner truths and examining the reasons for its modern growth. For Christians, it demystifies Paganism, offering respectful answers to the most common criticisms levelled at Pagan beliefs and practices.

1-56718-228-3
264 pp., 6 x 9, illus. $14.95

Paganism

An Introduction to Earth-Centered Religions

RIVER AND JOYCE HIGGINBOTHAM

If you want to study Paganism in more detail, this book is the place to start. Based on a course in Paganism that the authors have taught for more than a decade, it is full of exercises, meditations, and discussion questions for group or individual study.

This book presents the basic fundamentals of Paganism. It explores what Pagans are like; how the Pagan sacred year is arranged; what Pagans do in ritual; what magick is; and what Pagans believe about God, worship, human nature, and ethics.

0-7387-0222-6
272 pp., 7½ x 9⅛ $14.95

To order, call 1-877-NEW-WRLD
Prices subject to change without notice

To Write to the Authors

If you wish to contact the authors or would like more information about this book, please write to the author in care of Llewellyn Worldwide, and we will forward your request. Both the authors and publisher appreciate hearing from you and learning of your enjoyment of this book and how it has helped you. Llewellyn Worldwide cannot guarantee that every letter written to the authors can be answered, but all will be forwarded. Please write to:

Llewellyn Worldwide
2143 Wooddale Drive, Dept. 0-7387-0824-0
Woodbury, MN 55125-2989, U.S.A.
Please enclose a self-addressed, stamped envelope for reply,
or $1.00 to cover costs. If outside U.S.A., enclose
international postal reply coupon.

Many of Llewellyn's authors have websites with additional information and resources. For more information, please visit our website at www.llewellyn.com.